HE LIE

Writing, Speaking, and Communication Skills for Health Professionals

THE HEALTH CARE COMMUNICATION GROUP

Stephanie Barnard

Paul J Casella

Catherine Coffin

Kirk T Hughes

J Willis Hurst

Janet S Rasey

Diane Redding

Renée J Robillard

Deborah St James

Steven C Ullery

Writing, Speaking, & Communication Skills for Health Professionals

YALE UNIVERSITY PRESS • NEW HAVEN AND LONDON

Designed by Nancy Ovedovitz and set in Scala
type by Keystone Typesetting, Inc. Printed in the
United States of America by R. R. Donnelley &
Sons.

Library of Congress Cataloging-in-Publication
Data
Writing, Speaking, and Communication
Skills for Health Professionals / the Health
Care Communication Group ; Stephanie Barnard
. . . [et al.].
p. ; cm.
Includes bibliographical references and index.
ISBN 0-300-08861-2 (cloth : alk. paper)
ISBN 0-300-08862-0 (paper : alk. paper)
1. Communication in medicine. 2. Allied health
personnel and patient. 3. Interpersonal
communication. I. Barnard, Stephanie. II. Health
Care Communication Group.
[DNLM: 1. Writing. 2. Communication.
3. Teaching—methods. WZ 345 C7345 2001]
R118.C6175 2001
302.2'024'61—dc21   2001022234

A catalogue record for this book is available from
the British Library.

The paper in this book meets the guidelines for
permanence and durability of the Committee on
Production Guidelines for Book Longevity of the
Council on Library Resources.

10 9 8 7 6 5 4 3 2 1

Contents

Preface

The way the team works as a whole determines its success. You may have the greatest bunch of individual stars in the world, but if they don't work well together, the team won't be worth a dime.
—Babe Ruth

For the past ten years I have had the good fortune to work with the authors of this book. Together we have taught more than three thousand courses on Writing and Speaking for Excellence to more than twenty-five thousand physicians, pharmacists, and other health care providers at every major medical center and university in North America.

Each contributor is a star in his or her own right. All are talented writers, editors, and educators with unique talents and styles. Yet I think each would agree that our success as a group has not been the result of any one person's individual talent, but rather of our ability to work together as a team with one common passion: the love of teaching and learning.

In 1990, when I was a medical writer at Bayer Corporation, Pharmaceutical Division, I began to teach writing and speaking skills to physician residents in academic medical centers. I quickly learned that while most of the participants were exceptionally bright, well educated, well trained, and highly motivated, few had had any formal training in writing or speaking. Yet many were being asked to write case reports, oral and poster presentations, grant applications, or original research. The assumption had always been, "They're bright; they'll figure it out." Indeed, most of them would figure it out—after much trial and error. My goal was to give the residents a few hints to help them improve their writing and avoid some of the pitfalls.

That first year, I bought a Travelpro suitcase and was on my way. I taught ten seminars that year. By the second year, the request for seminars had quadrupled. I soon found I was on the road almost every week, racking up frequent-flyer miles and greeting pilots by their first names. I recognized that I was going to need some help. Dr David Albala, a urologic surgeon practicing at Loyola Medical Center outside Chicago, suggested that I call Catherine Coffin, a manuscript editor with whom he had worked at Dartmouth-Hitchcock Medical Center in New Hampshire. I met Cathy the next week and knew right away that she had a wealth of information about medical writing and publishing that would be valuable not only to the physicians but also to me. In addition, she had a quick wit and an adventurous spirit—two qualities necessary for any true road warrior.

Soon, *both* Cathy and I were on the road every week. Then, in 1992, I met the author Abraham Verghese MD, who was leading a short session for physician writers at the Iowa Summer Writing Festival. I told him I was looking for an enthusiastic person who could teach writing and speaking skills to physicians. The next day, Abraham introduced me to Paul Casella, who was teaching poetry, creative writing, and composition at Kirkwood College. Paul was a graduate of Dartmouth and the Iowa Writer's Workshop but had had experience producing medical videos, slides, and grant applications. At our first meeting, Paul told me he was really a poet but that he had learned early on that if he wanted to be a poet, he needed a day job. Soon Paul joined Cathy and me in his new day job and became our expert one-on-one speaking coach. Over the years, Paul has trained hundreds of physicians, pharmacists, and other health care providers—not only in this country but throughout Europe—to be more effective speakers and leaders.

In the next couple of years, the demand for the seminars continued to grow and the face of health care began to change. More and more physicians and pharmacists were asking for courses on business writing, on marketing their practices, on leading effective meetings, and on team building. In 1997 we found Stephanie Barnard, who owns a health care public relations firm. Her southern charm and abundance of information on "the business of health care" made Stephanie an instant hit with her audiences. With her expertise, we were able to add Communicating for Excellence seminars to our Writing and Speaking for Excellence courses. As part of that series, Stephanie developed courses including Business Writing, Writing a Business Plan, Patient and Physician Communication, Ethical Marketing, and Leading Effective Meetings.

As our team of four traveled around the country, we found one request coming up repeatedly: Could we teach others to teach? We were learning that while many physicians, pharmacists, nurses, physician assistants, health care executives, and managers were being asked to teach or train others, most of them had had no training in curriculum development, adult learning, or teaching. Where, I thought, will I find someone who not only can teach but also teach others to teach?

As it turned out, I didn't have to look far. Kirk Hughes and I met at Atticus Bookstore in New Haven, Connecticut. A mutual friend of ours taught at Yale and suggested that Kirk might be interested in joining us. Kirk had taught English, science writing, and speech and was intrigued by our group and its work. Since Kirk's doctoral research had included study of "the rhetoric of science" and "theories of teaching," we talked about incorporating some of his ideas into a new course. Within the month, Kirk had bought a laptop and a rolling suitcase and was on the road with the rest of us. His enthusiasm, energy, and wealth of information put him in high demand.

In fact, by 1998 the time between the request for a seminar and the date we could meet the request had grown to about five months. While I was meeting dozens of people who had the information and experience necessary to teach a seminar and who wanted to join the group, none seemed to have the flexibility, charisma, and panache that Cathy, Paul, Stephanie, and Kirk have—a style that has become a trademark of the group.

In the summer of that year, I was in Seattle waiting to give a seminar to some fellows at the University of Washington when I first saw Janet Rasey teach a course on grant writing. Immediately, I saw a potential addition to our group. Janet knew all the ins and outs of grant writing, but equally, if not more importantly, she communicated the information to her audiences in a way that both motivated and entertained. Later that day, I met with Janet to see if she would be interested in working with us. Since Janet had a full-time research position, she was available only on a limited basis. She soon became our "weekend grant-writing expert," traveling not only throughout the United States but also in Canada.

Renée Robillard soon joined us as another part-time trainer. She had been a medical editor with the *New England Journal of Medicine* and had worked as a medical writer for a surgical instrument company in Arizona. When Renée became a member of our group, she was teaching English at a community college in Sacramento. With her twenty years of experience in the field of medical writing and publishing, Renée has been instrumental in developing two advanced courses: Writing for Publication and Researching the Medical Literature. These courses have been in great demand at many medical centers and universities.

Our group became complete following a one-day writing and speaking seminar I was giving at Emory University for the Georgia chapter of the American College of Physicians. As is often the case, someone in the audience asked me to recommend books on writing, speaking, and teaching that might be helpful. One of the books I like to suggest is *The Bench and Me,* by J Willis Hurst. It is a concise book, full of excellent information about science, teaching, writing, and speaking. Much to my surprise, a gentleman in the first row thanked me for my kind words about his book.

It was in that way that I first encountered Dr Hurst, an avid reader, writer, and teacher who is the former chair of the Department of Medicine at Emory. Over the next year, I had the pleasure of talking several times with Dr Hurst, and it was from those meetings that we came up with the idea of this book.

Writing, Speaking, and Communication Skills for Health Professionals encompasses the years of experience, collaboration, and teamwork that created the Writing and Speaking for Excellence seminars. It is not intended to be a textbook; for a comprehensive guide to grammar, punctuation, and word usage, you will need another book. The authors' intentions are to address some of the most frequently asked questions, comments, frustrations, and problems they have heard from medical writers, speakers, and teachers—and to offer practical solutions. Not all chapters will be of interest to all readers.

This book contributes to an ongoing conversation with scientists and health care practitioners throughout the United States about the connections between strong communication skills and excellence in the medical and biological sciences. Lecturers, teachers, editors, and university faculty members alike have observed how poor communication skills can obscure even the most important scientific information. Ineffective seminars, lectures during grand rounds, and conference talks alienate nonspecialists, bore students, and dishearten the very practitioners we most need to encourage toward collaboration and problem solving. This book is a wake-up call for improving medical communication skills. The contributors offer little by way of theory and much in the way of practical suggestions. They urge that the current explosion in specialized bench research be accompanied by ongoing attention to clear explanation of the results.

In addition, the book argues that medical training must be ongoing, lifelong, and responsive to technological advances in the culture at large as well as in science. Rather than ending with school, ongoing training must be part and parcel of one's professional identity. *Docere*, the Latin root of our English word "doctor," means to teach, yes. But the best people in medicine are also constant learners: they refine their communication and teaching skills as rigorously as they pursue their science.

The five parts of this volume address communication skills that are essential to a wide range of twenty-first-century health care practitioners. Part I (Reading Science) focuses on ways to organize the complex technical data that health practitioners encounter in clinics and in the scientific literature. Robillard and Ullery extend this critical awareness of medical data by offering handfuls of pragmatic suggestions for time-efficient assessment of journal articles in their chapter, "Reading the Medical Literature."

Parts II and III discuss the publication and presentation tasks facing most health care practitioners. Hughes's "Grammar Tips for the Information Age" (Chapter 2) and Casella's "Creative Process" (Chapter 3) suggest practical ways of getting research projects off the ground and into the clear and accurate language that readers can understand. Coffin and Rasey share years of editorial and grant-review expertise in chapters that address four publication genres: the journal article (Chapter 4), the research grant (Chapter 5), the scientific poster (Chapter 6), and the curriculum vitae (Chapter 7). Similarly, Casella and Hughes outline practical ways to sharpen the delivery of conference and seminar papers (Chapter 8) and to improve learning in classroom teaching (Chapters 9 and 10).

This book concludes with several chapters that consider changes in the business of health care. The complexities of contemporary health care systems create communication challenges as never before. Part V reviews some of the ways individual departments in complex organizations can improve both the service they give and the service they get (Chapter 11). "Building Your Practice" (Chapter 12) outlines key steps that smaller practices can take to develop an edge in increasingly competitive markets. Likewise, Barnard's practical meeting skills (Chapter 13) and business-writing suggestions (Chapter 14) can trim hours of wasted time and effort from professional workweeks.

Finally, as you read this compact book, you will see that the diversity of this group is its strength. Each speaker uses his or her own experience to guide health care professionals toward more effective communication—sometimes gently, sometimes emphatically, always with humor. Each unique voice speaks in concert with the rest, and all share a common goal: furthering the commitment to excellence in communication.

ACKNOWLEDGMENTS

Special thanks go to Helena Bauernschmitt, our editor at ArcMesa. Without her good humor, eye for detail, and dedication, this book would not have been possible. She contributed ideas, pointed out omissions, and with kindness and graciousness corrected our mistakes and kept us on schedule. For all of the above, plus her friendship, we are grateful.

We also thank Bayer Corporation for its continued support of our work, as well as the talented and helpful people at Yale University Press, including Jean Thomson Black, Heidi Downey, Nancy Ovedovitz, Vivian Wheeler, Jenya Weinreb, and Manushag Powell.

Of course we are also appreciative of the thousands of physicians, pharmacists, and other health care professionals who have attended our seminars; their professional commitment and caring have been an inspiration to us all. Much of what follows is a result of their participation and contribution.

Finally, we warmly thank our families for putting up with our bizarre schedules and numerous absences. They have made coming home the best part of the job.

Deborah St James

Part One

Reading Science

1

Reading the Medical Literature: Assessing Reports on Clinical Intervention Studies

Renée J Robillard

Steven C Ullery

The ability to read the medical literature critically is a skill that has become increasingly important for health care professionals for three main reasons. The first is the enormous proliferation in medical information. The number of medical, allied health, nursing, and pharmacy journals published on paper and on-line has increased dramatically; health-related websites, many of which do not contain peer-reviewed data, have multiplied; and interest in medical news has blossomed in the popular media in response to baby boomers' concerns about health and aging.

The second reason is the growing sophistication of patients about health issues, resulting largely from their acquisition of medical information from sources other than their physicians, especially the news media and the Internet.

The third is the expanding influence of cost-containment initiatives in health care. Increasingly, third-party payers are requiring that the treatments they pay for be as effective and as inexpensive as possible. Often, evidence for efficacy and cost saving is found in the medical literature, reflecting an approach to medical practice called evidence-based medicine, which emphasizes the need to move beyond clinical experience and physiologic principles to rigorous evaluation of clinical actions.[1]

Unfortunately, even the medical information published in leading medical journals can be irrelevant, inconclusive, unoriginal, confusing, misleading, poorly presented, or a combination of these distressing characteristics. Reading the medical literature therefore becomes a reader-beware situation: to promote the health of your patients and to protect yourself against problems caused by giving flawed clinical advice, you must not simply believe everything you read. But many health care professionals have little training in critically appraising medical articles. Even those who faithfully attend journal clubs may not feel completely confident about their ability to assess what they read.

In the past few years, several worthwhile guides to reading the medical literature have been published (see notes). This chapter consolidates some of the information in those publications, concentrating specifically on clinical intervention studies, that is, investigations in which researchers treat patients for a condition and then assess the results of the treatment. The intervention may be a drug, an operation, psychological therapy, or an educational program. Excellent sources of information on evaluating other kinds of studies (investigations of screening or diagnostic tests, meta-analyses and systematic reviews, economic analyses, observational cohort studies of prognosis or exposure to an agent, epidemiologic cross-sectional surveys, and case-control studies) include the books by Greenhalgh, Crombie, and Elwood and the "Users' guides to the medical literature," a series of *JAMA* articles by the Evidence-Based Medicine Working Group.[2] In addition, the website of the Evidence-Based Medicine Resource Center (http://www.ebmny.org) has an extensive bibliography of print and electronic publications on finding and interpreting the most useful clinical literature.

SELECTION OF ARTICLES

Health care professionals read scientific articles to update their general knowledge of a discipline, to acquire information for research, or (most frequently) to answer a specific clinical question. Those still in training may read because they have been assigned articles in a course. Because your time to read is limited, you want to avoid wasting it on publications that do not meet your needs. Yet computerized database searches of the literature may yield hundreds of articles, most of which will not provide substantive information on the topic in which you are interested. It is therefore important to limit the number of articles that you must find and review to get the high-quality information you want. Fortunately, there are several new ways to do this relatively quickly and efficiently, many of which were reviewed by Hunt et al.[3] These include consulting "prefiltered" evidence-based resources such as the journal *ACP Journal Club*, the collection of the Cochrane Library, and the series *Clinical Evidence;* and using the free Web-based PubMed system to make searching more productive.[4] The medical librarians or information specialists at your institution are the best sources of information on all the searching resources available where you work and how to use them; brief descriptions of some of these resources are given below.

The purpose of *ACP Journal Club* (and its computer-searchable CD-ROM form, *Best Evidence*), which is published bimonthly by the American College of Physicians–American Society of Internal Medicine (ACP-ASIM), is to "select from the biomedical literature articles that report original studies and systematic reviews that warrant immediate attention by physicians attempting to keep pace with important advances in internal medicine" and to provide commentary on each article.[5] More than 150 top journals are reviewed to identify articles that qualify as the "best literature" according to an extensive set of criteria (for example, 80 percent follow-up for a randomized trial). These articles are then abstracted, and commentary on each is provided by an expert who discusses the context of the article, any methodologic problems with the study the article describes, and recommendations for clinical practice. Authors of the articles are given the opportunity to review the abstract and commentary before publication.

The Cochrane Library, which is available on both CD-ROM and the Web, includes the Cochrane Database of Systematic Reviews, the Database of Reviews of Effectiveness, the Cochrane Clinical Trials Registry, and a handbook for reviewing medical literature. The material in the Cochrane Library is provided by the Cochrane Collaboration, an international group that prepares, maintains, and disseminates systematic reviews of health care interventions in all fields. For the database of systematic reviews, Cochrane Collaboration reviewers search MEDLINE, EMBASE, and other sources for reports on the most important randomized studies of a topic. The reports selected are then reviewed according to strict and stated criteria. Before you do a MEDLINE search on your topic, check to see whether a Cochrane review of it has recently been written. If so, it could save you a great deal of time and effort in your search for answers to clinical questions.

Clinical Evidence is a printed book-length "compendium of evidence on the effects of common interventions"[6] that is produced by the ACP-ASIM and the BMJ Publishing Group. It is updated and expanded every six months. *Clinical Evidence* is not a textbook or a book of guidelines; it simply provides summaries of the "best" available evidence on clinical interventions or else states that there is no good evidence. The summary page for each clinical topic provides a list of questions addressed in the summary, the interventions covered, and whether or not they have been found to be effective. The publishers of *Clinical Evidence* believe that the series is complementary to the Cochrane Collaboration's systematic reviews, in that it takes the information provided by those reviews and other "high-quality" sources and puts it in one place in a concise format that is easy for busy clinicians to consult.

PubMed, developed by the US National Center for Biotechnology Information at the National Library of Medicine, is a Web-based search tool for accessing medical literature citations and abstracts and providing links to full-text journals at websites of journal publishers. The bibliographic information in PubMed comes primarily from MEDLINE, but PubMed is easier to use and yields more comprehensive results than older MEDLINE search engines. Instead of doing a simple text-word search for the term(s) you enter, PubMed automatically adds the officially designated MEDLINE Medical Subject Heading (MeSH) term to your entry, then "explodes" the MeSH term to include other relevant MeSH terms less specific than the one associated with your entry.

PubMed also allows you to save citations from searches on your computer, import search results into your bibliographic management program, and "link out" to outside sources of information on your topic. With PubMed's "preview/index feature," you can preview search results before they are displayed, build search strategies by adding one or more terms at a time, add terms to a strategy from specific search fields, and select terms from an index to build search strategies. PubMed also has a "limits" feature for refining a search (according to date of publication, age and sex of patients, type of study—for example, clinical trial—and human or animal) and a "history" feature that lets you combine searches or use the Boolean operators AND, OR, and NOT. When you find a citation with PubMed that appears to be just what you are looking for, you can click on a "related articles" link on the same screen to retrieve closely related references.

One of the most useful features of PubMed for clinicians is its "clinical queries" option. This feature has built-in search filters designed to greatly reduce the number of citations retrieved and to help locate high-quality studies. Four study categories are provided—therapy, diagnosis, etiology, and prognosis—and you can indicate whether you want your search to include most relevant articles and probably some less relevant ones (a "sensitive" search) or to include mostly relevant articles but probably omit a few (a "specific" search).

For example, in the therapy category, clicking on "sensitivity" will retrieve articles on your topic associated with the terms "randomized control trial" or "drug therapy" or "therapeutic use" or "all random." Clicking on "specificity" will yield articles described by the terms "all double and all blind" or "all placebo." Detailed information on PubMed's clinical queries feature is provided on the Web at http://ncbi.nlm.nih.gov:80/entrez/query/static/clinical.html.

CLINICAL INTERVENTION STUDIES

Randomized control trials (RCTs), controlled (but not randomized) clinical trials, case series, and case reports are all clinical intervention studies. The RCT is considered to provide the strongest evidence, the case report the weakest. Remember, however, that not all RCTs are unbiased (see Questions about Methods), primarily because many trials that are labeled RCTs have defects in design that prevent them from fulfilling the strict criteria for RCTs. Those criteria are the focus of this chapter.

Studies of drugs (and, in some cases, of medical devices), especially investigations that are performed to fulfill regulatory requirements, may be divided into three or four phases, which are done in order.[7] The purpose of a phase I trial of a drug is to determine a dose range that is well tolerated and produces no major side effects. Only small numbers of patients or healthy volunteers are enrolled in this kind of trial and there is usually no control group. A phase II trial is designed to provide preliminary information on whether a drug has any therapeutic value at all, that is, on whether it is effective in alleviating disease when used at a tolerable dosage. A phase II trial may or may not be controlled, but even if it is, the number of patients enrolled is usually too small to detect any but the largest treatment effects. A phase III trial is usually an RCT. When well designed, it provides definitive evidence of the efficacy of a drug and detects the most common side effects. It is this kind of study that persuades a regulatory agency to approve a drug for sale. Once a drug is in general use, a phase IV trial (also called postmarketing surveillance) may be conducted to track use of the drug in thousands of patients or more. Because of the large numbers involved, phase IV trials can detect the more uncommon side effects of drugs.

In an RCT, patients are randomly assigned to study groups that receive either a new clinical intervention or a placebo (that is, no active intervention agent); the new intervention or an older, generally effective standard intervention; or a new intervention, a standard intervention, and a placebo. "Blinding" or "masking" of some kind is generally done. The two or more study groups are followed for a specified time and compared with respect to certain outcomes (end points) selected before the beginning of the study. An RCT is the gold-standard clinical intervention study—although for ethical or economic reasons, not all forms of therapy can be assessed with an RCT, especially a placebo-controlled RCT. For example, because treatment of breast cancer is known to be more effective than no treatment, it would not be ethical to assign some patients with breast cancer to a no-treatment placebo group when assessing a new chemotherapy regimen for the disease. Like other patients, those enrolled in an RCT must be treated according to accepted standards of care.

A controlled clinical trial is similar to an RCT except that the subjects of the study are not randomly assigned to study groups. Instead, they are placed in one or another group because of a patient-related characteristic, such as the hospital or medical practice from which they received care or an intervention choice made by patients (for example, to be given or not to be given an anesthetic agent during labor and delivery).

A case series is a nonrandomized, retrospective (archival) study of the results of an intervention in a limited number of patients. A case report describes the response or nonresponse to an intervention of just one patient. These kinds of studies do not include a formal control group, although informal comparisons with historical controls or published investigations may be made. At best, case series and case reports suggest a testable hypothesis; the information they provide should not be used in selecting therapy for other patients.

QUESTIONS TO ASK ABOUT
AN INTERVENTION STUDY

Let us say that your search of the literature on the clinical issue in which you are interested, assisted by consulting prefiltered resources, is now finished, and you have downloaded or photocopied the published reports on the best RCTs that seem relevant to the issue. You are now ready to examine closely the reports on your desk. This kind of scrutiny is most easily done by asking a series of questions about each paper. The questions can be divided into categories according to the section of the paper in which the answers will most likely be found. You can generally answer the preliminary general questions by looking at the paper's title, list of authors, Abstract, and Introduction. Perusal of the Methods section should answer your questions about the design of the study and the statistical analysis that was done. The Results section is usually the place to go for answers about outcomes, follow-up, and statistical findings. The clinical implications of the study, the consistency of its results with those of earlier studies, and the study's limitations are best discerned by examining the paper's Discussion section.

Preliminary General Questions

Is the topic of the paper somewhat original?

Few biomedical papers describe truly groundbreaking investigations but, as Greenhalgh notes, research may enhance our knowledge of a clinical issue by providing a larger or longer study, more rigorous methods, or findings in a different patient population. Does the paper you are examining look as if it offers a new approach to the issue it addresses?

Do the authors have a solid track record?

If you attend conferences in your field often and do a fair amount of professional reading, you may have an impression regarding whose work is careful and whose is substandard. On the other hand, some excellent papers may have been written by authors unknown to you. You can always do an author PubMed search to find out what the authors have written about similar topics and what journals (prestigious or not) have published their research.

Is one of the authors a statistician, or is a statistician's contribution acknowledged?

The fact that a statistician was involved does not guarantee soundness of the study design, but it does provide evidence of dependability. The universal availability of personal computers and statistical software for them has produced a great many do-it-yourself statistical analyses, especially by researchers who do not have easy or inexpensive access to a professional statistician. Although statistical software can efficiently crunch numbers and output means, standard deviations, and P values, it cannot replace the wisdom provided by a statistician in designing a study and choosing the most appropriate statistical analyses.

Who sponsored the study?

Government agencies and private impartial foundations cannot provide all the research funding sought today. Therefore, many studies are funded by a pharmaceutical or medical-device company, or other organization with a special interest in the findings. The leading scientific journals have policies requiring disclosure of sources of funding for research studies reported in them. Manuscripts describing industry-sponsored studies are peer-reviewed by consultants to the journals in the same manner as other manuscripts. If they pass muster, and if the topics they address are considered by the journals' editors to be of interest to readers, the manuscripts are published. It is then up to you to decide whether the corporation acknowledged as having provided funding for a study may have influenced the findings in any way. This decision should be based on a close reading of the article.

Occasionally, authors do not disclose funding sources to a journal's editors. This is extremely risky because the authors' professional reputation will be severely compromised if the editors and the authors' colleagues discover this omission later. If you know that the research described was supported by a for-profit organization or that the authors have another (especially financial) relationship with such an organization that is not disclosed in the paper, consider why the relationship was hidden and whether that should affect your view of the paper.

Is the site of the study described sufficiently similar to where you work?

Although you sometimes read a paper for general information about an issue, you most often read for special information that *you* can use immediately to help *your* patients. If you practice family medicine in a village clinic in Central America, it may not be worth your time to read about a new screening test that uses magnetic resonance imaging, because your patients probably do not have ready access to this technology. Similarly, a paper describing the efficacy of a new antihypertensive agent in a study that enrolled only white patients may not be of much interest if most of your patients are African American. An article on a drug that may prevent second heart attacks may not be useful if you practice in the student health service of a university. As Dans and colleagues note, when clinicians are considering whether a study is applicable to their practice, they "first must decide whether the biology of the treatment effect will be similar in patients they are facing; second, their patients' risk of a target event which the treatment is designed to prevent; third, the adverse effects that may accompany treatment; and fourth, their own ability to deliver the intervention in a safe and effective manner."[8]

What was the aim of the study? What hypotheses did the researchers test? Are the conclusions reached (assuming they are valid) important to you?

In the Abstract or the Introduction section of a paper (or both), the aim of the study, according to Crombie, should be "phrased as a hypothesis to be tested or as a question to be answered. The absence of such a statement can imply that the authors themselves had no clear idea of what they were trying to find out. If this were the case it is likely that they did not find out much of interest."[9] In addition, the question asked in the study must be appropriate for the issue being addressed and relevant to your practice. You may discover that the study did not ask the "right" question. For example, a Dutch study published in the *New England Journal of Medicine* that compared conventional open anterior surgery for inguinal hernia repair with laparoscopic surgery was criticized in an accompanying editorial for addressing "the wrong clinical question," in that it compared *tension-creating* conventional open repair with *tension-free* laparoscopic repair.[10] Because most North American surgeons use *tension-free* conventional open repair, however, the editorialists pointed out that the question in which US and Canadian surgeons are most interested—whether tension-free laparoscopic repair provides better results than tension-free open repair—was unfortunately not asked by the study. Of course, if you are a surgeon who has never used laparoscopic techniques to repair inguinal hernias and you have no intention of ever doing so, you may choose not to read about the Dutch study simply because you consider it irrelevant to your practice.

Questions about Methods

Evaluating the Methods section of a paper describing an intervention study is the most important part of your critical analysis; according to Greenhalgh, "strictly speaking, if you are going to trash a paper, you should do so before you even look at the results."[11] It may also be the most intimidating part of your appraisal, chiefly because the Methods section usually contains the information on study design and statistical analysis. You may wonder whether, as a nonstatistician, you can really determine whether the study was designed properly and the data analyzed appropriately. Indeed, if you have little or no statistical training, you may not know whether the researchers should have used a Mann-Whitney U test instead of a Kruskal-Wallis test. But that does not mean that you have to accept their choice without question. You can always ask a statistician what she or he thinks, or you can read about statistical tests in a statistics textbook or one of the many handbooks of statistics for nonstatisticians.[12] However, you can usually detect some signs of questionable methods by asking questions that are more general than whether the correct statistical test was employed.

The purpose of most of your questions about a study's design and methods is to determine how well the researchers were able to minimize bias. Bias is a systematic (as opposed to random) error that results in favoring one outcome over another. The several categories of bias include selection bias, measurement or information bias, and confounding bias. *Selection bias* occurs when groups of patients are established or selected in ways that affect the outcome of a study. For example, the patients selected for study group A in the trial of a new chemotherapy agent have a better response to the new drug than those in study group B because they were recruited primarily from community hospitals, whereas most group B patients were from tertiary care centers and therefore had more advanced disease. *Measurement bias* occurs when the ways of assessing patients in the study groups are consistently dissimilar. For instance, follow-up monitoring in a study of vascular graft patency after femoropopliteal bypass consists only of clinical examinations in study group X, whereas monitoring in group Y includes both clinical examinations and ultrasonographic assessments. The study finds that the patients in group Y have graft failure sooner than those in group X, but it is only because they have been evaluated more thoroughly. *Confounding bias* occurs when extraneous, unrecognized variables distort the study's results by being responsible for an observed association or by masking an association. For example, in a study indicating that a new antihypertensive agent reduces blood pressure significantly, the results are affected by the confounding factor that the patients in whom the agent was apparently effective also lost weight during the study. Sound research studies use data-analysis techniques that control for possible confounding variables.

How were the patients chosen? Were they sufficiently similar to your own patients for the study to be of interest?

The inclusion and exclusion criteria for enrolling patients in the study should be given in the Methods section of the paper you are evaluating. Without this information you cannot determine whether the study's results might be applicable to *your* patients. The patients in the study may have been generally sicker or generally healthier than your patients; they may have belonged to ethnic, socioeconomic, or age groups different from those of most of your patients; or they may have received different attention during the study than what you routinely give your patients. The study's subjects, unlike your patients, may have had nothing wrong with them other than the condition being addressed or, also unlike your patients, they may not have been smokers or consumers of alcohol.[13] Keep in mind, however, that well-designed clinical research often requires that the subjects of a study be somewhat unlike "usual" patients. For example, a study of the effects of heredity on the development of lung cancer might exclude smokers, to eliminate the possibility that lung cancer in the subjects with a putative lung cancer gene was caused by smoking rather than by the gene.

The subjects in a study should be chosen with the most important clinical issues in mind. A trial of a new treatment for osteoporosis that excluded women or an investigation of a novel technique for repairing groin hernias that excluded men might seem to have limited usefulness.

Was consent to participate in the study obtained from the patients? Was the study approved by an institutional review board?

The editors of the leading biomedical journals require that most papers they publish contain an ethics statement, usually in the Methods section. In articles about studies with human subjects, the ethics statement generally includes a description of how those subjects were informed about the aims of the study, the possible risks of participating, and the measures taken to protect patient confidentiality before, during, and after the study. Generally, the name of the local ethics committee that approved the use of human subjects (often an institutional review board, or IRB) is given. If the ethics statement and the rest of the Methods section in a paper describing a clinical study do not convince you that the patients' rights and safety were well protected, or if the paper has no ethics statement, you may decide that it should not be in the competition for your reading time.

Was the assignment of patients to study groups truly random?

Some clinical studies cannot include randomization because of ethical issues. In general, human beings cannot ethically be given a disease (the common cold may be an exception) to study the effects of a treatment, nor can a treatment that is known to be effective be withheld to study another therapy. Moreover, RCTs are generally much more expensive and time-consuming than other studies and may require enrollment of a prohibitively high number of patients. However, if one or more RCTs on your topic have been done, you will probably want to focus on them rather than on nonrandomized studies because randomization is one of the best ways to minimize bias.

The Methods section of a report on an RCT should indicate how, when, and by whom the random assignment of patients was done and how, when, and by whom the randomization code was broken (that is, the patients were revealed to be in either the intervention or the nonintervention group). Today, careful researchers randomly assign patients to study groups by using a computer-generated list of random numbers. Unacceptable methods of randomization include use of the last digit of a patient's date of birth or medical record number, toss of a coin, sequential assignment, and date of a patient's visit to a clinic. These methods do not produce true randomization, chiefly because clinicians in the study may know in which study group patients would be placed before they make the final decision to enter them into the randomization process. Subconsciously or not, the clinicians may then keep patients they believe will benefit from the intervention from being place in the nonintervention group.

Was the study blind?

Like randomization, blinding is important in minimizing bias in an RCT. Patients who know they are receiving a new treatment, or clinicians who know they are administering one, may believe they have observed an improvement in the patients' condition even if one has not actually occurred. A study may have a single-blind, double-blind, or triple-blind design, depending on how many of the three partners in the investigation (that is, patients, clinicians, and data analysts) do not know which subjects are receiving which treatment (active or placebo) during the study's observation period. Generally, the greater the number of partners without this knowledge, the less biased the study. Of course, it is not always possible to blind one or more of the parties. For example, a study comparing two kinds of knee operations could not include blinding of the surgeons to the type of procedure performed. A study comparing radiation with chemotherapy in treating breast cancer could not blind either the patients or those administering the treatment. Both studies, however, could include blinding of those who analyze the clinical outcomes—perhaps primary care physicians or nurses.

The Methods section should indicate how the blinding was done (for example, by giving some patients placebo pills that looked and tasted like the pills containing the active agent that was studied), who had control of the blinding code during the trial (that is, who knew which patients were receiving a placebo and which the active agent), and when the blinding code was broken.

Were enough patients studied to reach valid conclusions?

Because clinical trials, especially RCTs, are expensive, time-consuming, and difficult to administer, researchers are motivated to enroll as few subjects as possible. However, studies with a large number of subjects tend to produce the most conclusive results become the effects of most interventions are small (rarely does an effect prove to be as dramatic as, say, treating appendicitis with surgery) and a large number is needed to discern a small treatment effect. Determining how many subjects are enough to answer the research question adequately requires making a sample-size (power) calculation before the investigation begins.

The specific type of power calculation done by a statistician varies according to the situation. Four factors are usually taken into consideration: the magnitude of the difference to be detected between subject groups, that is, the difference that is clinically important; the risk of an alpha (type I or false-positive) error, that is, of concluding that a treatment is effective when it really is not; the risk of a beta (type II or false-negative) error, that is, of concluding that a treatment is ineffective when it really is effective; and the characteristics of the data, especially the outcome measures, such as the rate of posttreatment events being tracked and variations among patients.[14]

A report on an RCT should include a justification of the study's sample size in the Methods section, the Discussion section, or both. Reports that do not mention sample size probably describe studies that enrolled too few patients. Such reports should be approached with caution; "underpowered studies are ubiquitous in the medical literature, usually because the authors found it harder than anticipated to recruit their subjects."[15] If you need to know for certain whether a study you are reviewing had an adequate sample size, a statistician may be able to do a power calculation for you by using data from the published report.

If a power calculation is given in the study report, you can check whether the stated probabilities that type I and type II errors occurred are close to generally accepted statistical standards. For a type I error, the alpha level is conventionally set at 0.05 to minimize the chance that a treatment a researcher finds to be effective really is not. For a type II error, the beta level is customarily 0.2; this is much larger than the alpha level because it is typically considered not as problematic to conclude that a truly effective treatment is ineffective than to claim that a worthless treatment is useful. However, the relative settings for these error rates depend on the objective of the study. For instance, if a disease is often fatal, if no satisfactory alternative treatments are available, and if a new intervention apparently does not have serious side effects, researchers might legitimately accept a relatively high risk of finding that a treatment is effective when it is not (large alpha error) in order to decrease the possibility of missing a useful treatment (small beta error).

Were the outcome measures (end points) appropriate?

Outcome measures indicate how a treatment helps patients. An ideal outcome measure (that is, one that is least likely to introduce bias) is well defined, specific, objective, widely accepted as being clinically important, directly observed by an independent observer, and recorded in a comprehensive database.[16] Outcome measures include death, prolongation of survival, disability, morbidity (disease recurrence or prevention), physiologic variables, physical and psychological comfort of the patients, patient satisfaction, and financial cost.

The outcome measures used in the study you are examining may vary enormously from the ideal. On the one hand, death is a well-defined, specific, objective, clinically important, and easily observed measure (though cause of death may not be). In contrast, recovery is ill defined, nonspecific, subjective, and difficult to record. Suppose a study found that a certain drug increased the concentration of a "beneficial" blood enzyme (that is, enzyme concentration was the outcome measure used) in seriously ill patients but did not prolong their survival. Despite the study's positive findings, you may not want to use the drug because you feel the enzyme outcome measure is not clinically important.

In evaluating another study, you may conclude that the ability to return to work is an inappropriate outcome measure because most of the subjects were retired. A trial of an analgesic agent in which male patients were asked only whether the drug decreased their pain may not reveal that the agent also caused erectile dysfunction. Thus, any recommendations the researchers make will be based on an incomplete documentation of outcomes.

Your clinical experience is the key to determining the relevance of the outcome measures used in a trial. If you are unfamiliar with the issue studied, you can review several similar investigations to see which outcome variables are usually assessed. Be skeptical about studies with end points that are radically different from those typically used.

It is also a good idea to check for claim inflation. For example, the Methods section of an article describing the outcome of a surgical procedure states that the researchers recorded only the time until patients were able to get out of bed on their own after the operation. This measure is relatively specific and objective because it is recorded on nursing charts. However, when you come to the Discussion section, you find that this measure has been inexplicably and hyperbolically transformed to mean "recovery from surgery." In another report, the Methods section states that the getting-out-of-bed-on-one's-own measure was used throughout the study to mean "recovery from surgery." This may be more honest—but is it clinically accurate?

Was follow-up long enough?

The duration of follow-up should be appropriate for the clinical question being addressed and sufficiently long to detect major adverse or beneficial events, or to give a strong indication that such events are extremely unlikely to occur in the future. A study of a medication used to relieve postoperative pain may correctly have a follow-up time of only a week or two, because that is roughly how long patients need to take the drug. In contrast, an investigation of an agent used for a chronic condition, such as an immunosuppressive drug given after liver transplantation, should include months or years of follow-up so that both long-term efficacy and long-term adverse effects can be tracked. Valid assessments of many surgical treatments, such as those for coronary artery disease, vascular disease, incisional hernias, herniated disks, many kinds of cancer, and osteoarthritis of the hip or knee, may also require years of follow-up. In some studies—for example, the trial of an antiobesity intervention—a lengthy follow-up is necessary to determine whether a treatment effect is sustained.

Again, your clinical experience will help you ascertain how much follow-up is sufficient. You can also examine reports on studies similar to the one you are examining, along with review articles, to get an idea of the length of follow-up generally used in investigations of the issue addressed.

Was the statistical analysis used appropriate for the study?

As mentioned earlier, without consulting a statistician, you may find it difficult or impossible to determine whether the correct statistical tests were used. But you can still ask appropriate questions about the data analysis and identify signs that it may have been incomplete or inaccurate.

1. Were the study groups comparable?

All reports of intervention studies in which at least two groups of patients were compared should describe the analysis done to determine whether the groups had similar demographic and other clinically relevant characteristics at the beginning of the study. If some or all of the characteristics were dissimilar, the report should state that the data analysis included a formal statistical adjustment to mitigate the differences. In some studies, even if randomization was done properly, the patients randomly assigned to one group may, by chance, turn out to be significantly older than those assigned to the other group; one group may, by chance, have significantly more men in it than women; or the patients in one group may, by chance, have significantly more severe disease at baseline than those in the other group. However, statistical methods can be used to adjust for such baseline differences between groups. Check to see that this adjustment was made, but remember that the stronger the relation between the basic characteristics of the subjects and the outcome of the study, and the smaller the sample size, the more the differences between the study groups will weaken any assumption made about treatment efficacy.[17]

Careful study reports usually contain a table or figure (perhaps in Methods, but often in the Results section) listing the basic characteristics of the study groups and "usually giving the mean or median for the principal measurements together with an indication of how the subjects vary (for example, the standard deviation or interquartile range)."[18] Reports with no reference to the comparability of study groups may describe trials in which the groups were not really comparable because of faulty randomization that resulted in bias in group assignment.

It is important to remember that a big difference in the number of subjects in the study groups does not necessarily indicate a flaw in the study's design. Several statistical methods will take care of this type of situation; an example is an analysis based on proportions. The researchers should explain the difference, however, because it may be related to the issue of study dropouts (see Questions about Results).

2. Was an obscure or exotic statistical test used? Were several statistical tests used? Was there a lot of subgroup analysis in a study with a relatively small sample size? Are the statistical tests mentioned in the Methods section the same as those discussed in the Results section?

Asking these questions will help you to judge whether a study's investigators engaged in the practice of P-value fishing, that is, analyzing and reanalyzing data until a significant P value (usually <0.05) emerges. Even if you know little about statistics, you can (simply because you have read many reports on clinical studies) recognize the names of the common statistical tests. If the study report "describes a standard set of data that has been collected in a standard way but the test used is unpronounceable and not listed in a basic statistics textbook, you should smell a rat."[19] The odor may be less offensive if the researchers carefully explain why they used the test and provide a reference for it.

You may also be suspicious if the data have been subjected to multiple statistical tests or if there is a large number of measured end points. Statistical software for personal computers makes it easy to enter data once and then perform one statistical test after another, regardless of the appropriateness of the tests for the data or the data-analysis method specified in the original study protocol. Crombie notes that "as more tests are carried out it becomes increasingly likely that spurious significance will result."[20] Researchers who use multiple testing should defend their actions.

The use of subgroup analysis, like the use of exotic statistical tests and multiple testing, is sometimes justified, especially in large studies and when it helps readers determine whether an intervention will be useful in their own patients (who may be mostly elderly, or members of a minority group, or generally sicker or healthier than most people with the disease studied). Subgroup analysis can be misleading, however, because it "increases the chance of finding effects in a particular group that are not present, in the long run, in nature."[21] Subgroup analysis is dishonest when researchers pretend that their study was designed to assess a treatment's effects in specific types of patients, whereas in reality the decision to examine what happened in categories of patients was made during a poststudy search for a low P value. Personal computers make subdividing data easy, and the more the data are subdivided, the greater the likelihood that chance alone will reveal some "apparently interesting effects."[22] Therefore, be especially cautious about a paper that begins by saying, for instance, that the study set out to investigate the efficacy of a fertility drug in a diverse group of women but ends with the enthusiastic claim that the agent significantly increased the number of pregnancies in thirty-five-year-old Hispanic women who had one previous pregnancy and lived in a rural area.

3. Was an intention-to-treat (ITT) analysis used? Was it used appropriately?

During the data analysis in a study with an ITT design, all patients are included in the group to which they were originally randomly assigned, even if they did *not* receive their assigned treatment (or nontreatment) because they stopped coming for office visits, did not take their medication consistently, did not have the operation for which they were scheduled, or were inadvertently given a placebo instead of an active agent (or vice versa). Often the subjects who do not comply with a study protocol are those who are doing especially poorly; thus, excluding them from the data analysis would introduce bias because only the results in the subjects who did well would be considered. An ITT analysis "preserves the value of randomization: prognostic factors that we know about, and those we don't know about, will be, on average, equally distributed in the two [study] groups, and the effect we see will be just that due to the treatment assigned."[23]

The ITT design was originally used in pharmaceutical trials in which a drug was compared with a placebo or no treatment; therefore, a large therapeutic effect in the patients given the drug was anticipated. In such a situation, an ITT protocol is a very conservative approach to data analysis. Because the subjects are analyzed in the group to which they were originally randomly assigned, any noncompliance with the treatment will serve only to reduce the possible observed differences between groups. Thus, when a large difference is observed despite these conditions, it is very convincing.

In other circumstances, however, an ITT protocol is not appropriate. In an investigation to determine whether two treatments have the same efficacy, an ITT protocol can make demonstrating "equivalence" easier. Consider a trial designed to show that a standard drug and a new drug for arthritis have equivalent anti-inflammatory activity. Such a study might be conducted if the new drug is much less expensive than the standard drug. Suppose an ITT protocol is used and that the new drug is really not as effective as the standard drug. Then any problems that occur in the randomization process (for instance, patients randomly assigned to receive the standard drug actually get the new drug) will enhance the ability to show that the drugs are equivalent by reducing the difference in outcomes between the two groups of patients. Thus, the trial will not correctly demonstrate that the new drug is inferior.

An ITT protocol is also not the best choice for a phase II trial, in which the principal objective is to ascertain whether the agent being studied has even a hint of therapeutic value. Also, if the goal of a study is to evaluate the safety of a treatment, an "as-treated" analysis is more appropriate than an ITT protocol.

Questions about Results

The Results section of a paper describing an intervention study usually contains tables and figures as well as text, and all should be examined carefully to help answer the following questions (as well as to see whether the numbers in them add up correctly!). As with the questions about methods, some of those about results relate to statistics. Again, even if you have limited statistical expertise, you can spot red flags indicating problems with the study's data analysis.

Do the Results section and the Methods section match?

The descriptions of a study's groups of patients, outcome variables, and clinical and statistical evaluations that appear in the Results section of a paper should match those given in the Methods section. This seems obvious, but sometimes researchers refrain from mentioning test results that did not appear to add much information to their findings. Yet the very fact that little information was obtained (the test results were perhaps inconclusive) might be quite important.

Was follow-up as complete as possible? Were all patients accounted for? Who dropped out of the study and why?

These questions should be asked because patients who drop out of a research study are usually different from those who remain in the study. If the dropouts are not accounted for, the study will be biased in favor of the results in the patients who completed it. Patients withdraw from studies for several reasons: incorrect entry into the trial (it is discovered only after enrollment that the patient did not meet the inclusion criteria), a suspected adverse reaction to the intervention being studied, loss of interest in participating, clinical reasons (for example, pregnancy), loss to follow-up (the patient moves), or death.[24] Patients who drop out cannot simply be forgotten; instead, researchers are obligated to try to find out exactly why they disappeared and to report their findings in the paper describing the study.

Some trials appear to have a substantial number of patients lost to follow-up. How can you tell if this number is excessive? Guyatt, Sackett, and Cook suggest that one should assume that all patients lost from the treatment group did badly and that all lost from the control group did well, and then recalculate the outcomes under these assumptions.[25] If the conclusions of the trial change, the study's claims may be based on weak evidence.

How are outliers handled?

An outlier is an unusually high or low value (representing, for example, a result on a laboratory test) that is most likely to appear in a table in the Results section of the paper you are reviewing. If you see such a number, check to see whether the authors explain or comment on it. Reasons for outlying results include individual variations among patients and errors in measurement, interpretation, calculation, or proofreading. In statistical analyses, a few outlying values "can pull against the bulk of the data, creating misleading effects."[26] Thus, if outliers are present, researchers should explain how they were dealt with during the data analysis.

Were changes made in the study protocol after the trial began, to save time or money or because of untoward events?

In general, intervention studies should not change horses in midstream or return to the stable before the end of the race. There are exceptions to this rule. One is a study that is stopped because the patients in the treatment group began to experience serious adverse effects clearly related to the therapy. A second is an investigation in which the patients in the standard-treatment or placebo group are obviously doing so much worse than those receiving a new treatment that it would be unethical to withhold the new therapy from them any longer. Sometimes a study is stopped because the patients in the standard-treatment group are clearly doing better than those in the new-drug group. For example, early in 2000, one part of a large National Heart, Lung, and Blood Institute study of treatments for hypertension was stopped because one of the drugs being tested (doxazosin, an alpha-adrenergic blocker) was observed to be less effective than a traditional diuretic (chlorthalidone) in reducing cardiovascular events.[27]

If a legitimate protocol change was made in a study, the reasons behind it should be thoroughly explained in the paper. Some studies are shortened or otherwise altered because a sponsor stopped sending money, a researcher needed to rush publication because he was up for tenure, or the only data collector in the study with whom the subjects felt comfortable quit her job and patient follow-up visits dropped precipitously. None of these are scientifically acceptable reasons for modifying a study protocol, and of course the paper is unlikely to say that the protocol *was* changed—for these or any similar reasons. However, if many data seem to be missing from the paper's Results section, or a high subject dropout rate (more than 15 percent) is noted, you may feel some skepticism about the study.

Are both P *values and confidence intervals reported?*

Most clinicians understand that a *P* value is a measure of the probability that an observed difference in outcomes between groups was a result of chance. A low ("statistically significant") *P* value suggests that there was a true difference, in that it indicates that it is unlikely that the researchers made a mistake by observing a difference where none existed. The traditional cutoff point for significance is 0.05; however, the value used is a matter of choice and is often lower.

Reporting only a *P* value in a study may be insufficient, however. In fact, according to Yancey, "when statisticians talk to each other . . .

they find the use of P values by medical researchers a subject for much raucous ridicule."[28] The problem is that a P value alone gives no information about the level and variability of outcomes in the study groups; it is simply an arbitrary cutoff between significance and nonsignificance (and is there really much difference between P = 0.05 and P = 0.06 or P = 0.04?). Thus, an increasing number of editors of biomedical journals (many of whom are using statistical consultants in their peer-review process) are requiring that researchers include an estimated effect of the treatment—an indication of the strength or weakness of the evidence—because, in fact, the true value for the difference between treatments could be as low as zero (that is, no difference). This estimation is often done by calculating confidence intervals (CIs).

A CI represents the precision of an estimate of a value obtained in a study. Usually, a 95 percent CI is used; it gives the range within which the researchers are 95 percent sure the true value lies. For example, in a trial of an antihypertensive agent, patients given the drug had a mean decrease in diastolic blood pressure of 15 mm Hg, whereas those given a placebo had a mean decrease of 5 mm Hg—a difference of 10 mm Hg. The researchers stated that the 95 percent CI around this difference was 3 to 17 mm Hg, meaning that they are 95 percent sure (by virtue of a statistical calculation) that the true difference was within this range. Because the range of 3 to 17 does not include zero, zero (no difference) is unlikely to be the true value; therefore, the drug probably was responsible for the decrease in blood pressure in the patients who received it. If the range had included zero, there would have been evidence that the drug produced no reduction in blood pressure.

Statisticians consider CIs more informative than P values and often suggest that both be presented in reports on intervention studies. Does this mean that if the report you are reading includes only P values, you should assume that the results of the study it describes are not valid? Not necessarily, although you might have more confidence in those results if the "significant" P value is set lower than 0.05. On the other hand, the presence of CIs might indicate a degree of sophistication about statistical analysis particularly and study design in general that helps to assure you that the researchers really knew what they were doing.

Are the effects of the intervention expressed in terms of benefits and drawbacks for your patient?

When you recommend a treatment to a patient, she or he usually does not want to know whether it has produced a statistically significant difference in an outcome measure in a clinical trial. Instead, your patient and all other patients want to know how much better off they personally will be if they take the treatment, particularly if it has unpleasant or potentially dangerous side effects. Writers of papers on intervention trials should do their best to help you help your patients to understand the risks and benefits to them of a certain therapy. For this reason, researchers should report *all* the adverse effects of a treatment they observed, perhaps in a table in the Results section. Most treatments have some adverse effects, although they may be minor. If researchers report that no adverse effects occurred, they should indicate that they conducted a careful search for such problems that came up empty, and they should describe that search.

Researchers can also present values for relative risk reduction, absolute risk reduction, and number needed to treat. Calculation of these values answers the following questions.

1. How large was the treatment effect?
Treatment effect can be represented by the absolute risk reduction, which is the difference between the proportion of subjects with an adverse outcome (death, morbidity) in the control group and the proportion with an adverse outcome in the treatment group; by the relative risk, which is the risk of an adverse outcome in patients in the treatment group relative to that in control patients; or by the relative risk reduction, which is the complement of the relative risk

and is expressed as a percentage. A relative risk reduction of 34 percent means that the treatment reduced the risk of death or other adverse outcome by 34 percent relative to that occurring in control patients.

2. Are the likely treatment benefits worth the potential adverse effects and costs?

This question can be addressed by calculation of the number needed to treat, which is the inverse of the absolute risk reduction and equals the number of patients similar to those studied who would have to be treated in order to prevent one relevant adverse event. Guyatt, Sackett, and Cook note: "We might not hesitate to treat even as many as 400 patients to save one life if the treatment were cheap, easy to apply and comply with, and safe. In reality, however, treatments usually are expensive and they carry risks. When these risks or adverse outcomes are documented in trial reports, users can apply the [number needed to treat] to judge both the relative benefits and costs of therapy."[29]

Final Questions

In the Discussion section of an article describing a clinical intervention study, the authors should tell you what their findings mean and what they do not mean. They should not simply reiterate their results: they should interpret them. Although researchers are entitled to some speculation about the meaning of their study, their primary responsibility is to satisfy you with their explanation of the clinical implications of their findings.

The principal purpose of an intervention study is to find evidence of causation, that is, that a treatment causes patients to get better or live longer. It is crucial to remember that a correlation or an association between a treatment and an outcome does not necessarily indicate causation. As Cohn observes, "Remember the rooster who thought his crowing made the sun rise? Unless an association is so powerful and so constantly repeated that the case is overwhelming, association is only a clue, meaning more study or confirmation is needed."[30] If a paper on a clinical trial does conclude with claims of causation, you may evaluate those assertions by asking the following questions.

Are the results plausible?

Do the results make biologic sense? Check to see whether the researchers have provided a biologic justification for their findings with respect to what is known about the disease process and the intervention agent. Fletcher, Fletcher, and Wagner relate the following story:

> Some years ago, medical students were presented a study of the relationship between the cigarette smoking habits of obstetricians and the vigor of babies they delivered. Infant vigor is measured by an Apgar score; a high score (9–10) indicates that the baby is healthy, whereas a low score indicates that the baby might be in trouble and require close monitoring. The study suggested that smoking by obstetricians (not in the delivery suite!) had an adverse effect on Apgar scores in newborns. The medical students were then asked to comment on what was wrong with this study. After many suggestions, some finally said that the conclusion simply did not make sense. . . . It was then acknowledged that, although the study was real, the "exposure" and "disease" had been altered for the presentation.[31]

The lesson of this tale is that readers of a research paper must remember to think outside or beyond that paper. That is, they must avoid getting so involved in the authors' methods, assumptions, and conclusions that they ignore their common sense and clinical experience regarding causation.

The timing of the treatment effect reported in a paper should also be examined for plausibility. For example, you may have some doubts about a study claiming that a new antibiotic eliminated all pathogens from the blood within six hours. In addition, in most situations, the treatment studied should be found to be effective in a wide range of subjects, that is, in patients of both sexes and various ages. If it is not, the evidence for causation is not consistent.

Are the results consistent with those of other studies?

Well-written study reports include a concise, relevant literature review in the Discussion section. Here the researchers discuss studies similar to theirs and indicate whether the findings of their study confirm or diverge from those of previous investigations. A study with results that are completely different from those of similar studies requires a particularly careful evaluation, especially if the other studies have a more powerful study design. If you suspect that the literature review is unbalanced (only studies with similar results are mentioned), you may find it helpful to read reviews on the topic addressed by the study to get a better overview of the findings of earlier investigations.

Have the authors discussed possible limitations of the study?

Few studies are definitive, because most have limitations that may have produced bias. Not all sources of bias in a given study are known or suspected by the researchers, but some certainly are. For example, the sample size may have turned out to be too small to answer the research question, according to the researchers' own power calculation; or the data-collection method may have introduced a possibly confounding variable. For instance, in a study of an appetite suppressant, it may be that most of the subjects who took the agent were weighed midmorning and most of those who took a placebo were weighed right after lunch. Thus, the time of the weighing may have confounded the study's finding that those who took the drug lost weight more quickly than those who did not.

Researchers should include an honest description of the limitations of their study in the Discussion section of their study report, mentioning such factors as selection bias, follow-up method and time, and sample size. If the researchers omit this explanation altogether or do not cover limitations, you may well question their findings.

Do the study's findings have clinical importance, regardless of whether they have statistical significance?

This question, one of the most important you can ask about a study, is a summary query related to several specific questions discussed earlier. A clinically important finding is one that has implications for patient care, particularly *your* care of *your* patients, whereas a statistically significant finding represents a conclusion that there is a low probability that an observed event occurred by chance. As Lang and Secic observe:

> Statistical significance essentially reflects the influence of chance on the outcome; clinical importance reflects the biological value of the outcome. In general, small differences between large groups can be statistically significant but clinically meaningless. A difference of 0.02 kg in the weights of two groups of adults is not likely to have any clinical importance even if such a difference would have occurred by chance less than 1 time in 100 ($P<0.01$) or even less than 1 time in 100,000 ($P<0.00001$).
>
> It is also true that large differences between small groups can be clinically important but not statistically significant. In a study of 20 patients in which even 1 patient dies, the death is clinically important, whether or not it is statistically significant.[32]

Other differences between clinical importance and statistical significance pointed out by Lang and Secic are that statistics are derived from groups, whereas medicine is practiced on individuals; statistical answers are probabilistic, whereas medicine requires committed decisions; and statistical analysis always requires measurement, whereas medicine sometimes requires intuition. A well-designed study incorporates a balance, so that clinically relevant differences are found to be statistically significant, whereas differences that are not relevant are found not to be significant.

YOU, YOUR PATIENTS, AND
FLAWED STUDY REPORTS

There remains a "wide chasm between what a trial should report and what is actually published in the literature."[33] Several reviews have described serious defects in many of the study reports published in top biomedical journals.[34] Medical journal editors and formal and informal groups of clinicians, researchers, statisticians, information specialists, university administrators, and government officials are currently addressing these problems in several ways: (1) by developing statistical and nonstatistical guidelines for reporting clinical trials and laboratory studies; (2) by taking steps to mitigate publication bias (the tendency for papers that report positive results to be accepted for publication more often than those reporting negative results); (3) by increasing the use of statistical consultants; (4) by articulating policies on ethics in scientific publications; and (5) by educating readers through the use of print and electronic media. In the meantime, it is up to you to carry the torch of biomedical literature evaluation to illuminate the risks and benefits of therapeutic options for the patients who depend on you.

NOTES

1. Guyatt G. H., and Rennie, D. Users' guides to the medical literature. *JAMA* (1993) 270:2096–97; and Oxman, A. D., Sackett, D. L., and Guyatt, G. H., for the Evidence-Based Medicine Working Group. Users' guides to the medical literature. I. How to get started. *JAMA* (1993) 270:2093–95.

2. Greenhalgh, T. *How to Read a Paper: The Basics of Evidence Based Medicine.* London: BMJ Publishing Group, 1997; Crombie, I. W. *The Pocket Guide to Critical Appraisal: A Handbook for Health Care Professionals.* London: BMJ Publishing Group, 1996; Elwood, J. M. *Critical Appraisal of Epidemiological Studies and Clinical Trials.* 2nd ed. Oxford: Oxford University Press, 1988; and Guyatt and Rennie, Users' guides.

3. Hunt, D. L., Jaeschke, R., McKibbon, K. A., for the Evidence-Based Medicine Working Group. Users' guides to the medical literature. XXI.

Using electronic health information resources in evidence-based practice. *JAMA* (2000) 283:1875–79.

4. ACP-ASIM Online. *ACP Journal Club:* Purpose and Procedure. Available at http://www.acponline.org/journals/acpjc/marapr99/ma99pp.htm; Cochrane Collaboration. Cochrane Brochure. Available at http://www.update-software.com/ccweb/cochrane/cc-broch.htm; BMJ Publishing Group. BMJ-*Clinical Evidence*. Available at http://www.evidence.org/homepage.htm; and National Center for Biotechnology Information, National Library of Medicine, National Institutes of Health. PubMed Overview. Available at http://www.ncbi.nlm.nih.gov:80/entrez/query/static/overview.html.

5. ACP-ASIM Online, *ACP Journal Club*.

6. BMJ Publishing Group, BMJ-*Clinical Evidence*.

7. Fletcher, R. H., Fletcher, S. W., and Wagner, E. H. *Clinical Epidemiology: The Essentials*. 3rd ed. Baltimore: Williams & Wilkins, 1996.

8. Dans, A. L., Dans, L. F., Guyatt, G. H., and Richardson, S., for the Evidence-Based Medicine Working Group. Users' guides to the medical literature. XIV. How to decide on the applicability of clinical trial results to your patient. *JAMA* (1998) 279:545–549.

9. Crombie, *Pocket Guide*.

10. Meakins, J. L., and Barkun, J. S. Old and new ways to repair inguinal hernias. *N. Engl. J. Med.* (1997) 336:1596–97.

11. Greenhalgh, *How to Read a Paper*.

12. Cohn, V. *News and Numbers: A Guide to Reporting Statistical Claims and Controversies in Health and Other Fields*. Ames: Iowa State University Press, 1989; Byrne, D. W. *Publishing Your Medical Research Paper: What They Don't Teach in Medical School*. Baltimore: Williams & Wilkins, 1998; Lang, T. A., and Secic, M. *How to Report Statistics in Medicine: Annotated Guidelines for Authors, Editors, and Reviewers*. Philadelphia: American College of Physicians, 1997; and Fletcher, Fletcher, and Wagner, *Clinical Epidemiology*.

13. Greenhalgh, *How to Read a Paper*.

14. Fletcher, Fletcher, and Wagner, *Clinical Epidemiology*.

15. Greenhalgh, *How to Read a Paper*.

16. Byrne, *Publishing Your Medical Research Paper*.

17. Guyatt, G. H., Sackett, D. L., and Cook, D. J., for the Evidence-Based Medicine Working Group. Users' guides to the medical literature. II. How to use an article about therapy or prevention. A. Are the results of the study valid? *JAMA* (1993) 270:2598–2601.

18. Crombie, *Pocket Guide*.

19. Greenhalgh, *How to Read a Paper*.

20. Crombie, *Pocket Guide*.

21. Fletcher, Fletcher, and Wagner, *Clinical Epidemiology*.

22. Crombie, *Pocket Guide*.

23. Guyatt, Sackett, and Cook. Users' guides II A.

24. Greenhalgh, *How to Read a Paper*.

25. Guyatt, Sackett, and Cook. Users' guides II A.

26. Crombie, *Pocket Guide*.

27. United States National Library of Medicine. Clinical alert: NHLBI stops part of study—high blood pressure drug performs no better than standard treatment. Available at http://www.nlm.nih.gov/databases/alerts/bloodoo.html.

28. Yancey, J. M. Ten rules for reading clinical research reports. *Am J Surg.* (1990) 159:533–539.

29. Guyatt, G. H., Sackett, D. L., and Cook, D. J., for the Evidence-Based Medicine Working Group. Users' guides to the medical literature. II. How to use an article about therapy or prevention. B. What were the results and will they help me in caring for my patients? *JAMA* (1994) 271:59–63.

30. Cohn, *News and Numbers*.

31. Fletcher, Fletcher, and Wagner, *Clinical Epidemiology*.

32. Lang and Secic, *How to Report Statistics*.

33. Begg, C., Cho, M., Eastwood, S., Horton, R., Moher, D., Olkin, I., Pitkin, R., Rennie, D., Schulz, K. F., Dimel, D., and Stroup, D. F. Improving the quality of reporting of randomized controlled trials. The CONSORT statement. *JAMA* (1996) 276:637–639.

34. Yancey, Ten rules; Altman, D. G. The scandal of poor medical research: We need less research, better research, and research done for the right reason. *BMJ* (1994) 308:283–284; Hall, J. C., Mills, B., Nguyen, H., and Hall, J. L. Methodologic standards in surgical trials. *Surgery* (1996) 119:466–472; Moher, D., Dulberg, C. S., and Wells, G. A. Statistical power, sample size, and their reporting in randomized controlled trials. *JAMA* (1994) 272:122–124; and Pocock, S. J., Hughes, M. D., and Lee, R. J. Statistical problems in the reporting of clinical trials: A survey of three medical journals. *N. Engl. J. Med.* (1987) 317:426–432.

Part Two

Writing Science

2

Grammar Tips for the Information Age

Kirk T Hughes

The sheer quantity of information that twenty-first-century medical science must deal with calls for writing that is streamlined, clear, and concise. While authority was once granted to those who possessed knowledge, now it lies more and more with writers who effectively filter information to fit the needs of a well-defined, specific audience.

MEDICAL WRITING: FACTS AND FALLACIES

Before we discuss how to improve your writing, let's look at some outdated fallacies about medical writing.

Fallacy: I'm a health care provider, not a writer. No one cares about my writing; they care about my science, my know-how, and my skill.

Fact: Writing is not a career; writing is a skill that all professionals need to do their jobs. Your writing is an essential part of communicating your know-how and your skill. Sometimes all a person knows about you is what you have e-mailed, written, or published. For this reason writing should be at the top of your list of carefully honed skills.

Fallacy: If a paper is published, it must be well written.
Fact: Many of the published medical and scientific papers we read are poorly written.

Fallacy: I'm just not a very good writer. I don't have the necessary talent.
Fact: Writing is a skill, not a talent. Like any skill, writing gets better with practice. All health care professionals can and should learn to write effectively.

Fallacy: Writing has nothing to do with science.
Fact: Strong writing requires the very same qualities of thought demanded by strong science: logic, precision, clarity, and thoughtful organization.

Fallacy: My (department chair, mentor, supervisor) is well published; he or she will fix my writing for me.
Fact: Weaker writing gets published all the time, for all kinds of reasons. The people in your department may have no more knowledge of effective writing than you do.

Fallacy: I shouldn't start writing until all my ideas are clearly organized in my head.
Fact: One of the best ways to generate clear ideas is by writing. Writing, rereading, and rewriting helps organize your thoughts and develop richer ideas.

Fallacy: I'm going into private practice. If I'm not in academia, I don't need to worry about writing and publishing.
Fact: Writing is an essential part of professional life—wherever you practice. Memos, letters to physicians, newsletters, and patient-education materials need careful writing as much as case studies, journal articles, and grants.

Fallacy: Most science is poorly written; that's just the way it is.
Fact: Scientific and medical writing does not have to be poorly

written. These days the cost of mediocrity is not being read. The time of writers and readers alike is too precious to be wasted on ineffective or disorganized writing.

As data bombard the professional from every direction, the most user-friendly writing gets right to the point, supports its claims, and achieves a transparent style that lets data shine. The strongest medical writing is—

- Reader based
- Purposeful
- Clear and concise
- Correct
- Streamlined

REWRITING FOR CLARITY

Effective medical writing rarely springs forth all at once as fully formed Athena sprang from the head of Zeus. The strongest writing develops in stages, through multiple drafts and generous rewriting. While properly punctuated, grammatically correct, and error-free writing is essential in the sciences, the writing must be tight and clear as well. The most experienced writers know how rewriting develops these very qualities. Rewriting at the level of the sentence, at the level of the paragraph, and then again at the level of the complete work takes correctness to the next level; rewriting makes science more readable.

Streamlining the Scientific Sentence

English is a "verby" language, and readers prefer active verbs to passive ones. Although English sentences come in a huge variety of shapes, difficult technical vocabularies beg for syntactic clarity. In the age of estrogen-induced neurosynaptic plasticity, myocardial infarction, and the vasoepididymostomy, less is more.

Compare the following. Each example is correct, but which do you think most readers prefer?

A. The payment to which a health care provider is entitled should be made promptly so that in the event of a subsequent billing dispute we, the health maintenance organization, may not be held in default of our billing contract by virtue of nonpayment to participating providers.

B. Please pay health care providers promptly. Then if billing disputes arise, our organization cannot be held in default of our contract for nonpayment.

Most readers choose B. Clarity often comes with fewer words.

The subject-verb pairing in the following three sentence shapes helps to clarify the sentence's idea with straightforward syntax. Rewriting at the level of the sentence focuses the writer's attention on subjects and verbs. It gives the writer an opportunity to listen carefully for accurate expression and to choose economical phrasing. Remember a helpful rule of thumb: one good idea deserves one good sentence. In each of the examples below, notice the circled subject phrases and underlined verb phrases.

"A" Assertion

Think of simple assertion sentences as one-part sentences with a subject + a main verb. Simple assertions define, put forth, and clearly state.

- Clinicians treat patients.
- Clinicians meet, interview, assess, consider, diagnose, and treat all kinds of patients in a surprising variety of contexts these days.
- Too many overzealous scientific writers use obfuscating technical terminology when straightforward words will do.

"B" SuBordinate

In two-part subordinate sentences, the main part of the idea (with its own subject + verb) is conditioned on or subordinate to the other. *Separate these unequal parts with a comma.* Introductory phrases and subordinating words and phrases such as "although," "because," "when," "given that" (marked here with ͜) all signal subordination. Notice which part of each sentence can stand alone; which cannot?

- Although clinicians primarily treat patients, (they) also do research.
- When we overload our staffs with too much work, (stress-related) (symptoms) start showing up in departments all across the hospital.
- Because of the poor performance of many health maintenance organizations (HMOs) that serve disadvantaged populations, (health) (policy makers) need to reconsider hidden costs behind the much-touted benefits.

"C" Coordinate

Two-part coordinate sentences compare or contrast; both halves of the sentence's idea are equal in importance. Both sides of the sentence have a subject + a verb, and writers tie them together either with a *comma,* a *conjunction* ("and," "but," "so"), or a *semicolon.*

- (Clinicians) treat, and (patients) get better.
- (Clinicians) use different methods of treatment; (patients) improve at various rates.
- (Our success) rates have shown improvement during the first two years of implementation, but (we) are convinced that further promotion of these three new procedures will lead to even more significant health benefits.

TIPS FOR REWRITING SENTENCES

- Rewrite each sentence until you can easily identify its shape as an "A" simple assertion, "B" subordinate sentence, or "C" coordinate sentence. This process helps prevent wordiness, confusing syntax, and an array of punctuation errors.
- Circle main subjects and underline verb phrases to help you notice whether your sentence asserts, subordinates, or coordinates. Consider breaking longer sentences into shorter ones and varying the sentence shapes you use.

- Rewrite important (or difficult) sentences in three new versions, and replace the original with the best of the three. This practice sharpens your sense of phrasing, and it shifts your attention from "fixing mistakes" to aiming for clarity.
- Notice how these streamlined sentence shapes encourage use of stronger active verbs rather than passive constructions. The following list gives a wide variety of active verbs especially useful for rewriting at the level of the sentence. Circle the six to twelve that are most appropriate to your writing. Consider copying them down and posting them prominently near your desk, so they will be at hand the next time you need them.

acted as	conducted	distributed	implemented
administered	consolidated	documented	improved
advised	constructed	drafted	increased
allocated	consulted	drew up	informed
analyzed	controlled	edited	initiated
arbitrated	coordinated	eliminated	installed
argued	corrected	enacted	instituted
arranged	corresponded	established	instructed
assembled	counseled	evaluated	interpreted
assisted	created	examined	interviewed
assured	delegated	executed	invented
audited	delivered	expanded	learned
balanced	demonstrated	financed	lectured
built	designed	followed	led
calculated	detected	forecasted	located
chaired	developed	formulated	logged
chartered	devised	forwarded	maintained
coached	diagnosed	founded	managed
collected	directed	generated	manipulated
communicated	discovered	guided	marketed
completed	dispensed	hired	mediated
composed	disproved	identified	monitored

navigated	proposed	researched	strengthened
negotiated	protected	resolved	studied
obtained	provided	restored	summarized
ordered	purchased	reviewed	supplied
organized	raised	revised	taught
oversaw	realized	routed	tested
performed	received	scheduled	trained
persuaded	recommended	screened	translated
photographed	recorded	secured	updated
planned	recruited	served	upgraded
prepared	reduced	set	was active in
presented	referred	sold	worked as
processed	repaired	solved	wrote
produced	reported	specified	
proofread	represented	stimulated	

REWRITING PARAGRAPHS

Writers develop the qualities of unity, coherence, and flow when they order their sentences into thoughtfully focused paragraphs.

Order

Consider the order of your ideas by critically assessing your outline. Most scientific articles follow variations of the Introduction, Methods, Results, and Discussion (IMRAD) outline. Within each of these sections, writers have choices about which point to put first, which to put second, third, and last. Rather than settling for a coherent order, consider making even small changes to emphasize the strongest parts of your ideas as you lead the reader through your data.

Unity

Reread your paragraphs sentence by sentence to ensure that every sentence contributes to development of the idea. If the idea expressed by a sentence is off the point, or better suited to another section, move it. If a sentence is repetitious or irrelevant to development of the paragraph's main idea, simply excise it. Editors and grant reviewers consistently identify needless repetition as one of the most prevalent manuscript errors.

Transitions and Coherence

Ideas hold together well when transitions signal the route from paragraph to paragraph. Transitions connect ideas, indicate relationships, and keep the reader's mind moving in tandem with the writer's. Useful transitions include the following:

- Addition: moreover, further, furthermore, besides, and, likewise, also, nor, too, again, in addition, equally important, next
- Comparison: similarly, likewise, in like manner
- Contrast: but, yet, and yet, however, still, nevertheless, on the other hand, on the contrary, even so, notwithstanding, for all that, in contrast, at the same time, although, otherwise, nonetheless
- Place: here, beyond, nearby, opposite, adjacent to, on the opposite side
- Result: hence, therefore, accordingly, consequently, thus, thereupon, as a result, then
- Time: meanwhile, at length, soon, in a few days, in the meantime, afterward, later, now
- Summary: to sum up, in conclusion, in brief, on the whole, in sum, in short, in other words, that is

REWRITING THE COMPLETE PIECE

At this point, nothing helps your writing more than putting it away for a time, then rereading it with fresh eyes. For many writers, rereading a piece from beginning to end helps test the organization and emphasis of the ideas. For medical and scientific writers, this is an appropriate time to consider additions that will make it easier for readers to skim your piece intelligently.

Titles, Headings, and Subheadings

Choose them wisely. Be specific. Consider adding subheadings to help readers navigate any lengthy segments of text.

Graphics

Format or reformat your piece to conform to journal style sheets, grant forms, or publisher instructions.

Beginnings and Endings

One well-published biologist explained to a group of her postdoctoral fellows that a conclusion is inadequate until it has been written in three different versions, then in a fourth that incorporates the best sentence from each of the previous three! If any part of your piece deserves special rewriting attention, it is your opening words or your concluding ones.

Proofread

Better yet, make friends, brew strong coffee, and ask associates to proofread for you. Very few of us can identify obvious errors in our own work. Remember, associates need not be professional editors to help with proofreading. Consider giving a friend one or two specific things to read for. Multilingual speakers might ask someone to review a piece just to check the articles (*a* and *the*) that are so difficult for some writers who are English Speakers of Other Languages. Perhaps you could ask different proofreaders to check different sections of your paper: ask one associate to check over the Abstract, another to proofread the Methods, and so on. This procedure usually encourages busy readers to get to your work sooner. Whether you are proofreading your own work or that of a colleague, consider using some of these tricks of professional copyeditors:

- Enlarge the type on the computer screen (the change in font size often reveals previously invisible errors).
- Read backward, sentence by sentence.

- Read out loud.
- Pay extra attention to names, dates, numbers, titles, and addresses.

COMMON PROBLEMS

Rewriting is the best approach to clear writing, and being aware of the most common problems while you rewrite will help you avoid them.

Long Sentences

Long sentences contribute to lack of clarity in medical writing. It is difficult for readers to keep track of antecedents, multiple modifications, and difficult technical terms when sentences are too long. Remember the rule of thumb that urges one idea per sentence. Notice how length alone makes the following examples difficult to work through.

Examples

Assessing the above curves, it was observed that SR-OX displayed characteristics of a slow-release preparation, with considerably reduced maximum plasma levels appearing primarily at three hours but with more sustained elevated levels at twelve hours.

Note: Science is complicated enough without using overly complex sentences to describe it. Lengthy sentences are one of the greatest deterrents to clear science writing.

While few complications are seen in patients undergoing treatment for the former, patients undergoing treatment for the latter frequently complain of a variety of symptoms, including incontinence, frequency, and low-grade fever. This especially is of concern.

Note: When too much is going on in a sentence, the meaning can get lost. Vague pronouns like "this" only confuse things more.

Although the McMillan et al. Long Term Care Association findings contradict those of several previous nursing home and geriatric care center studies reporting higher risks of increased morbidity for patients with minor bacterial infections or who arrived with previous existing infections—they are virtually identical to the findings of recent cross-sectional studies including those by Linahan, Walsh, and Cooper et al.

Note: At 61 words, the sentence above is a challenge to the best reader. While many of the most artful writers in English use complex and lengthy sentences (Emerson, Twain, and James, for example), William Zinsser is right to suggest in *On Writing Well* that now "among good writers it is the short sentence that predominates." A wise and well-published department chair put it this way: "I love long sentences—especially Mark Twain's. A page or so read aloud to my kids at bedtime, and they're fast asleep—guaranteed."

Misplaced Modifiers

Misplaced modifiers are phrases that confuse what or who is being described. Writing in the passive voice usually increases this error, while using active verbs helps avoid it. The trick is to place the describing word as close as possible to the word it describes.

Examples

Confusing: By using an antipsychotic, Dr Smith was able to treat the patient effectively.

Clearer rewrite: Dr Smith effectively treated the patient by using the antipsychotic haldoperidol.

Confusing: While eating lunch in the cafeteria, the CAT scanner malfunctioned.

Clearer rewrite: While the technician was eating lunch in the cafeteria, the CAT scanner malfunctioned.

Confusing: Walking to the clinic, the missing pills were found.

Clearer rewrite: While walking to the clinic, I found the missing pills.

Confusing: To evaluate the feasibility of the study, the pilot data will be compared with previously published results.

Clearer rewrite: To evaluate the feasibility of the study, we will compare the pilot data with previously published results.

Misused Words

Medical writing often includes words and phrases that are misused. Below are some of the more common errors.

Examples

The patient was not toxic when she arrived.
Note: Patients can't be toxic; their condition may be.

Researchers must look at specific coronary symptoms in samples with and without a history of high cholesterol.
Note: Samples, like cases, don't have symptoms, patients or people do.

Please join Dr Schmidt, Dr Rossberg, and myself in wishing this project the best of success.
Note: "Myself" should be changed to "me." Many people are confused about when to use "I" and when to use "me," so they throw in "myself."

Hematologists must take the preventative measures specified in the guidebook.
Note: The correct word is "preventive."

We studied the effect of propranolol on the blood pressure of the heparinized rats.
Note: "Endorphinized," "heparinize," "coumadinize," and "surgerized" are not words! While they often serve as useful laboratory shorthand when speaking with colleagues, avoid them in your writing.

Amoxicillin can affect a cure.
Note: "Affect" and "effect" are frequently confused, for both words function as nouns and verbs. While amoxicillin can positively affect and contribute to comprehensive treatment of an ear infection (which might also include bed rest, fluids, and the like), it might also effect a cure.
"affect" (v) = to influence. The drug can affect weight gain.

"affect" (n) = behavior, outward appearance. The pediatrician noticed the child's inappropriate affect; the girl cringed every time her uncle spoke.

"effect" (v) = to bring about. Fluoxetine can effect dramatic personality changes.

"effect" (n) = outcome. What is the effect of trazodone on sleep?

Most often, writers use "affect" as a verb and "effect" as a noun. Here is an easy way to keep the spelling straight:

*a*ffect and *a*ction share their "a"; *e*ffect and *e*nd point share their "e."

Biopsy the lesion.

Note: Biopsy is a noun, not a verb.

The disease rarely impacts women over the age of forty-five.

Note: The word "impact" is misused as a verb. Usually it is best replaced with "affect" or "effect." For example, The disease rarely *affects* women over the age of forty-five.

The patient presented with rhabdomyolysis, i.e., an acute, fulminating, potentially fatal disease of skeletal muscle.

Note: The Council of Biology Editors (CBE) suggests that medical writers replace Latin abbreviations with plain English whenever possible.

"i.e." stands for the Latin *id est* (meaning "that is"), used to amplify the meaning of the previous clause.

"e.g." stands for the Latin *exampli gratia* ("for example"), used before a list of examples of the previous clause.

"et al." stands for the Latin *et alia* ("and others"); it continues to be used in reference lists to save space when referring to works with multiple authorship, for example. "Miller et al., 1987."

Passive Voice

In sentences in the active voice, someone or something performs the action of the verb. Thus, the following order is usual: subject, verb, object. Sentences in the passive voice lead off with the object.

Active voice: Dr Stuyvesant wrote the Methods section.

Passive voice: The Methods section was written by Dr Stuyvesant.

The active voice gives writing a sense of direct strength and energy. The passive voice slows things down. The active voice is not only stronger than the passive voice; it is 20–30 percent shorter. The prevalence of passive voice, too, is based on some outdated fallacies.

Fallacy: The active voice is self-promoting and shows a lack of humility.

Fact: If you are responsible for doing the work, there is nothing wrong with saying so. "We determined . . ." is stronger than "It was determined that . . . ," and "The study shows . . . ," is stronger than "It was shown by the study that . . ."

Fallacy: It is not good science to use the active voice. The scientist should stay out of the work.

Fact: Good science is logical, well designed, clear, and concise—as is good writing. Overuse of the passive voice results in confusing and convoluted prose because it promotes misplaced modifiers and separates subjects from their verbs.

Fallacy: Using the passive voice makes the writer less accountable—especially if something goes wrong.

Fact: Accountability is rarely reduced to matters of simple phrasing. Saying "The procedure was performed using . . ." doesn't make you any less accountable than saying "The investigators performed the procedure using . . ."

To change passive voice to active voice, reread the sentence. Identify the doer and the action (circling the subject and underlining the verb). Place the subject and verb next to each other, and make any other changes necessary for clarity.

Change: The conference was convened by Dr Jones.

To: Dr Jones convened the conference.

Most often, the words these changes leave out will be nonessentials: "is," "was," "by," "of," "that."

Passive voice does have appropriate uses; here are some occasions when it is preferable.

Examples

If the doer is unknown.

The patient was left just outside the emergency room.

Note: In this sentence we don't know who left the patient, nor do we care. The sentence remains clear, concise, and accurate.

If for discretion's sake, the subject should remain nameless.

The patient was never given his afternoon meal.

If the receiver of the action is more important than the doer.

Melissa Tolan, M.D., was named chair of the Department of Cardiology.

Wordiness

Avoid using long words when simpler words will do. Reading your writing out loud is an excellent way to check for wordiness. If it sounds pretentious or stilted when you say it, rewrite it.

Instead of:	*Use:*
accomplish	do
a limited number	one
an overwhelming amount	most
proportionally	some
in the near future	soon
is of the opinion	believes
make a statement saying	say
make an adjustment in	adjust
at this point in time	now
owing to the fact that	since
in spite of the fact that	although
is in violation of	violates
in the event of	if
to a large extent	largely
irregardless	regardless
take into consideration	consider

Words ending in -ality, -ation, -ize, -ization, -ational, and so forth often make sentences more complex than they need to be. Ask yourself if these suffixes can be removed without damaging the sentence; if you can use a shorter form, you probably should.

Instead of:	*Use:*
We made an application of	We applied
Researchers made the determination	Researchers determined
Nurses should provide appropriate information	Nurses should inform

Punctuation and Grammar

Appropriate punctuation and correct grammar significantly contribute to ease of reading. Given the difficulty of many medical and scientific technical vocabularies, proper punctuation helps guide readers through the sentences, paragraphs, and pages of what are often complicated ideas. Developing the habit of systematic rewriting does much to avoid grammatical errors. Knowing some of the most common errors can help as well.

Commas

Place commas after introductory phrases in subordinate sentences. These often include a verb or start with the words when, if, because, although, despite, since, or after.

Example

As you requested, I included the patient's X rays with the chart.

Because she understood the basic science, the pediatrician's explanation was more accurate.

Do not insert the comma when the clause comes at the end of the sentence.

Example

The pediatrician's explanation was more accurate because she understood the basic science.

Using the last comma in a series before "and" is a matter of style. While the *American Medical Association Manual of Style* says to put it

in, the *Washington Post Deskbook on Style* says to leave it out. In scientific and medical writing, the serial comma helps to avoid confusion.
Example
The patient complained of fever, muscle aches, and fatigue.

With dates that include the month, day, and year, put a comma after the day. When one of the three elements is missing, you may omit the comma.
Examples
His date of birth is February 15, 1972.
The study section met twice in October 1999.

With "and," "but," "so," and other conjunctions, use a comma only when there is a subject and verb both before and after. If the two parts of the sentence do not both have their own subject, omit the comma.
Examples
The committee members were all present and voted 12–2 to fund the study.
The committee members were all present, and they voted 12–2 to fund the study.

Semicolons

Use a semicolon to connect two parts of a coordinate sentence (in place of a comma and a conjunction); there should always be a subject-verb pair on each side of the semicolon.
Example
She graduated on Tuesday afternoon; she began work in the clinic Wednesday morning.

When you use the words "however," "therefore," "moreover," or "consequently" to connect two parts of a coordinate sentence, put a semicolon before and a comma after. When these words are used as interjections within a sentence, set them off with commas on both sides.
Examples
We had no intention of purchasing the equipment; however, we wanted to know everything we could about what was available.

Dr Hutchinson was a well-known expert in the field. He was, more-over, one of the most respected physician-teachers in the hospital.

Use semicolons in a series where other elements are already separated by commas.

Example

Dr Stein will present this colloquium three times: November 19, 1999; January 14, 2000; and March 1, 2000.

Colons

Colons introduce long lists and series. A complete sentence (subject + verb) must come before the colon.

Example

Here is just a partial list of the basic science that the next century's physicians can be expected to know: anatomy, physiology, organic chemistry, genetics, molecular biophysics, biochemistry, epidemiology, and biostatistics.

Hyphens

Hyphens join two or more words that serve as a single modifier before a noun. Do not use hyphens with modifying "-ly" adverbs.

Examples

He arrived at the ER with a self-inflicted gunshot wound.

She was moderately obese.

Quotation Marks with Other Punctuation

Periods and commas go inside the last quotation mark.

Example

Patients are often confused by the term "remission."

Question marks go inside quotation marks in every case except one: when the sentence begins with a question but ends with a quotation that is not a question.

Example

Did Dr Burton really say, "We need to develop more elaborate laboratory protocols"?

Semicolons and colons always go outside quotation marks.

Examples

The insurance company said, "The payment has been sent"; however, it had not.

Please remove the containers marked "hazardous waste": container 1, container 3, and container 16.

Exclamation points almost always go inside quotation marks.

Example

The attending physician in the ER yelled, "STAT!"

Subject-Pronoun Agreement

Pronouns must agree with their subjects. The word "each," like the word "someone," is singular and requires the use of "his" or "her." One effective way to sidestep the problem is to make the subject plural.

Change: Each study participant recorded their own data.

To: Each study participant recorded his or her own data.

or

Study participants recorded their own data.

Subject-Verb Agreement

Verbs, too, must agree with their subjects. Even if a phrase comes between subject and verb, the verb needs to match its main subject.

Change: The hip fracture, along with heart disease and pneumonia, are the top three threats to the health of America's older adults.

To: The hip fracture joins heart disease and pneumonia as one of the top three threats to the health of America's older adults.

Parallelism

The parts of a sentence that are parallel in meaning should be parallel in structure. In bulleted lists, it helps when writers respect parallelism with each item. Start all phrases consistently with verbs (or nouns) but don't mix them. In the example below, "rewrite," "use," and "proofread" satisfy conditions of parallelism as strong verbs.

Example
Medical writers need to—

- Rewrite regularly
- Use strong active voice
- Proofread carefully to catch punctuation errors.

Numbers and Dates

Use Arabic numerals when directly connected to symbols and abbreviations.
Example
The baby weighed 5 lbs 6 oz.
Use Arabic numerals any time you include numbers in a series.
Example
The ages of the patients in the pediatric study were 5, 7, 9, and 11.

Eponyms and Abbreviations

Technical names that are derived from names are called eponyms. Capitalize an eponym (as you would the name), but do not use the possessive when describing surgical and diagnostic instruments, materials, or solutions.
Examples
Cohn cardiac stabilizer, Foley catheter, Liston-Stille forceps.

Do use the possessive with eponyms that describe particular treatments or tests.
Examples
Balfour's treatment, Miller's method, Rosengard's diet.

Do not capitalize words derived from eponyms like fallopian or eustachian.
Example
The surgeon removed the diseased fallopian tubes and ovaries.

Plurals of all capital-letter abbreviations do not use apostrophes; for example, ECGs, EEGs, MRIs.

Example

The patient's ECGs showed many irregularities.

Grammar and Spell Checks

Grammar and spell checks on the computer are a boon to proofreaders everywhere; they are especially valuable in catching typos such as transposed letters that authors easily miss in their own writing. Save your computerized proofreading tools, however, for when you have completed a draft and you will probably find them far less distracting than at earlier stages.

Unfortunately, few standard programs include medical terms in their word lists. Keep a medical dictionary handy so that you can check the number of *rs* in hyperreninemic hyperaldosteronism. Nor will most spell checks catch "there" misspelled as "their" or "they're." As helpful as spell check programs can be, there is still no substitute for your own careful proofreading.

New on-line writing resources are being developed regularly. The BioTech Life Science Dictionary, for example, includes a free searchable database of about nine thousand technical terms at ⟨biotech.chem.indiana.edu⟩. Commercial medical editing programs such as Spellex often offer quick spell checkers on their websites (see ⟨spellex.com⟩), and they sell comprehensive medical, pharmaceutical, dental, and legal dictionaries on CD-ROMs ranging in price from $100 to $400. The resources below provide more on-line resources.

RESOURCES FOR WRITERS

Printed Style and Writing Guides

The best reference book is the one you have read. While these are some of the more helpful professional standards, also consult the style sheet of any journal to which you may be submitting your manuscript.

AMA Style Manual Committee. *American Medical Association Manual of Style: A Guide for Authors and Editors.* 9th ed. Baltimore: William & Wilkins, 1997.

The industry standard for medical writing.

CBE Style Manual Committee. *Scientific Style and Format: The Council of Biology Editors Manual for Authors, Editors, and Publishers.* 6th ed. New York: Cambridge University Press, 1994.

Especially good on international-style science writing.

Day, R. A. *Scientific English: A Guide for Scientists and Other Professionals.* Phoenix, Ariz.: Oryx Press, 1996.

A concise, useful, and readable guide focused on writing.

Schwager, E. *Medical English Usage and Abusage.* Phoenix, Ariz.: Oryx Press, 1990.

An excellent guide to medical word usage; as enjoyable to read as it is meticulous.

On-line

Style manuals are increasingly becoming available on-line for keystroke access to whole hosts of information. University and professional associations are exceptional at identifying, ordering, and keeping current the most well-designed websites. The following is a brief, but dependable starter list.

American Medical Writers Association

www.amwa.org

Includes a helpful collection of medical and technical writing links. A few keystrokes will get you to NIH, NSF, or excellent technical writing centers at locations such as Rensselaer Polytechnic Institute and the University of Colorado.

Biotech at Indiana

biotech.chem.indiana.edu

Includes a free on-line dictionary of terms in the biological sciences. Spellings and definitions are available with a few keystrokes.

Harvard Experimental Medicine

expmed.bwh.harvard.edu

The best comprehensive list of links to the sciences currently on the Web. Includes links to dictionaries and thesauri, an on-line *Elements of Style* (Strunk's classic), and field-specific science links.

Plain English Campaign

plainenglish.co.uk
Directed at legal writing, government writing, and the Securities and Exchange Commission, these on-line style guides include "before and afters" that demonstrate the power of rewriting while giving lots of useful tips.

University of Minnesota

www.biomed.lib.umn.edu
One-page style guides for the AMA, APA, and CBE at a university website designed with the distance learner in mind.

Web Style Guide

info.med.yale.edu/caim/manual
The on-line version of Patrick J Lynch and Sarah Horton's excellent foray into the next wave of publishing venues provides helpful models of just how effective writing can look on-line.

3

The Creative Process

Paul J Casella

In their view of the "creative process," too many people focus on the "creative" part and virtually ignore the "process" part. While there is a certain mystery to creativity that we may never understand, there are surefire ways to approach that creativity—the process—that can allow it to flourish. This chapter addresses strategies and ways of thinking about writing so that you can use your own writing, as William Zinsser puts it, "as a tool for thinking."[1]

Zinsser also says, "Take care of the process, and the product will take care of itself."[2] Rather than use writing solely as a means to record ideas, you must trust your writing to allow *it* to reveal your ideas *to you*.

A PAGE A DAY, EVERY DAY

To fully benefit from the process of writing, you must write at least one page every day in a log of your ideas. Not seven pages on Sunday: one page a day, every day, to make a record of your thoughts over time. This log is not a diary; it is a record of your professional observations, whether you understood what was happening or not. If a particular topic doesn't immediately inspire you, then write about the most interesting thing that happened that day, the funniest thing, the thing that made the most sense, the thing that didn't make any sense at all: try to fill your writing with an itinerary of the mystery that surrounded you that day. By writing daily, you will be able to gain insights that are otherwise unavailable to you.

The Weather Channel Analogy

When you watch the weather channel (or the weather report on the evening news), often the forecaster will compile what looks like a satellite view of the earth. Then the weather map is put in motion, and you can see twelve hours of weather condensed into a seven-second loop. This time-lapse record of the movement of the clouds reveals the various pressure fronts and precipitation patterns, making it possible to forecast the next day's weather. If you were in a space ship hovering over North America, would you get the same insight into the weather *in real time* that you get in the seven-second loop? No—the weather moves too slowly.

The insight into the weather that you get from the seven-second loop is the same kind of insight that you can get into your thoughts when you read your daily log. You condense months of thoughts into a couple of hours. You will notice that certain topics keep reappearing. You can identify patterns in your thoughts and in your approaches to specific situations—material that will allow you to examine more closely the issues that surround you. At the very least, this condensation of your thoughts will direct you to areas in which you are most interested and enthusiastic, areas that can benefit from your full attention.

Walking across the Brooklyn Bridge

In the fall of 1987, I worked as a paralegal on Wall Street for a year before going on to graduate school. Because I was a writer working as a paralegal, I had to find a way to write. So I bought a microcassette recorder and carried it with me wherever I went. Every day I would have to file papers at the courthouses in Brooklyn, so every day I would take the subway to the Borough Hall stop, file my papers, and walk back to the office over the Brooklyn Bridge talking into my recorder the whole time. I was no crazier than the rest of the maniacs walking around New York talking to themselves. The transcriptions of those tapes ran to more than four hundred pages. After editing out the junk, I came away with forty or fifty pages of condensed, tight, interesting material—material I was proud to share with my colleagues.

Wax Pencils in the Shower

Can any of us sit down at a desk, pencil and pad at hand, and say "I'm ready for a good idea now" and get a good idea? Certainly not. When do good ideas occur to us? What are we doing when we get them? Usually our good ideas occur to us when we are doing *something else:* driving a car, performing surgery, working out, tossing and turning in bed, taking a shower. Cordell Jepson suggests that if your best ideas occur to you in the shower, you should get a set of wax pencils and scribble madly on the tile.[3]

To best use writing as a tool for thinking, you should never be more than a few steps from your notebook, tape recorder, or computer. Be ready to interrupt what you are doing for a few seconds to jot down your good idea. You will not be able to force creative ideas into being, but you *can* be sure to record them as they come. You can facilitate an awareness of your insights, and with practice recognize them more easily.

The Wright Brothers' Approach

The main reason the Wright Brothers were able to successfully put an engine on their glider and make it into a self-propelled airplane was their unique approach to problem solving. When they encountered a problem they were unable to solve, one brother would take one side of the issue and the other brother took the other side. They would argue. And when they reached an impasse, the brothers would switch positions and continue their debate.

By keeping a journal, you are in a sense creating a conversation with an imaginary sibling, your intellectual twin. The process of putting your ideas into a symbolic language—writing—and then reinterpreting them—reading—is to effect this dialogue. Argue with yourself as a means to flesh out your ideas.

THE INCUBATION OF IDEAS

My friend Abraham Verghese told me how he wrote his first book: "I got up every morning at 4:00 A.M., sat at the computer, and wrote. I wrote for three hours, showered, went to the hospital, rounded with the residents, had my day. And some days, somebody would say something that would trigger an idea that would solve a problem I had been struggling to write about that morning. I know it was not divine intervention. I know it was because I had been sensitizing myself to the issue by writing in the morning."[4]

This experience demonstrates what cognitive psychologists call the incubation of ideas. You should write not only for the ideas you've had, but for those that may begin to take shape. You can help to foster understanding about an issue by writing about it. Sometimes you can make things happen by writing about them enough.

The trust you should have in your writing is, to a degree, the kind of trust you may have in your religious faith. You should maintain a state of preparedness, so that when inspiration comes you are prepared to receive it. That means more than having your journal at your side. It means practicing your writing, revising for meaning and emphasis and clarity, and keeping your writing skills sharp so that you can record ideas when they occur to you and bring them into focus.

Turn off the Computer Monitor

At the 1994 meeting of the American Medical Writers Association, one roundtable discussion addressed ways to encourage the writing process. The most novel suggestion I heard that hour was that authors who write on the computer should actually *turn off* the monitor as they type their ideas, so that they do not get distracted by issues such as spelling and paragraph structure. Those are editing concerns.

One popular word-processing program inserts a wavy red line under every word that it considers misspelled. I find this feature to be an unfortunate innovation. As a writer, whenever I see the wavy red line, I stop what I am typing—indeed, stop what I am thinking—grab the mouse, click on the word, correct the spelling, then try to pick up where I left off. Often I struggle to remember my train of thought, and many times I cannot. I know that the wavy red line distracts me and inhibits the flow of my ideas. Consider turning off the monitor when you are writing your early drafts.

It is important, then, that we separate the two major parts of the writing process: the intuitive part from the editing part, the idea-making part from the clarifying part. Don't let small editing issues get in the way of bigger thinking issues while you are still busy thinking. Save the editing for later, after you have exhausted all your possible ideas.

Writing Is Rewriting

Writing is rewriting. Writing is 10 percent inspiration, 90 percent perspiration. If you begin a project knowing that it will take a number of drafts before it even *begins* to look like something you will want to share with your colleagues, it will be much easier to get material down on paper. Grant-writing consultant Audrey Shifflett suggests to her authors that they "get over the perfect draft syndrome."[5]

Writing Is Recursive

When it *is* time to edit, as you refine and revise your ideas so that they are as precise and as clearly stated as possible, you may decide that you need to go back and do more thinking. This is an encouraging sign. Editing your words has helped you recognize possible areas for clarification. In this sense, writing is a recursive activity. You think, write, refine, and revise as many times as necessary to improve your ideas and make your message available to your readers. Some argue that a piece of writing is never finished, that it can always be improved.

TIME FOR FEEDBACK

After a few revisions, you no longer are your own best editor. You are too close to the material to be able to see gaps in the reasoning or awkward turns of phrase. Your natural bias as author may prevent you from addressing issues that others may find it necessary to address. It is time for a more objective set of eyes to read your manuscript and provide feedback.

It is best to solicit editorial feedback from people you trust, people who are acquainted with the content, people who are unafraid of letting you know what they really think. It is particularly helpful if you have an agreement with a colleague: you edit my manuscript, I'll edit yours.

Be sure you make your editor's job as easy as possible. Double-space the pages of your draft in a font that is at least 14 point, with plenty of room in the margins for comments. Going to run your manuscript by your mentor? Consider using only the left half of the page, so that he or she has plenty of room to write suggestions.

Do not despair if your draft is returned full of red marks, or if the journal has rejected your submission or given you a conditional acceptance with twenty-five topics to address. Be positive: you have been given an opportunity to improve your thoughts, thoughts that once published will be an official part of the scientific literature, thoughts for which you will be intellectually responsible. Be glad that your dedication to the process of writing has caught these issues before publication. View this moment as an opportunity to think even more profound thoughts. If you approach your next revision with this attitude, it becomes much easier to complete it, and you stand a better chance of addressing the needs of your readers and improving the quality of your information.

Journal editors ask me to remind potential authors that they *want* authors to succeed: they want to publish solid, important, timely information that will further understanding and improve treatment and benefit world health. The fact that considerable editorial time is spent rejecting manuscripts doesn't mean that editors want to reject yours. Your job as an author is to make your writing as clear as possible so that the reader's job of interpreting your ideas is as easy as possible. And your first readers are the editors and reviewers of the journal.

A WAY TO BEGIN

To get you started writing, I suggest you open to the first page of your daily journal (or open a new computer file), and write your first entry in response to the following. It is a real Request for Submissions for a real book I am editing, and I welcome your submissions.

Request for Submission

How do we get ideas? *The Genesis of Ideas* will be a collection of short essays from thinkers in diverse fields who discuss how they got their best ideas.

Please consider writing and submitting a piece that traces the thinking behind the formulation of a specific idea. How did the idea come about? What events or situations helped foster the idea? What encouraged the idea; what hampered it?

I am looking for stories packed with details so that future idea-makers can experience your creative process and learn from it.

Please submit manuscripts to

Paul J Casella, ed.

The Genesis of Ideas

1620 Morningside Drive

Iowa City, IA 52245

NOTES

1. Zinsser, W. *Writing to Learn*. New York: Harper & Row, 1980.

2. Zinsser, W. Personal communication. 1996.

3. Jepson, C. Personal communication. From presentation at Creativity in Research Workshop, San Antonio, November 13, 1997.

4. Verghese, A. Personal communication. March 21, 1995.

5. Shifflett, A. Personal communication. May 6, 1998.

4

The Scientific Journal Article: Approaching the First Draft

Catherine Coffin

I had always believed that giving an oral presentation about giving an oral presentation was the most anxiety-producing aspect of my job as a communication consultant. Now I know otherwise: that notion was replaced by the prospect of writing a chapter on writing a scientific journal article. So many excellent sources are already available; what could *I* add? My work with medical professionals struggling to write about their clinical and laboratory research has taught me that getting through the first draft of a manuscript is often the most difficult part of getting work published. So I have chosen to focus on that preliminary process.

My recommendations in this chapter are geared toward the inexperienced author, but I hope that published writers will benefit also. If your work is not getting published as often as you wish, or not in the journals to which you aspire, perhaps some of my suggestions will help you to meet those goals.

THE IMPORTANCE OF EXCELLENT WRITING SKILLS

At a conference of emergency medicine researchers that I attended a while back, I was intrigued by the large-scale response to the keynote speaker's question, "What is the most difficult part of doing research?" Although the most frequent answer was "Writing up the results," later that day the number of participants in my writing workshop was much lower than I had expected. Most professionals do not enjoy writing; rather, we like having written. We like having completed a project. We like having something finally published. But we do not like what we have to do to get there. At least we have the motivating force of "publish or perish" to goad us. The answer to "Why bother to write well; what's in it for you?" includes our desire and need to document our work in a respected journal in our field of study.

Beyond the realm of writing for publication, professional success and image are also in part determined by writing ability. Your writing often gives the first impression someone has of you and your work, your abilities, and your qualifications; it may determine whether you are invited to be a conference speaker or are interviewed for a new position. A person may not observe you hard at work, but does see an e-mail message, for example, that is poorly organized and contains incomplete sentences, incorrect grammar and usage, and misspellings. The recipient will probably assume that you are a careless communicator or that you lack intelligence. If you are hoping to receive research funding, the task of writing a grant application may be so daunting that you delay the process until close to the deadline and do not get the priority score necessary for funding. Professional success is not necessarily determined by a high grade-point average, a degree from a prestigious school, or the number of hours worked, but rather by excellent communication skills, including professional writing.

What is good writing? How do you know it when you see it? Imagine that you have just read a scientific abstract written by a colleague and you think, "This is well written." What does that mean? Most medical professionals will answer that the writing is clear, well organized, and flows. What does "clear" mean? What does a well-organized abstract look like? And how in the world do you define "flow"?

Excellent medical or scientific writing can be described as writing that is concise, correct, complete, consistent, convincing, and reader based (appropriate for the intended reader). If your writing is not scientifically correct, it does not matter whether it has all the other desirable attributes; your manuscript will not be published in a peer-reviewed, well-edited journal. (Usually, the term "manuscript" refers only to the physical representation—the pages or computer file—of your "paper" or "report," which represents the actual scientific content. In this chapter I use the terms interchangeably.) If we assume that your science is sound, you can begin to improve your writing by concentrating on achieving clarity and conciseness.

Achieving Clarity

Suppose I write in an abstract, "It is not uncommon for patients who undergo this new procedure to experience significant headaches." What does "not uncommon" mean? What is a "significant" headache? Left undefined, these terms mean different things to different readers. To achieve clarity, aim for using the most precise words and phrases possible so that you do not leave your ideas open to interpretation. It is not sufficient for you to understand what you are saying; rather, each reader's full understanding is the most important consideration. My example illustrates the difference between what may be acceptable in spoken medical communication and what is acceptable or appropriate in formal medical writing. If I use the phrase "not uncommon" in a face-to-face conversation with a colleague, that person can gain clues to my intended meaning by my gestures, facial expressions, and the tone of my voice, and can question me for clarification. Your readers do not have that opportunity.

Beware also of the tendency to lose clarity when the information you are writing about constitutes bad news or negative results. Refrain from writing sentences such as "The procedure is not without considerable danger." Double negative constructions are confusing, and your attempt at obfuscation (whether intentional or unintentional) will be seen as such by reviewers and editors. For further assistance on how to write more clearly and correctly, refer to Chapter 2 or to one of several classic books on rhetoric (see Resources).

Good News, Bad News, and Myths

Writing is a skill, not a talent. It can be learned, but you must practice to become proficient. No one is born a superb writer, although I have worked with two physicians—only two—who I believe were born with the gift of excellent language skills. These individuals have had scientific journal articles published without revision, a very rare occurrence. For the rest of us, only regular practice improves our writing. By itself, reading about good writing will not improve your ability. Some medical faculty members assign their residents frequent, short writing tasks, such as a response to a controversial journal article, in the form of a letter to the editor that is never mailed. This type of exercise provides the writing practice necessary to improve your skills, without the anxiety associated with submitting your work for review.

In addition to practice, regular reading of high-quality writing by others helps you to write better yourself. Not only will your vocabulary improve, but you will also begin to identify ways to organize ideas, construct logical arguments, and use effective transitions between paragraphs and sections. (For recommendations of well-written scientific papers to read, see Byrne's *Publishing Your Medical Research Paper.*)

Another suggestion for improving your professional writing is to challenge some of the myths you may believe about writing, namely that bigger words and longer sentences are better, and that if you use them in your writing you will look smarter. Think back to your high school years. When the teacher announced a writing assignment, what was the next question someone in the class asked after "When is it due?" It was probably "How long does it have to be?" If the teacher expected a ten-page paper and you did not have enough material to fill ten pages, you probably resorted to finding bigger words in a thesaurus and crafting longer sentences filled with lots of adjectives, repetition, and redundancy.

This secondary school flashback illustrates why you and many other professionals have difficulty writing clearly and concisely. You spent many years perfecting a technique that often rewarded you with a good grade, even though you may have had little that was worthwhile to say. Now you need to consider that scientific journals value conciseness, if only because they can publish the same number of articles on fewer pages if the articles are shorter. Similarly, editors and readers alike appreciate shorter words. If you have the option of using a short word or a long word (say, "use" or "utilize"), choose the shorter word. You are more likely to spell it correctly and use it correctly. The most admired writers are those who can explain complex scientific ideas with the fewest and shortest words possible.

COMMON WRITING PROBLEMS

Getting Started

Many authors agree that the most difficult part of writing a scientific paper is getting started. We procrastinate because the dread of staring at the blank page or computer screen while surrounded by piles of books, reprints, and note cards is overwhelming. In addition, if we predict that we need two hours to complete a writing task, the work gets put off because very few of us have two free hours in which to write without interruption.

The goal is to make the task easier by using short periods and by turning off your internal editor. One technique is called freewriting, which results in quantity, if not quality, of words, the premise being that it is always easier to edit than it is to write from scratch. Set a timer for twenty minutes; your goal is to write about your topic without pausing to check your spelling, grammar, data, and references. (If English is not your native language, consider freewriting in the language with which you are most comfortable; the only goal at this point is to get words on paper.) Because you have turned off your internal editor—the voice that insists you stop to make certain that what you have written is perfect—at the end of twenty minutes you will have a significant amount of material. By reviewing your rough draft for its main ideas and supporting details, you will gain insight into how to organize your material. (This aspect of freewriting is especially helpful for those of us who are not proficient at creating outlines before we begin to write.) After several freewriting sessions, you will have accumulated sufficient text to motivate you to complete your first draft.

Overuse of the Passive Voice

One reason that you may have trouble writing clearly is that you have read a lot of *un*clear writing. Many scientific textbooks are poorly written or inconsistently edited. Just because a piece of writing has been published does not mean it is well written. If you have to read a sentence several times to detect its meaning, usually it is not because you are too tired or not intelligent enough, it is because the writing is substandard or the writer has overused the passive voice.

One of the ways you can improve your writing is to write more often in the active voice. Active and passive do not refer to tense (that is, to past-tense or present-tense verbs); rather, writing done in the active voice makes it clear to the reader who or what is performing the action in your sentences.

Examples

Passive voice: The clinical data for 404 patients with Type 2 diabetes and left ventricular hypertrophy who underwent acute ACE inhibitor therapy between January 1997 and December 1999 at the University of Oklahoma Health Sciences Center were analyzed.

Active voice: The University of Oklahoma Health Sciences Center (or We) analyzed the clinical data for 404 patients with Type 2 diabetes and left ventricular hypertrophy who underwent acute ACE inhibitor therapy between January 1997 and December 1999.

Passive voice: It is concluded that this method can detect pulmonary edema and congestion.

Active voice: This method detects pulmonary edema and congestion.

A common misconception about the active voice is that it requires writing in the first person (that is, starting sentences with "We" or "I"). Although writing in the first person is one way to write in the active voice, there are other ways, as my examples illustrate. For busy professionals who are looking for timesaving tips and who need motivation, writing more frequently in the active voice will make your sentences (and your documents) shorter. The abstract that you hope will result in a trip to the convention in Hawaii next February might fit inside the nonreproducible blue-lined rectangle on the abstract submission form without your resorting to the smallest typeface allowed and overusing abbreviations and acronyms. Also, you will have fewer grammatical errors, such as dangling participles (see page 49) and other misplaced modifiers.

Writing will be easier because you are thinking in the active, not the passive, voice. For example, if you were asked to describe something you did yesterday, you would be more apt to say, "I went to the medical school to teach a class," than "A class was taught by me at the medical school."

Too Many Nouns

Another way to create more concise writing is to include more verbs than nouns in your sentences. Abstract nouns, including words that end in the suffixes -tion, -sion, -ing, or -ment, slow down your reader and impede the flow of the writing. Of the following two sentences, which is more clear and has better flow?

1. Our findings have resulted in an improved understanding of the probable types of transmission, as well as a means of identification of patients at risk for infection.
2. From our findings we understand better how the infection is transmitted and how to identify patients at risk.

Most readers will choose the second as the better sentence without realizing that the first sentence contains more nouns than verbs and the second contains more verbs than nouns. Verbs are the action words of the English language; using them abundantly usually results in shorter, clearer, more interesting writing. In the first drafts of your documents, underline all the words that end in the four suffixes I have singled out. Most likely, these abstract nouns can be changed back to the verbs from which they were created. In the sample sentences above, I changed "understanding" to "understand"; "transmission" to "transmitted"; and "identification" to "identify."

STRUCTURE AND ORGANIZATION

Beyond being clear and scientifically and grammatically correct, excellent medical writing is also well organized. For lack of a template to follow, many prospective authors of journal articles organize their writing based on the order in which things happened in their study, or the way in which they think about their material. This structure corresponds to the IMRAD format of the scientific research method: Introduction, Methods, Results, and Discussion. It is an order appropriate for the structure of the entire document, but not for the paragraphs that constitute the sections. More important, this model does not consider the order in which the reader expects the information, which may differ from the order in which you think about your topic.

If you do not know the specific needs of your audience, you might use a method based on the needs and expectations of readers in general. To understand this concept, imagine that when you arrive at your office you are greeted by a stack of documents that you must review for an upcoming meeting. You are pressed for time; how do you skim the material? You probably read the beginning and ending sentences of each paper, followed by the section headings and the first sentence of every paragraph. Why? Because you expect that the places you choose to read first are where the writer has put the most important information. Do the same for your readers; they will expect it of your writing.

Accordingly, in any document:

- Place the most important information at the beginning and end.
- Include the next most important information at the beginnings of sections and paragraphs (remember topic or theme sentences?).
- Place specific influential information at the ends of your sentences if you wish to persuade readers most effectively. Read the following two sentences to realize that the information at the end influences your interpretation.
  1. Although the treatment has significant side effects, it is highly effective.
  2. Although the treatment is highly effective, it has significant side effects.

WRITING FOR PUBLICATION

Abstracts and Their Titles

In terms of organizing a piece of medical or scientific writing, the initial obstacle for many presents itself in the form of an abstract. A well-written scientific abstract is a distillation of much thought, research, work, and data. It can be difficult to write because it needs to be so brief. The task is made easier by learning some of the jargon that is used to describe the components of an abstract and a full-length paper.

Although the final version of the title should be the last thing you write, you need to start with a working version. Skim the contents page of a medical journal and most likely you will find *indicative* titles of the articles (for example, a comparison of Drug A and Drug B in treating Disease C), which indicate what the study is about. In contrast, an *informative* title tells readers about the study's results and conclusions (Drug A reduces anorexia in the elderly). An informative title usually includes a verb and is similar to a newspaper headline.

The majority of medical journals publish indicative titles; as readers locate a specific article, they leaf through pages containing advertisements. In addition, most investigators are reluctant to make the bold statement often associated with an informative title (for instance, Lorazepam prevents recurrent alcoholic seizures). However, if you are making your way now to that medical convention in Hawaii, you may notice more informative titles than indicative titles on the abstracts printed in the list of presentations in the meeting guidebook. You will be skimming these reports of research or case studies to determine which presentations you plan to attend and which posters you are likely to view. Therefore, to write the first draft of a title, review titles already published in journals in your field or in the published proceedings of previous scientific meetings, as well as any instructions and sample abstracts provided by your specific organization or publication. (For detailed information about composing a scientific title, including the use of questions and subtitles, refer to the books by Browner, Byrne, and Zeiger, respectively, listed in Resources.)

Abstracts themselves may be indicative or informative. An abstract accompanying a review article may only indicate what the paper is about, offering a preview of the paper's content with sentences such as "X is discussed," and "Y and Z are compared." An informative abstract is a stand-alone summary of the paper, one that includes specific information about methods and results. An abstract written as one paragraph without headings is considered *unstructured*. A *structured* abstract includes headings such as Objective, or Background; Methods, or Materials and Methods; Results; and Conclusion (abstracts are too brief for a full Discussion section).

Three distinctions may be made between an abstract you are writing to accompany a journal article and one that you are submitting by itself for presentation at a scientific meeting. Meeting abstracts may include (1) a small table of data, a figure such as a line graph, or a few references; (2) more detailed information about the experimental methods and more actual data than an abstract for a journal; and (3) more implications about the importance or use of the research results than a journal abstract would contain. These differences reflect the notion that a meeting abstract may never be published as a full-length paper, and therefore it is necessary to include more data, detail, and implications.

Authorship of a Journal Article

Authors are not the same as writers. As a manuscript editor, I may help a scientist write a paper, but I do not deserve authorship because I do not meet all the necessary criteria. True authorship implies responsibility, and every prospective author should become familiar with the Uniform Requirements for Manuscripts Submitted to Biomedical Journals (see Resources). Among other qualifying criteria, each author listed on your manuscript should (1) be able to publicly defend the content of the study (for example, if called on in a gathering of peers to explain why there were only six patients in the study's control group, each person listed as an author could answer the question); (2) have read and agreed to the final version of the manuscript before it is submitted; and (3) have contributed significantly to the design of the study or the analysis of the data (one reason that statisticians often can claim authorship). The bottom line is that "gift" authorship (being listed as an author when you do not meet the eligibility criteria) is considered fraud. Researchers should not receive credit for work they were not directly responsible for doing. Establishing authorship at the outset—before any significant writing occurs—allows the primary (first) author to delegate responsibility for drafting specific sections of the paper. Another guideline to consider (albeit tongue-in-cheek) is "Never have more authors on your paper than you have patients in your study"; often there is a questionably long list of authors for a relatively limited study, such as a case report.

You may choose to recognize colleagues who contributed to the research endeavor but do not deserve authorship in an Acknowledgments section at the end of the manuscript. Check the "Instructions for Authors" of your target journal for guidelines. Some journals require that you obtain a letter from those you acknowledge, granting permission to thank them in print.

I recognize that it is difficult or unrealistic for a student, resident, or junior faculty member to negotiate with more senior physicians or faculty who insist on being listed as an author when that designation is undeserved. One must acknowledge the political nature of negotiating authorship and insist that academic training programs include realistic discussions of how to handle the process. Various professional organizations, such as the International Committee of Medical Journal Editors and the Council of Science Editors, continue to review the pertinent issues and have made various suggestions for dealing with the problems. Furthermore, the compulsion to pad one's curriculum vitae (CV) with a long list of publications may be decreased by the use of some form of citation analysis. For example, when assessing a CV as part of an appointment or promotion decision-making process, committees may use the impact factor of the Science Citation Index (produced by the Institute for Scientific Information) to assess the quality, rather than the quantity, of the list of papers.

Content and Organization (IMRAD Format)

Introduction

How then, and in what order, do you write the sections when you are ready to begin? Which section of the abstract or paper should you attempt to write first? Choose the easiest one, which will probably be the Methods or the Results, because you should be well versed on how you did your research and probably have created tables and graphs from the data you have collected. However, the sections are discussed here in the order in which they will appear in your manuscript.

The Introduction may be called the Background or Objective (especially in a structured abstract), or it may not have a heading. Start with a statement of the problem you have studied. Try to be as precise and informative as possible. For example, "Alcohol abuse is a serious problem among teenagers in the United States" is not as specific as "Alcohol plays a role in at least 95 percent of violent crimes on American college campuses." A statement of the problem gives your readers an idea of why you undertook the study. After informing your readers about the existing problem (hence the use of present-tense verbs; see Table 4.1), tell them what others have already done to study the problem or to try to solve it. For example, "Currently, three United States government-funded pilot studies are looking at ways to approach the problem of teenage alcohol use," followed by a concise description of only the most important references that highlight the problem and document what has been published. (Resist the temptation to regurgitate the literature in your introduction; just because you read many papers while reviewing the topic does not mean your readers need to know about all of them. It is your job to condense what is most pertinent and important.) Waiting to write this section until after you have drafted the rest of the paper may help you to write the limited introduction that most journals require; you do not truly know what your are introducing until you have written the rest of the paper.

After your statement of the existing medical or scientific problem and the relevant background information, you should include the reason for your investigation. Here is your opportunity to convince readers that despite other investigations and published work, the problem remains unresolved. To continue with the example of teenage drinking, you could write, "Physicians, psychologists, parents, teachers, and law enforcement officers disagree about the best approach to reducing alcohol abuse on U.S. campuses. Therefore, we designed a randomized, double-blinded, triple-somersaulted [I'm making this up!] study to determine which program, if any, was most successful in reducing alcohol consumption, crime, and academic

Table 4.1 IMRAD organization of scientific journal articles.

Section	Question answered	Verb tense
Introduction	Why?	Present tense for research question
Methods	How?	Past tense
Results	What found?	Past tense
Discussion/ Conclusion	So what?	Present tense for answer to research question

problems." Some journals publish the answer to your research question near the end of the Introduction; others prefer that the answer appear only at the beginning of the Discussion, Conclusion, or Comment section. In either case, use present-tense verbs for most, if not all, of the Introduction because what you are writing about, the problem, currently exists. Sentences that describe previous work done by you or others can be written as "Others have shown that . . . ," which is a form of the present tense.

Methods

The most common logical organization for the Methods section (or Materials and Methods, or whatever a journal chooses to label it) is chronological: you tell readers how you studied the problem in the order in which you did the research. Most Methods sections of clinical papers need information about the following: study design, setting, participants, interventions (what you did to the participants), main outcome measures (how you measured your interventions), methods of data analysis (statistical methods used), and patient consent procedures or institutional review board approval for the interventions; see Chapter 1 for details. In other words, the Methods section of a clinical abstract or a full-length paper should provide your readers with answers to the following: What did you do? To whom did you do it? Where did you do it? How did you measure what you did? How did you analyze your measurements? If the experimental methodology is complex, you may wish to use subsections with descriptive subheadings.

As always, the best guideline for how to organize this or any other section of your paper is to follow the style used in similar types of published studies. Writing and publishing a medical paper can be likened to applying for a new job: to land the job, you prepare your CV or résumé, cover letter, personal appearance, and interview comments according to what you know about the hiring institution. Moreover, your attempt to have your work published can be compared to creating and marketing a new consumer product. No company is going to invest until testing shows that your product matches consumer taste and demand. You should "test" your product (research paper) by having knowledgeable colleagues evaluate its appropriateness for your chosen market (the target journal's audience).

Most, if not all, of the Methods section should be written in the past tense (for example, "We studied ..."). In addition, much of this section can be written in the passive voice because it is not usually necessary to know who or what did what. "Chest radiographs were reviewed for evidence of lung damage" is fine; after an initial mention, your readers do not need to know that a particular radiologist interpreted the films.

Results

Several medical journal editors have told me, with some seriousness, that the ideal Results section of a paper would read, in its entirety, something like "See Figures 1 to 3 and Tables 1 and 2." Although no one likes to read an abundance of numbers and numerals in narrative form, you would never get your paper published with a one-sentence section. Rather, the Results should answer the question "What did you find?" and include the evidence and data you have collected to answer the research question(s) posed in the Introduction. This section should include little, if any, interpretation of your findings; only the actual results of all of your methods are appropriate. Interpretive sentences usually contain present-tense verbs—an indication that they belong in the Discussion section instead. For example, "The mean number of weekend alcohol-related injuries on college campuses with more than 10,000 undergraduates was 13" would be appropriate as a result, whereas "The decreased mean number of weekend injuries shows that the new program was effective" represents an interpretive comment about the findings that is best placed in the Discussion.

To determine the order in which to present the material in the Results, consider the way you yourself skim an article, a book chapter, or a report. You probably read the beginning of each section and paragraph before the middle or end. Therefore, when you present your results, think about your readers' expectations and place the most important result(s) first, followed by the less important results. Using the example of alcohol abuse by college students, you would want to place information about one abuse-reduction program's ability to reduce violent crime on a college campus by 70 percent before the data describing a mere 3 percent improvement in the same students' academic performance. You may decide to organize this section with subheadings that are identical to the ones you have used in the Methods section. The nature of your research project (complicated experimental methods, several experiments, or multiple medical centers) ultimately will determine the structure and content of your Results. Always consider using illustrations, figures, or simple tables to replace (not duplicate) numbers and numerals in the text. (Consult Mary Helen Briscoe's *Preparing Scientific Illustrations* and other texts for detailed information.)

Discussion or Conclusion

By the time you reach the "D" of the IMRAD formula, the Discussion section, you may no longer see the forest for the trees. Reread the question(s) you posed in your Introduction: the objective(s) of your study, the purpose, the "why." Resist the temptation to begin this final section with information about the relevant literature or with details about the data given in the Results. Instead, recall what it is your readers expect at the beginning of a Discussion (or a Conclusion or a Comment section in some journals and abstracts): namely, the answer to the question(s) the study was designed to answer. For example, if your study's objective was to determine whether a newly developed drug or a procedure (X) is safe and effective in treating a disease (Y) in a particular population (Z), your answer—the beginning of your Discussion section—should address the safety and efficacy of X in treating Y in Z. One way to ensure that you accomplish this is actually to write the following type of sentence at the start of your first draft of the Discussion: Drug X is _____ or is not _____ (check one) safe and effective in treating Disease Y in Population Z.

Rarely will your answer be this simplistic, but this technique should help you focus on your readers' needs and expectations and on structuring your comments in a way that provides the answer to the studied question, followed by how your results support this answer and the meaning and significance of the results. Next, you will need to include references to and comments about any previously published or ongoing work that supports and provides credibility to your claims, followed by work that does not agree with or limits the significance of your findings. Here you must admit to your study's own weaknesses, which might be too many control subjects lost to follow-up (see Chapter 1).

End the Discussion with the implications of your findings and results. Acknowledge that busy clinicians and researchers most likely will skip to the end of the article to discover how your findings will help them to diagnose, treat, or manage patients or to continue their own research. They prefer to see specific recommendations, or generally useful suggestions or information. A statement for the end of the Discussion of the alcohol abuse example might be, "Stiffer enforcement of underage drinking laws, an increase in substance-free dorms and fraternities, and college-sponsored alcohol-free concerts can reduce campus crime and alcohol-related hospital admissions while improving student academic performance." When reporting the implications of your research study, you may use what are called "hedging" verbs. Instead of writing that your research will or should alter the way all colleges handle alcohol-related incidents, for example, you might write, "Our research might perhaps/possibly could [choose only one!] change the way college administrators view their role in managing student alcohol abuse."

Writing a Case Report

Because your initial desire or assignment to "write it up for a journal" may not coincide with any current research project, you may be tempted to write a case report, or a case report plus review of the relevant literature. Begin by realizing that most clinical journals receive more case reports than any other type of manuscript, so the adage "Many are sent, but few are chosen" should be taken to heart. Not only must you have a case that is unique and interesting, but it should also present new information that will be useful to others in your field. Journal editors and readers want case reports that will alter or improve how they think about diagnosing and treating a disease or condition. The fact that you think you have a valuable case to report does not mean that the rest of the world wants to read about it.

Although the structure of a case report is more like a story or a sequential retelling of events, you can still apply the logic used to write research reports in the IMRAD format (the paper's final section headings will differ):

- Start with a description of the medical problem. Include a clear, concise explanation of why the case is unique or unexpected. Usually, only one or two paragraphs are needed to justify reporting the case. Include the possible causes of the problem, with a limited number of references to relevant literature. (*Introduction*)
- Write a concise case description with relevant data, a chronological "story" in which you include information about the patient's medical history, presentation, physical examination, social history, and family's medical history, as well as the laboratory tests and procedures used. In other words, what did you do to analyze the problem and what did you find? (*Methods and Results*)
- Discuss your findings (the evidence for your diagnosis and assessment of the problem). Argue for the case's importance; include the extent of your literature search to lend credibility to your state-

ments. Also include possible alternative explanations for case features. (*Discussion*)

- End with a conclusion and recommendations for readers who may encounter a similar patient (may not be required).

SUMMARY

Good medical writing is a process that involves thinking, planning, and rewriting. The result is a paper that is clear, concise, correct, complete, convincing, and well organized. Getting started is often the biggest obstacle, and procrastination has prevented some of the brightest professionals from publishing. Write the easiest sections of your document first, using short (twenty-minute) sessions. Turn off your internal editor in order to produce a rough draft. In science we are fortunate to have an organizational structure to follow: IMRAD—Introduction, Methods, Results, and Discussion. Within these sections organize your information based on your readers' expectations and the intended journal's style. Aim for simplicity and clarity in your sentences by using the active voice often, and more verbs than nouns. Use only language in your writing that you use when you are speaking. Study published articles similar to yours for a sense of section, paragraph, and sentence style. Finally, use recommended books for self-study; consult an author's editor; or join a writing group. Above all, read often and widely to discover writing to emulate.

RESOURCES

Books

Many excellent books are available to help the medical writer. Although a comprehensive list is not possible here, the following are useful resources.

Albert, T. *Winning the Publications Game: How to Get Published without Neglecting Your Patients.* Abington, Oxon, England: Radcliffe Medical Press, 1997.

AMA Style Manual Committee. *American Medical Association Manual of Style: A Guide for Authors and Writers.* 9th ed. Baltimore: Williams & Wilkins, 1998.

Briscoe, M. H. *Preparing Scientific Illustrations: A Guide to Better Posters, Presentations, and Publications.* 2nd ed. New York: Springer-Verlag, 1996.

Browner, W. S. *Publishing and Presenting Clinical Research.* Baltimore: Williams & Wilkins, 1999.

Byrne, D. W. *Publishing Your Medical Research Paper: What They Don't Teach in Medical School.* Baltimore: Williams & Wilkins, 1998.

Chicago Manual of Style: The Essential Guide for Writers, Editors, and Publishers. 14th ed. Chicago: University of Chicago Press, 1993.

Cook, C. K. *Line by Line: How to Edit Your Own Writing.* Boston: Houghton Mifflin, 1985.

Council of Biology Editors Style Manual Committee. *Scientific Style and Format: The CBE Manual for Authors, Editors, and Publishers.* 6th ed. New York: Cambridge University Press, 1994.

Davis, M. *Scientific Papers and Presentations.* San Diego: Academic Press, 1997.

Day, R. A. *How to Write and Publish a Scientific Paper.* 5th ed. Phoenix, Ariz.: Oryx Press, 1998.

Elbow, P. *Writing without Teachers.* 2nd ed. Oxford: Oxford University Press, 1998.

Goodman, N. W., and Edwards, M. B. *Medical Writing: A Prescription for Clarity.* 2nd ed. Cambridge: Cambridge University Press, 1997.

Hall, G. M., ed. *How to Write a Paper.* 2nd ed. London: BMJ Books, 1998.

Huth, E. J. *Writing and Publishing in Medicine.* 3rd ed. Baltimore: Lippincott, Williams & Wilkins, 1998.

Iles, R. L. *Guidebook to Better Medical Writing.* Olathe, Kans.: Island Press, 1997.

International Committee of Medical Journal Editors. Uniform Requirements for Manuscripts Submitted to Biomedical Journals. *JAMA* (1997) 277:927–934, or visit the American Medical Association's website (www.ama-assn.org).

Johnson, E. D. *The Handbook of Good English.* New York: Washington Square Press, 1991.

Joseph, A. *Put It in Writing: Learn How to Write Clearly, Quickly, and Persuasively.* New rev. ed. New York: McGraw-Hill, 1998.

Lamott, A. *Bird by Bird: Some Instructions on Writing and Life.* New York: Anchor Books Doubleday, 1994.

Nelson, V. *On Writer's Block: A New Approach to Creativity*. Boston: Houghton Mifflin, 1993.

Penrose, A. M., and Katz, S. B. *Writing in the Sciences: Exploring Conventions of Scientific Discourse*. New York: St. Martin's Press, 1998.

Porush, D. *A Short Guide to Writing about Science*. New York: Harper Collins College, 1995.

St. James, D. *Writing and Speaking for Excellence*. Boston: Jones and Bartlett, 1996.

Schwager, E. *Medical English Usage and Abusage*. Phoenix, Ariz.: Oryx Press, 1991.

Strunk, W., Jr., and White, E. B. *The Elements of Style*. 4th ed. Boston: Allyn and Bacon, 1999.

Weissberg, R., and Buker, S. *Writing Up Research: Experimental Research Report Writing for Students of English*. Englewood Cliffs, N.J.: Prentice Hall, 1990.

Williams, J. M. *Style: Ten Lessons in Clarity and Grace*. 5th ed. Chicago: University of Chicago Press, 1996.

Zeiger, M. *Essentials of Writing Biomedical Research Papers*. 2nd ed. New York: McGraw-Hill, 1999.

Zinsser, W. *On Writing Well: The Classic Guide to Writing Nonfiction*. 6th ed. New York: Harper Reference, 1998.

Zinsser, W. *Writing to Learn*. New York: Harper & Row, 1988.

Professional Biomedical Writing and Publishing Organizations

American Medical Writers Association
40 West Gude Drive, Suite 101, Rockville, MD 20850-1192
Tel.: 301-294-5303; fax: 301-294-9006
e-mail: amwa@amwa.org
website: www.amwa.org

Council of Science Editors
11250 Roger Bacon Drive, Suite 8, Reston, VA 20190-5202
Tel.: 703-437-4377; fax: 703-435-4390
e-mail: CSE@CouncilScienceEditors.org
website: www.CouncilScienceEditors.org

Institute for Scientific Information
3501 Market Street, Philadelphia, PA 19104
Tel.: 800-336-4474 or 215-386-0100
website: www.isinct.com

5

How to Ask For a Research Grant

Janet S Rasey

The task of obtaining a research grant, particularly your first one, can seem overwhelming. As with most large jobs, it is easier to contemplate when broken down into steps.

1. *Before you write:* Doing your homework first makes for efficient, directed writing when you finally put your hands on the keyboard (or your pen to the paper, if the old-fashioned approach stirs your creativity), and it gives you confidence that your efforts will pay off.
2. *As you write:* Preparing the application is easiest when you understand what points about yourself and your work you need to communicate, and what section of a typical biomedical proposal best allows you to make those points.
3. *After you've written:* After a grant leaves your hands, it must pass the scrutiny of reviewers before it can be funded. If, before you submit your proposal, you understand what reviewers want, you dramatically increase your chances of success.

BEFORE YOU WRITE

I call this the Know/No Stage of grant writing, because you need to know several things before you start to write; perhaps the most important is that there is *no substitute for a good idea*.

Know the Grant Makers

As with any audience to whom you write or speak, understand its composition in order to deliver your ideas and requests effectively. To obtain financial support of your work, you first need to know who funds grants in science and medicine. These sources are often "received knowledge." From your coworkers, you will know about the National Institutes of Health (NIH) and the National Science Foundation (NSF). If your field is cardiology, you have certainly heard of the American Heart Association. If you are an oncologist, you are aware of the many types of career development and research awards made by the American Cancer Society.

While the possibilities are legion, the best ways to identify grant makers are through the Internet and by networking with your colleagues and others in your institution. On-line, these three funding databases are the best general sources: IRIS (Illinois Research Information System), SPIN (Sponsored Programs Information Network), and COS (Community of Science). Each requires an institutional subscription, so check with your establishment's sponsored projects office or medical library. Each database has an intuitive Web-based search interface and will yield useful data for even a novice searcher.

Other important sources of funding information often include—

Your institution's Office of Sponsored Projects, or equivalent
Your institution's medical library
The acknowledgments section of other papers (who funded those authors?)
Publications and on-line services of the foundation center
Professional organizations, particularly for start-up grants

Know the grant makers' priorities. Several years ago I was shocked when I realized that the NIH does *not* exist to fund my research! The purpose of the NIH is to improve the physical and mental health of the people of the United States, and it chooses to accomplish that mission by funding research in medical centers, universities, and research institutes. The NIH fortunately employs a broad definition of "health related." *It is impossible to overemphasize the importance of proactively learning grant makers' priorities.* The most successful grant writers are often those who actively seek out the program office of their target grant maker and discuss their research ideas and plans. By being known to that program officer, they will have an advocate at the granting agency who often can provide additional information when the grant is reviewed.

Successful grant writers learn the explicit or implicit budget limits of their targeted grant maker, and they also get their application in on time. Many grant opportunities state maximum budgets, but implicit limits also often exist. Don't make yourself look naive by trying to do the research on a shoestring, and don't look greedy by asking for too much. A scientific research administrator at NIH recently told me, "Here's how to commit R01 suicide: come in with a budget of $300,000 a year." Senior investigators can credibly ask for more money than junior investigators.

Know Your Colleagues

In our research careers, colleagues are invaluable team members as well as sources of ideas and expertise. When you get ready to write a grant proposal, remember that coworkers can identify grant makers and may know which individual is likely to review your proposal after it is submitted. They also can review drafts of your proposal. The time to identify potential evaluators is before you start writing.

Know Yourself

"Know yourself" takes on a special meaning when you prepare to write a grant proposal. Beginning grant writers often find it useful to ask, "What is the 'big picture' of the research I want to do? What are the fundable subunits?" You can act on the answers by writing a one-page abstract of what you want to do, in language understandable by an intelligent nonexpert. This summary can form the basis of a letter of intent or a preproposal, items often required as the first step in the application process. Developing the big picture also helps you think of projects that might be broken out and funded with a small amount of money from one or more start-up grants. Many investigators have successfully launched their careers by patching together small grants from a variety of grant makers. This versatility makes them look like go-getters when they are ready to write a major application, and the approach also allows them to collect valuable preliminary data.

Another part of knowing yourself is to ask, "What do I do well?" Be prepared to prove whatever you say by providing preliminary data, listing your publications in the biographical sketch, referring to your work in the background sections, and getting letters of recommendation with sufficient detail and specific examples of your achievements for career development awards. Actions speak louder than words; preliminary data and other evidence of experience are critical parts of a grant application.

The converse of the above question is, of course, "What don't I yet do well?" In answer, you will need to find consultants or collaborators to help with new methods and problems, or perhaps learn new techniques to generate preliminary data before the proposal is submitted.

Be honest with yourself about how you manage your time. Many quotations about time have a message for grant writers:

"There is no *time* like the present." (Start your proposal today, not tomorrow.)

"*Time* is money." (Spending only a brief time writing the application usually means no money.)

"When you remodel your house, it will take twice as much *time* and money as you expect."

If you are the kind of person who likes to give yourself plenty of time to complete a project, recognize that writing a grant proposal will take far longer than you estimate, just like that house remodeling job. If you get a kick out of pushing deadlines, however, accept the likelihood that by submission date you will have a number of frustrated coinvestigators.

Be Sure You Have a Good Idea

Of all the homework to be done before you start to write, nothing is more important than developing a good idea. Poor writing can obscure a good idea, but no amount of skillful prose can disguise a bad one. What attributes do you assign to a good idea? I've asked that question many times in grant-writing seminars for physicians and biomedical scientists, and the answers usually include adjectives such as innovative, creative, exciting, testable or doable, and clinically relevant.

For a grant, a good idea needs to meet two additional criteria. First, the grant maker also must think it's good, and find your idea relevant to his or her mission. Second, *you* need to find the idea exciting and convey that enthusiasm in your writing. Do you like the idea enough to work on it, and the offspring it will generate, for three to five years? If a grant announcement is so specific that you must shoehorn your idea into the guidelines, chances are you won't sound very interested in doing the work—or won't enjoy doing it if you get the money.

AS YOU WRITE THE PROPOSAL

Consider how hard it would be for a journalist to write an enlightened, balanced op-ed piece on a political issue if she thought her job was to continue to be an investigative reporter. The physician or scientist who has published clinical or technical papers but has never written a grant application faces a similar challenge—shifting her mindset about the kind of writing she needs to do. As Robert Louis Stevenson said, "Everyone lives by selling something." The successful grant writer, to a large extent, lives by selling his ideas: a successful grant is a *marketing document*. This fact can be summarized in a simple equation:

A winning grant application =
a good idea + effective communication.

Authoring scientific or medical papers differs markedly from writing a successful grant application. Compare the parts of a typical biomedical paper to the layout of a research grant (Table 5.1). Consider the order in which most of us read a scientific paper: the Abstract first, the Discussion second. Persons who read a paper this way want an overview, then the bottom line or main ideas. The kind of "bottom-line" thinking that leads many persons to read the Discussion immediately after the Abstract pervades the minds of grant reviewers. It is no accident that most grants begin with an Abstract. The Background section, which comes early in a grant, is comparable to the Discussion of a paper, which comes at the end. Conversely, the Methods in a grant usually come last, unlike the Methods and Materials section of a paper (which comes right after the Introduction).

Get the important ideas in your proposal up front, near the beginning of each section. Follow the old adage: "Tell them what you are going to tell them. Tell them. Tell them what you have told them."

Virtually all successful biomedical or scientific research applications have certain attributes. Whether you do bench science or clinical research, reviewers expect you to think like a scientist. They want you to—

Ask *questions*
Formulate *hypotheses* based on those questions
Design *experiments* that test the *hypotheses*.

We often assume that this line of reasoning is natural for a biomedical scientist with a PhD, but less common for the physician without formal laboratory training—a physician who may have a more pragmatic approach to designing projects aimed at improvements in patient health care. The major deficiency in clinical research projects headed by principal investigators holding the MD degree lies in the technical methodology (62 percent of proposals in

Table 5.1 Comparison of sections of a scientific paper and a grant application.

	Scientific paper	Scientific grant application
Purpose	Describes what you've already done	Describes what you plan to do
Parts	Abstract	Abstract
	Introduction	Specific Aims
	Methods and Materials	Background and Significance
	Results	Progress Report/Preliminary Data
	Discussion	Experimental Design and Methods
	Conclusions	
	References	References
		Budget and Justification
		Biographical Sketch(es)
		Other Grant Support
Final goals	Construct a logical set of conclusions about your data and ideas	Get the important idea up front!
	Convince your readers that you have done careful work	Convince your readers that you will do careful work
		Get the money by selling your ideas

one large sample). The second most common problem is the absence of hypothesis-driven questions (45 percent of proposals). Interestingly, grant applicants who hold the PhD degree and propose clinical research make the same mistakes but at a slightly higher rate.[1]

Most grants that fail to get funded share some common features. A few years ago I conducted a national survey of NIH Study Section members, the investigators who provide peer review of NIH grant applications. One of my open-ended questions was, "What is the most common correctable fault in grants that fail to get a fundable priority score?" The most frequent answer (44 percent of the respondents) was "lack of focus," "unfocused," "needs focusing," or some other variant. Some time later, after I had finished my own second term on an NIH Study Section, I reviewed many of the critiques I had written and found that I too had cited "lack of focus" as a fault of many research grants that had interesting ideas but failed to be funded. Recall the earlier observation that no amount of good writing can shore up a weak idea, whereas poor writing (which often is unfocused writing) can obscure a good idea. Lack of focus is a particular problem for beginning grant writers, but fortunately it is readily obvious to those who review your draft proposals.

If a grant application lacks hypothesis-driven experiments *and* is unfocused, a reviewer may say, "This grant is a fishing expedition"—the kiss of death for a proposal!

Another real problem for many grant writers, beginning and experienced, is that they do not give themselves enough time. Six months before the due date is not too early to start working on a major grant, such as an NIH R01 proposal. Less time is required for smaller grants, but do not underestimate the challenge of describing your project clearly in five pages as opposed to twenty-five.

Successful grant writers know they cannot do it all alone, and they find reviewers for drafts of their proposals. Equally important, they leave enough time for these individuals to make their review—at least two weeks for the draft of a major NIH research grant. I often ask grant writers to identify the attributes of persons they would like to have to review their draft proposals; the answers always include variations on the following:

An expert in the field, to make sure that the techniques are correct and that the methods and literature citations are current

An "intelligent nonexpert," who can read the proposal for clarity and focus

A good scientific editor (especially important if English is not your first language)

Someone who has enough time and will invest it in you.

Parts of a Grant

With these general attributes and caveats in mind, it is useful to look at the different sections of a grant and identify winning strategies as well as problems to avoid.

Abstract

The Abstract is usually the first and may be the *only* part of a grant that some reviewers read. Liane Reif-Lehrer, author of *Grant Application Writer's Handbook,* says of the Abstract, "You never get a second chance to make a first impression."

A well-constructed Abstract serves as a mini outline of the proposal. If it has all the necessary parts, it will give a snapshot of the whole application. It should include a general statement of the problem being addressed, an outline of the specific aims and methods to be used, the expected outcomes, and the long-range significance.

To illustrate these points, let us compare two abstracts for a research grant on osteoporosis.

Abstract 1

Osteoporosis is a debilitating condition involving bone loss and affecting many postmenopausal women in the United States and throughout the world. A major consequence of osteoporosis in older women is fracture of the hip, an expensive and debilitating condition. Our research group has long experience investigating drugs that may reverse bone loss in osteoporosis and was one of the first groups to conduct controlled clinical trials with alendronate and related drugs. We also have long experience with new techniques to measure bone density and so are uniquely qualified to undertake the proposed work. Little work has been done to date comparing alendronate to estrogen replacement therapy, and we propose to make such a comparison in older women in a community-based setting. Standard combined ERT will be compared to alendronate. Appropriate placebo controls will be done, and we will be careful to enroll enough patients to guarantee

Table 5.2 Strengths and weaknesses of Abstract 1.

Strong points	Weak points
General problem to be studied, osteoporosis, is stated and presented as important.	Applicant gives no specific data to back statement that osteoporosis is an important medical problem.
Specific gap in knowledge about treatment is identified (no comparison between alendronate and estrogen replacement).	Applicant does not indicate how alendronate and estrogen replacement will be compared.
	Abstract is short on particulars: no Specific Aims given, no hypotheses stated, no expected results outlined.
	No reference is made to long-term goals or to how the data might be used.
	Applicants state they are experienced or expert without supporting data and give no specifics about future work.
	Undefined abbreviations (ERT, DEXA) are used; may be clear to investigators in osteoporosis but not to other readers.

statistical significance of our results. Bone density in hip and femur will be measured with DEXA at various times after initiation of treatment. In a selected subset of patients we will compare DEXA to the newer ABC and XYZ methods for assessing bone density, which may become important techniques in the future.

Table 5.2 reveals the strengths and (several) weaknesses that emerge when we apply the successful grant-writing criteria.

Compare Abstract 1 to Abstract 2, a proposal on the same topic.

Abstract 2

Osteoporosis is a widespread condition associated with more than 250,000 hip fractures each year. Although more than 90 percent of these fractures occur in individuals over 70, little information is available on the effectiveness, benefits, and side effects of therapy for osteoporosis of the hip in elderly women. We postulate that in women aged 65 and over: (1)(a) bisphosphonate therapy will maintain femoral bone mass, (b) estrogen replacement therapy will independently aid in maintaining hip bone mineral density, and (c) the combination of bisphosphonate and estrogen replacement therapy will have an additional positive effect in maintaining femoral bone mass; and (2) bisphosphonate will have the unique complementary benefit of increasing femoral and radical bone strength estimates. To investigate these hypotheses, we will conduct a four-arm, double-blind, placebo-controlled study in community-dwelling elderly women age 65 years and over. Initially, all participants will complete a two-month "run-in" phase of daily oral combined continuous estrogen-progesterone therapy to optimize compliance and reduce dropout following subsequent randomization. Following this run-in period, 368 women will be randomized to receive daily oral therapy with (1) bisphosphonate therapy (Alendronate 10 mg), (2) standard combined continuous estrogen-progesterone replacement therapy (Premarin 0.625 g and Provera 2.5 mg), (3) standard combined continuous estrogen-progesterone replacement therapy (Premarin 0.625 mg and Provera 2.5 mg) and bisphosphonate (Alendronate 10 mg), or (4) a placebo. The major outcome variable will be hipbone mineral density as assessed by Dual Energy X-ray Absorptiometry. We will follow bone density of the femoral neck, total hip, trochanter, intertrochanter, and Ward's triangle in addition to vertebral, radial, and total bone density and indices of bone metabolism at six-month intervals for two years. We will estimate femoral and radial bone strength as predicted by integrated measures of density and cross-sectional moments of inertia. We will investigate whether such therapy (1) will prevent

Table 5.3 Strengths and weaknesses of Abstract 2.

Strong points	Weak points
Applicant states that osteoporosis is important and uses figures to back up the statement.	Applicant gives more detail than is needed (actual drug dose, number of patients).
Applicant gives hypotheses (postulates) and outlines the study's aims.	Abstract is too long for current NIH format (although appropriate at time the grant was submitted).
Basic design and methods, as well as types of measurements to be made, are clearly outlined.	
Applicant explains how the data would be used.	
Applicant avoids obscure abbreviations.	
Abstract gives a snapshot of entire proposal.	

or reverse femoral bone loss, (2) will maintain or increase bone strength estimates, (3) has differential effects on hip, vertebral, or radial bone mass, (4) has differential effects on cortical and trabecular bone density, and (5) alters indices of bone mineral metabolism. Furthermore, we will determine if the response to therapy can be predicted by indices of bone mineral metabolism or vitamin D receptor alleles. Data derived from this study should provide the basis for an effective intervention to stabilize or increase femoral bone mass and reserve architectural integrity in elderly women.[2]

The second Abstract (see Table 5.3) provides clear information about the project and certainly fulfills the criterion of giving a snapshot of the proposal. A reviewer who read only this Abstract would understand the problem being investigated and why it is important.

He would understand the questions and the hypotheses behind them, as well as the overall design, specific aims, and methods to be used. The kinds of data to be collected and the long-term application of the information are laid out. Finally, this Abstract invites the reader to delve into the full proposal. Had I read this Abstract while reviewing applications for NIH, I would have been eager to read the full proposal and would have expected a well-crafted document from which I would learn something new.

Specific Aims

Reviewers often read the Abstract of a grant application first and the Specific Aims next, but some go directly to the Specific Aims. For either kind of reviewer, it is useful to construct the Aims to stand alone. Pretend the reader has only that page of the proposal. What will she learn? Numbered Aims that are preceded by an overview paragraph and accompanied by hypotheses give a clear picture of what you are going to do, the context in which your work fits, and the ideas being tested. The Abstract, in addition to giving abbreviated versions of the Aims, provides shorthand answers to the questions, "Why are we doing this?" and "Where will it lead?" The Specific Aims section needs to provide a fuller answer to the question, "What are we doing?"

To communicate clearly what you will do, consider the meaning of the two words *Specific* and *Aim*. To be specific means to avoid generalities. Don't talk around the subject by saying that you will characterize or describe a phenomenon, or determine the relationship between two processes. *Aim* is a verb as well as a noun. Your proposed work needs to point to a particular outcome. A Specific Aim that will collect data with no explanation of the hypotheses being tested or indication of how the data will be used sounds like a fishing expedition. Whenever possible, state a hypothesis for each Aim.

Consider a grant opportunity that might be offered through an internal fund in a large general hospital. The hospital wishes to encourage physicians, nurses, and pharmacists to write small proposals for studies that will improve patient care and compliance as well as reduce expenses. A pharmacist might write the following Aims for a proposal in response to such an announcement.

Example A

Specific Aims

Acyclovir is commonly used to treat HSV infections, but its effectiveness is limited by bioavailability. We propose to compare acyclovir to the new analog XYZ for preventing oral infections from HSV in severely immunocompromised patients.

Specific Aim 1: Compare acyclovir (t.i.d., 400 mg/dose) to XYZ (once/day, 500 mg).
A. Serum levels
B. Incidence of oral mucositis

Specific Aim 2: Determine if XYZ is more cost effective than acyclovir.

These Aims start from what probably is a fundamentally good idea for the type of grant program the hospital offers, but they are too brief and vague (Table 5.4). Now let us assume that the writer of this proposal consulted with a savvy colleague who has written many successful proposals. The applicant applied the advice and revised his Specific Aims. The new version (Table 5.5) is improved.

Example B

Specific Aims

Acyclovir is used to treat severely immunocompromised patients, as it significantly reduces the incidence of HSV infections when administered throughout the neutropenic period. Acyclovir has limited bioavailability and requires frequent dosing. The acyclovir prodrug, XYZ, recently proven effective in animal models, also allowed higher serum levels of acyclovir to be obtained (Phase I patient studies). We propose to compare XYZ to acyclovir in preventing oral HSV infections in patients undergoing bone marrow transplant.

Table 5.4 Strengths and weaknesses of Example A.

Strong points	Weak points
Introductory paragraph gives reason for the study.	Introductory paragraph is too brief, uses undefined abbreviations. What types of patients will be included? What is XYZ and why might it be better that acyclovir?
Basic study design is simple and can be conveyed in the Aims as stated.	Aim 1 does not really explain how the two drugs will be compared (inference that serum levels of active drug will be measured, and patients examined for incidence of oral mucositis).
	The term "cost effective" is not defined; can have different meanings in different contexts.
	Applicant does not state hypotheses.

Specific Aim 1: Compare serum levels of acyclovir in patients receiving oral acyclovir three times/day, 400 mg/dose, vs. patients receiving oral XYZ once or twice per day, 500 mg/dose.

Hypothesis: Serum levels of acyclovir in the groups treated with XYZ will be equivalent to or greater than levels in patients receiving acyclovir, owing to the greater bioavailability of XYZ.

Specific Aim 2: Compare degree of mucositis, using a standard scoring scale, and frequency of HSV infections, determined by weekly oral cultures, in patients receiving acyclovir (t.i.d., 400 mg) or XYZ.

Hypothesis: Acyclovir and XYZ will have equivalent effects, provided the treatments give equivalent serum levels.

Specific Aim 3: Compare the cost effectiveness of acyclovir and XYZ.

Table 5.5 Strengths and weaknesses of Example B.

Strong points	Weak points
Introductory paragraph frames research problem well. Applicant identifies patient population (bone marrow transplant patients), explains that XYZ is an acyclovir prodrug that revealed useful attributes in prior studies.	Introductory paragraph does not define animal models of infection used in preliminary studies with XYZ.
Hypotheses are stated for each Aim.	
Endpoints to be assessed in patients, and how measured, are clear.	
"Cost effective" is defined implicitly in terms of total drug cost.	

Hypothesis: XYZ will be more cost effective because, even though more expensive per dose, fewer doses per patient will be required for equal effect.

Here are two more examples of "before and after" Aims from a renewal request on an NIH research grant (see Table 5.6).

Example C

Specific Aims

The Specific Aims outlined below represent a change in focus for this grant, based on wanting to pursue some new observations made during the current funding period. These preliminary observations, and the reason for the new direction, are discussed below.

1. Further elucidate the role of DNA and chromosome (both interphase and mitotic) damage and early mitochondrial changes in drug-induced apoptosis in LK77 cells.

2. Determine the role of protein phosphorylation in the regulation of drug-induced apoptosis in the LK77 cells.

Table 5.6 Strengths and weaknesses of Example C.

Strong points	Weak points
Brief; easy to read.	Too brief; does not take advantage of the full page recommended for Specific Aims in an NIH grant.
	Does not start with a statement of broad objective. Introductory statement is vague. Uses terms like *elucidate* and *determine* without specifying what will be shown or investigated.
	Gives no idea which endonucleases will be isolated or what aspects of protein phosphorylation will be studied. What will be done with this information?
	No hypotheses stated.

3. Isolate and characterize constitutive endonucleases potentially involved in drug-induced apoptosis and necrosis.

Example D

Specific Aims

Apoptosis has recently been shown to account for 80 percent of cell death in leukemia cells treated with _____ , the new class of potent antileukemic agents. Our laboratory has become actively involved in synthesizing and characterizing new drugs in this class. We thus propose to investigate the following Aims in the LK77 leukemia cell line and two variants that are resistant, respectively, to Ara-C and methotrexate.

Specific Aim 1: Investigate the role of early DNA double-strand breaks (DSBs) and DNA-protein cross links in the induction of apoptosis in LK77 cells and their variants.

Table 5.7 Strengths and weaknesses of Example D.

Strong points	Weak points

Hypothesis: New drugs in the _____ class that produce mostly DNA DSBs will induce apoptosis more effectively than drugs that produce more DNA-protein cross links than strand breaks.

Specific Aim 2. Compare early mitochondrial changes (changes in membrane potential, increased mitochondrial proliferation) in LK77 cells treated with strand-breaking vs. cross-linking drugs in the _____ class.

Hypothesis: DNA strand-breaking drugs will kill more cells by apoptosis, which will be associated with earlier mitochondrial changes.

Using the blank form in Table 5.7, try to critique these revised Aims, using the principles outlined above.

Background and Significance

The Background and Significance section lays the background for the work you propose; it sets the stage upon which your ideas and experiments are displayed to full advantage. It serves a function similar to the Discussion in a scientific or medical paper in that ideas and results, those of others as well as your own, are discussed, compared, and brought together. Unlike a manuscript, the goal here is not to put new findings in a tidy box; it is to identify the gaps that your proposal will fill, the still-unanswered questions you will answer. Show how existing work lays the groundwork but does not go far enough. Begin by stating the problem you will address, and do so at the beginning of this section.

The Background and Significance section includes a selective review of the literature, but it is both more than and less than a traditional literature review on the topic of your research. It is *less* in that it cannot be exhaustive, and should not be. You demonstrate your judgment by the papers you choose to cite. The review is *more* than a literature review in that you are stating and defining problems. You use the literature and your own data to accomplish this and emphasize the links you are going to forge.

Use the four Cs of writing the Background section to shape this part of the proposal:

Compare and *contrast* the work reported by others. Don't just catalog what has been done, evaluate it.

Cite the literature judiciously. You cannot include everything, but remember that authors you do not agree with might be reviewing your grant. They need to be cited, respectfully.

Critique what you read, again respectfully; not all papers in the literature are equally valuable.

Preliminary Data

If a colleague or even a program officer tells you, "Preliminary data are optional," view this advice with considerable skepticism. No proposal was ever hurt by appropriate preliminary data. For NIH research grants, preliminary data are as optional as breathing.

One of the main reasons for presenting preliminary data is to demonstrate your expertise with the techniques you are going to use.

This is particularly important for new investigators without a track record of publications, for any researcher who is changing directions (for example, from physiology to molecular studies), and for projects that require teamwork to accomplish a study (such as complex positron emission tomography imaging protocols or clinical trials of treatment of addiction involving social workers, psychologists, and pharmacists as well as physicians).

Another reason for including preliminary data is to show that your hypotheses are supported by your initial studies. If you are developing anticancer drug combinations based on a proposed new mode of action, it would be helpful to have in vitro data documenting cell killing in cells resistant to more conventional chemotherapeutic agents. The dissection of the mechanism of cell death, confirmation in a wider variety of cell types, and efficacy in animal tumor models would then be seen as feasible goals of the project.

Which data should be included? Present only those that are pertinent to the proposed work. Beginning investigators who have few data may be tempted to include information that does not directly support the proposal under construction. Avoid this pitfall unless the data make the point that you know how to perform a new or challenging technique, which you will use when your grant is funded. The preliminary data should be weighted toward material that has not been published previously. Published data can be cited in the Background section and, if included in the Preliminary Data section, should be very closely linked to the proposed project.

How many preliminary data are enough and how many are too much? This is a difficult question to answer, so seek guidance from colleagues in the same field. You need to balance the expertise and feasibility of the preliminary data with a demonstration of need; you don't want the grant maker to believe you've accomplished so much that you don't need the money!

You say a great deal about yourself in the way you present preliminary data, almost as much as in your biographical sketch or CV. If you advance your data clearly and professionally, you send the message that you will carefully execute the studies for which you are requesting money. Sloppy data suggest sloppy work, and data presented unclearly imply that you think unclearly, too.

By the time you write up your preliminary data, you will know the material like an old friend. Try to have sympathy for your reviewers, who probably are seeing your data for the first time. (Recall that, all else being equal, happy reviewers usually are favorable reviewers.) Because these data are so familiar to you, this section of the grant particularly needs careful reading by an intelligent nonexpert.

- Organize the preliminary data into sections with headings.
- End each section with a short summary that states the significance of the work.
- Use graphs or pictures instead of text whenever possible. Most scientists are visually oriented, and it is still true that one picture is worth a thousand words.
- Use brief but descriptive figure legends, and make sure that the labels on your graphs are consistent and can be understood by the nonexpert. The graphs themselves should be intelligible without the need to scour adjacent text to decipher them.
- Use appropriate statistics based on replicate experiments.

Experimental Plan and Methods

In this part of the grant you get down to an expanded version of what you propose, as well as describing how you will do it. You need to give both an overview of your research strategy and the details of what you propose to do. This section is important for several reasons:

> To convince the reviewers that you have a clear overview and see the connections between the different parts of the research.
> To anchor the reviewers once again in what you are doing.
> To provide a framework for the details that follow—your description of methods and experimental systems.

An overview can be presented in a paragraph or two, but sometimes a flow chart or time line adds clarity to the text.

The details of Methods can be organized in many ways, but often it is effective to list the approach for Specific Aim 1, followed in order by Aims 2, 3, and so on. Repeat each Aim as it appears in the Specific Aims section, to orient the reader. Some techniques or systems may be common to several or all Aims (for example, cell lines and culture conditions, a rodent disease model, or a diagnostic test or assay). These items could be grouped in a general Methods section, separate from the specifics for each Aim. After reviewing hundreds of grants, I prefer to see a general Methods section after the plan for each Aim. I am more interested in seeing first how the general research design plays out in each Aim than I am in the fine points of the Methods. However, "the devil is in the details," and you need to provide enough explanation to convince the reviewer that you really know how to carry out the proposed studies. How much detail is enough? I often get this question from beginning grant writers, and there is no simple answer. You need to convey credibility but not appear to be so bogged down in details that you are unable to see the big picture.

Here are some considerations in determining how much detail is enough.

> An investigator with a strong track record may remain credible while writing more general descriptions, even for new techniques, because reviewers are convinced she will be able to do the work.
> If your Preliminary Data shows expertise with a new technique, you do not need as much detail as with an approach you will initiate after the grant is funded.
> If a particular methods paper is well known and respected in your field, cite that and provide specifics on changes you would make.
> Page limits restrict the amount of detail, so the writer of a ten-page proposal is held to a different standard than the person writing an NIH grant with a twenty-five-page research plan.

Finally, ask the individuals who review drafts of your grants to advise you.

Explaining how you will do the work must be supplemented by examples of the kind of results you expect and how you will interpret them. If you have proposed a clinical trail and hypothesized that Drug A is better than the conventional treatment, Drug B, what benefits do you expect to see, and how long do you expect to follow your patients in order to observe those benefits? If you, as a medicinal chemist, propose to synthesize several analogs to a drug, which structural changes do you expect to increase potency and which to decrease it? Do you expect changes in toxicity in addition to altering the drug's primary effect? If you say that you will synthesize ten congeners and run them through an in vitro screening test, you have embarked on the classic fishing expedition. You don't want to go there!

Because grants fund research rather than applied technology, studies may not work out the way we expect or they may just plain fail. You make yourself look like a realistic and savvy investigator when you anticipate pitfalls and explain how you will deal with them. Any medicinal chemist worthy of his HPLC columns will understand that a synthesis strategy that looks elegant on paper may fail in the flask, or work well on a small scale but not when scaled up. As a backup, the chemist may need to suggest a less elegant, multistep path to the desired product. The researcher who develops transgenic mouse embryos recognizes that some will not survive until birth, while others will display unexpected phenotypes incompatible with the proposed studies. How will she deal with these untoward and expensive outcomes?

AFTER YOU'VE WRITTEN

Throughout this chapter I have made reference to what reviewers look for, because they are the primary audience for whom you write. In writing, as in speaking, it is critical to understand who constitutes your audience, and what they expect. In this final section we will dissect the reviewer's perspective in more detail.

Now is an appropriate time to review some of the principles we have covered, principles that were included because they highlight features reviewers look for in a grant application.

As a self-check, fill in the missing words in the following statements:

Reviewers expect you to have a good _____ (1) _____.

A winning grant application = a good _____ (1) _____ + effective communication.

Reviewers expect you to formulate or state _____ (2) _____.
They want you to design _____ (3) _____ that test the _____ (2) _____.

Reviewers expect you to _____ (4) _____ your writing.

The most common problem of beginning grant writers is lack of _____ (4) _____.

Now look at the end of the chapter for the answers.

Here are some more elements reviewers look for:

Reviewers expect you to show productivity and knowledge of proposed techniques.

Reviewers expect you to follow the instructions and stick to the prescribed format.

Reviewers generally are not picky persons; but they are too busy to decipher a grant when the applicant alters the format and ignores the guidelines.

Reviewers are turned off by careless errors (typos, misspelled words, mislabeled figures).

"If the applicant can't write the grant carefully, how carefully will she do the work?"

To pull this together, think about the questions reviewers ask themselves, implicitly or explicitly, and the parts of a typical research grant where these questions may be answered (see Table 5.8).

Table 5.8 Summary of the questions reviewers ask, and where in the grant application they will look for the answers.

Questions	Answers
Who are you? (Translation: Can you do the work?)	Your biographical sketch or CV and your publications help answer this question. As you become more experienced, your overall track record tells who you are, and sometimes a grant proposal lacking in detail can be rescued by the investigator's reputation. (Do not count on this!) For both beginning and experienced PIs, the Preliminary Data/Progress Report section conveys a great deal about who you are. Remember that actions speak louder than words.
What are you going to do?	The Specific Aims section answers this one. A satisfactory Abstract also presents a brief version of the Aims, and the Experimental Design and Methods section expands on them.
Why is it worth doing?	Answering this question is *the* main goal of the Background/Significance section and what sets it apart from a literature review. An Abstract mentioning the long-term goals of the work touches on this point.
Why do *you* want to do it?	This question is related to, but not quite the same as, the preceding one. Presumably you want to do a research project because it is worth doing, interests you, and fits your expertise. The Background, your biographical sketch and publications, and your Preliminary Data all help answer this question.
How are you going to do it?	The Experimental Design and Methods section answers this one.

Table 5.8 Continued.

Questions	Answers
Where will the work lead?	The Abstract should project your view of where the work is likely to lead. The order of Specific Aims (particularly if the last Aim is more speculative than the others) can indicate the expected direction. When the Background section talks about unsolved problems, and how your work can fill the gaps, you are explaining to reviewers where you think the work will go. The Experimental Design and Methods section, by the order of the studies and the discussion of expected results, also suggests the long-term outcome.
How much will it cost?	The Budget, of course. Unless instructed otherwise, strive to write a complete, detailed budget justification. You say a lot about how carefully you work and plan by the way you justify the funds you are requesting.

FINAL THOUGHTS

As you prepare to write your grant, remember the following fundamentals of grantsmanship:

Study the grant makers before you start. Their goal is to fund work that furthers their mission. Your mission is to understand their mission.

A good idea is necessary but not sufficient. Poor writing can obscure a good idea, but no quantity of well-crafted words can mask an inadequate idea.

A successful grant application is an exercise in communication and a marketing document for your ideas.

Getting experienced grant writers to review drafts of your proposal is one of the most important ways in which you can increase your chances for success.

Understanding what reviewers look for is critical to writing a successful grant application.

A final word: The only people who don't make mistakes are the ones who don't do anything. If your grant fails to get funded the first time, don't quit. Revise and resubmit.

Answers to the fill-in-the-blank statements: (1) idea; (2) hypotheses; (3) experiments; (4) focus.

NOTES

1. Cuca, J. M. NIH grant applications for clinical research: Reasons for poor ratings or disapproval. *Clin. Res.* (1983) 31:453–461.

2. Greenspan, S. L. Femoral osteoporosis in elderly women. Taken from NIH CRISP database; grant Ro1AG13069.

6

Planning and Preparing an Effective Scientific Poster

Catherine Coffin

Other sections of this book discuss the importance to your career of developing excellent written and oral communication skills. But sometimes you will choose to present your material in poster form. Many communication skills will be required: you need to be a researcher, planner, writer, graphic designer, and presenter.

Scientific posters are "display boards on which scientists show their data and describe their experiments" for recently completed research, or for research in progress but not yet published.[1] Posters are a visual, concise, appealing form of communication that allows medical professionals to share with their colleagues their original scholarly work, clinical investigations, and interesting case presentations. Some medical posters describe management topics or new programs or projects rather than research findings; such posters usually are not presented at a scientific meeting. The increase in desire to participate, and the resulting crowded agendas of biomedical meetings and conferences, do not allow time enough for all the ten- to fifteen-minute oral presentations desired.[2] Beginning in the mid-

1970s, posters, once relegated to the hallways, moved inside the convention hall and became significant components of professional meetings, along with oral presentations, symposia, and workshops.[3]

THE CHOICE: ORAL PRESENTATION OR POSTER?

The process of creating a poster starts with writing an abstract to be submitted for review by the program committee of the scientific conference in which you are interested. Often at this stage you must decide whether your research is better suited to presentation in an oral format (sometimes referred to as a platform or podium presentation) or as a poster. Develop a sense as you are writing of whether you wish to have your abstract accepted as an oral or poster presentation, or either—and because you're reading this chapter, you have probably decided on a poster! If you have never produced a poster, you might want to attend a scientific poster session, view those currently on display in the hallways of your institution, or seek out colleagues who have successfully created posters.

If you remain uncertain whether to submit your abstract for selection as a poster or an oral presentation, consider the following factors:

Perceived prestige

Because of limited time and display space, there are usually fewer oral presentations than posters at scientific meetings. Therefore, oral presentations tend to be considered more prestigious.

Complexity of data

Oral presentations are ideal for describing two or three main points or research results, whereas a poster is better for more complex experimental results and ideas.

Expertise, time, and cost

Generating a poster usually requires greater expertise than preparing a laptop presentation and more money (anywhere from $50 to

Table 6.1 Comparison of presentation at a scientific meeting by poster or orally with projected visual aids.

Poster presentation	Oral/slide presentation
Viewers can concentrate on part that most interests them.	Everyone looks at the same slides or other visual aids.
Viewers can determine time to spend studying material.	Speaker determines length of viewing time by audience.
Viewers may have diverse interests.	More experienced scientists may not attend.
Viewers can interact individually with presenter.	Speaker has little interaction with audience.
Viewers are not comfortably seated.	Audience is seated and may or may not be comfortable.

$1,000 or more) than the 35-mm slides you would probably use during a talk. Determine whether you have access to the necessary hardware and software (laser printer, word-processing and presentation graphics packages) for generating content, producing copy, and aiding design, or whether you will have to seek the help of professionals.

Desired audience

A poster may attract a more diverse audience than an oral presentation. The more experienced or senior investigators in your specialty may not attend your talk, but they may well view your poster. According to a survey of physicians presenting at a national internal medicine meeting, posters met their needs better than oral presentations "for feedback and criticism and for networking and developing collaborative projects."[4] However, the researchers admitted that oral presentations offered more "national visibility" and furthered their goal of sharing knowledge with their colleagues. Perhaps the ideal format is a session during which investigators present a short oral review of their posters. This format can provide the desired increase in visibility.

In addition to the above considerations, Table 6.1 presents some factors to consider relative to how the audience is affected by each presentation medium. Both types of communication may take place in a noisy, crowded, distracting environment. As your poster will be one of many, so may your presentation be one of many on a given day.

WRITING THE ABSTRACT

Preparation for a scientific meeting starts with a well-written abstract that is due six to twelve months in advance, with notice of acceptance as an oral presentation or a poster three to six months before the meeting. Reviewers look for the following characteristics:[5]

Timely, useful, important, original, and relevant information
Clear, concise description of the research project
Appropriate and credible study design and methods
Specific results and conclusions, described clearly.

You may increase your abstract's chances of being accepted if you select a content category that you anticipate will have the fewest submissions, write an abstract that corresponds to a theme of the meeting, or select a timely topic in your field.

When writing an abstract, consider the following:

- A well-written scientific abstract is clear, concise, correct, complete, consistent, and convincing. As with any medical writing, your abstract should be appropriate for the intended audience.
- Format the abstract according to the submission instructions, whether structured (with headings such as Introduction, Methods, Results, and Conclusion/Discussion—the IMRAD formula) or unstructured (one or several untitled paragraphs). See Chapter 4 for more detailed information.
- An abstract for a meeting may include more data and more detail about the experimental methods used than an abstract accompanying a journal article.[6] You may also choose to include more implications about the importance of your study, along with a reference, table, or figure. To determine if this is acceptable, refer to the specific instructions provided by the meeting organizers.

- The best title contains ten words or fewer, can be displayed on one or two lines on your poster display, and can be seen from approximately ten feet away.[7] Be sure it is informative, interesting, and attention getting; it may be in the form of a question. Think about how your title will look in large type and prominently displayed before you attempt to be overly creative! Put yourself in the place of the audience: would the title attract you to the poster?
- Authorship should follow the guidelines discussed in Chapter 4. If the instructions do not say otherwise, you may choose to include the authors' first names instead of first initials only; when displayed on the poster, they aid interaction with viewers.
- Edit for common writing problems such as wordiness, incorrect spelling and punctuation, and lack of clarity. Refer to an appropriate style manual for questions about usage (see list of Resources in Chapter 4).

PLANNING THE POSTER

The scientific program committee has accepted your abstract as a poster presentation. Now what? You should—

Review the instructions provided by the meeting organizers. This may sound like simplistic advice, but you do not want to arrive at the convention hall with a poster 4 feet high by 8 feet wide, to fit into a 3 × 6 space. Will a background be provided, and if so, what color is it? Is it corkboard or fabric covered? Will your poster be displayed on a tabletop or a tripod, or will it be mounted on a rolling easel or a wall? Is a mural (one large photographic piece) recommended, or should you use separate poster, mat, or foam-board sections? If the instructions are unclear or incomplete, now is the time to call the meeting organizers.

Think about how to present your information in a visual way. This task is often a difficult one for scientists, but an effective poster contains fewer words than pictures. Consider visiting a children's science museum to see how information has been designed to attract and appeal to a moving (and impatient) audience. Pay attention to other uses of nonscientific graphic illustration for ideas about how to present scientific information. For example, the next time you are on an airplane, look at the safety card in the seat pocket in front of you to review how the information is presented without using words.

Get help early. Locate people who can assist you with designing illustrations and formatting text if you have little expertise in this area. Most medical centers have biomedical communication professionals who may be able to assist you; consult with them early in the poster-production process. At the very least, have the title block of your poster (the piece containing your research project's title, authors, and affiliations) professionally done. You also need to determine if your department or institution requires that a specific logo or insignia be displayed on your poster.

Create a checklist and follow it. As with any project that requires several steps and procedures, a checklist may help you separate the work into manageable tasks. See Table 6.2 or create your own list.

Practice your presentation. Just as you would practice your oral/slide presentation for a scientific meeting, hold a dress rehearsal for your poster presentation. Answer questions from your colleagues and practice explaining and defending the content of your poster.

WRITING THE TEXT

After you have done the initial planning of your poster's content and design, the next step is to write the text portions. Keep in mind that a scientific poster is different from a scientific journal article (see Table 6.3).

Follow the IMRAD format that you used for the abstract submission, but remember that a poster is not a journal article tacked to a wall. According to one source, each picture you use is worth four thousand words: "one thousand you don't have to write, one thousand you don't have to proofread, one thousand you don't have to put on your exhibit, and one thousand your reader doesn't have to read."[8]

Table 6.2 Poster presentation checklist.

- Review your abstract to determine the main points you want to make with your poster.
- Create a rough layout using graph paper, a bulletin board, or desktop publishing software. Identify areas for the title, text, and illustrations.
- Write the text for all your poster sections. Develop appropriate headings for each section.
- Outline any detailed material not appropriate for the poster, to be used in a handout for interested viewers.
- Design the photographs, charts, tables, and other graphic elements for the Results section.
- Experiment with different colors, shapes, and arrangements of the poster parts. Ask several colleagues for suggestions.
- Edit all the text.
- Recheck all data in the tables and figures.
- Revise any handouts to be used.
- Duplicate (usually photocopy) handouts.
- Review the meeting instructions a final time to ensure compliance with all guidelines.
- Produce the final versions of all text and illustrations for your poster sections or single-unit photographic mural, and bring the materials to any production personnel assisting you.
- If your poster contains separate pieces, photograph or sketch the final layout to use as a guide for quick setup at the meeting location.
- Decide how you will pack, carry, or send the poster components or mural. Remember Murphy's Law when traveling: never pack your poster in checked luggage. Consider mailing poster components ahead by a reliable courier.
- Collect and pack office supplies (scissors, tape, rubber cement, Velcro™, pens, markers, stapler, etc.) for emergency touch-ups. Put these with your handouts and business cards.
- Finally, visualize yourself talking with the audience and explaining your poster. Anticipate possible questions and practice the answers. Rehearse with your colleagues before the meeting.
- Be patient and try to enjoy the experience of the poster session. Do not be disappointed if not many attendees talk to you. At least a few will be interested, but they may not get to your poster until the end of the session.
- Study other posters at the meeting for design techniques to use in the future.

Table 6.3 Comparison of a scientific poster and a journal article.

Poster	Journal article
Text supports figures	Figures support text
Mostly illustrations (several kinds)	Mostly text; illustrations limited in number, kind, and color
Emphasis on Results; brief Discussion, which uses numbered items or bulleted lists of Conclusions	More emphasis on Discussion than Results
Little text; 50 percent white space	Lots of text
Not a publication of record, not exhaustive; does not need detailed statistical analyses; few or no references	A publication of record; needs detailed statistical analyses and references

In the Introduction section of the poster, provide a succinct overview of your findings. Justify the importance of your study and include your research hypothesis. Include a clear objective or overview that includes the purpose of your study and answers the question, "What is the one thing I want viewers to learn from my poster?" or "Why did I do this project?" Consider writing this section with bulleted statements instead of paragraphs of text.

Do not cite references in the Introduction or in a list elsewhere on the poster. A poster is not a formal publication, and, therefore, few or no references are required.[9] In addition, few viewers will choose to read a list located in small type at the bottom right-hand corner of your display.

In the Methods or Study Design section, consider using a flow chart, diagram, or bulleted statements instead of a verbose description of a clinical protocol. An example of bulleted writing in a fictional Methods section is as follows:[10]

- Elderly inpatients with no history of cardiac disease
- Randomized, controlled clinical trial

- IRB-approved
- Six weeks per treatment regimen
- Cardiac catheterization every three weeks; laboratory evaluation every week
- Intention-to-treat statistical analysis used

If the above information were to be written in complete sentences in paragraph form, approximately four times as many words would be needed. A flow chart or diagram is also preferable to paragraphs of text.

When preparing the Methods and other sections of your poster, remember that your audience will be on their feet and will spend only a few seconds (at best, a few minutes) looking at your work. The way in which you show your findings will determine their interest. If your poster presents a new method or technique, the Methods section may be more prominent than the Results section. Finally, there is no need for the detailed statistical analyses on the poster that there would be in the Methods section of a scientific journal article.[11]

In the Results section (usually the most important part of the poster), you do not have to include everything that happened in your study. Highlight the major facts; viewers will be able to question you for any details while you are standing next to your display. Remember that the Results should be visual and colorful and include as few words and as many illustrations as possible—photographs, charts, graphs, models, or maps. Each figure or illustration should be able to stand alone; in other words, each figure legend should be self-explanatory. There should be no references to these figures in the text of the other poster sections, because a viewer should not have to move back and forth between sections.[12]

For any of the text sections of the Results, use short, simple statements that allow your audience to scan the information quickly. Use precise, descriptive language: "Mean weight loss for the patients receiving treatment was 9 kg" is much better than "The treatment had a positive effect on weight loss."[13]

As with the other principal sections of the poster, consider presenting your results in diagram form or with bulleted writing. Notice how the bulleted version below is easer and quicker to comprehend than the sentence version:

Complete sentence format: "The treatment produced reductions in fever, decreases in swelling, increases in appetite, weight gain, sharper responses to stimuli, and better coordination."[14]

Bulleted statement format: "Treatment produced favorable changes in [patients']—

- temperature
- appetite
- responses to stimuli
- swelling
- body weight
- coordination."[15]

A Discussion section may not be needed. Instead, consider writing a bulleted list of Conclusions; number this list only if you want to imply an order of importance or discovery. If you decide to write a Discussion, consider a few ideas from Robert Day.[16]

- Briefly describe any relationships or generalizations shown by your data.
- Mention any exceptions, variations, lack of correlation, or study limitations.
- Include indications of how your results support or agree (or limit or disagree) with findings from similar studies.
- Emphasize what is important about your results (that is, how your work will help the laboratory or clinical work of others).
- Be certain to answer the research question(s) posed in your Introduction. For example, if you set out to study the safety, effectiveness, and cost savings of a new procedure, your Discussion/Conclusion should address all these issues.

DESIGNING ILLUSTRATIONS AND LAYOUT

As you begin to prepare the layout (visual presentation) of your poster, reflect on what bothers you most about poster displays you have viewed. The following complaints are often cited:[17]

Text is too small or too difficult to read easily.

Too much unnecessary data and text are included.

Organization is confusing; there are no informative headings.

Glare from lamination or glossy paper makes reading and studying difficult.

Research is not worthwhile; science is not great.

A poster's content is the crucial consideration, but the layout can add to or detract from its clarity. A successful layout organizes information in a way that attracts viewers. It maps out a visual path for readers that makes the message as clear as possible.[18] An attractive layout gets the attention of passers-by and helps your poster stand out in the crowd. Here are some tips to help you achieve the best layout.

- Consider the poster's purpose, audience, and setting.
- Include your abstract on the poster only if the meeting instructions require it.[19] Your colleagues will have a copy of the abstract in the printed schedule of oral and poster presentations for the meeting.
- Allow for 50 percent white space (any area without text or pictures) to rest the eye and visually organize the elements.[20] Less white space between, or the same color background behind, two elements makes them look related. To avoid having your viewers focus on the edges of your poster components, use Velcro™ instead of pushpins or tacks to attach the pieces to the background.
- Use "visual grammar" and a logical arrangement. That is, organize your sections the way people read: left to right and top to bottom in columnar fashion, using three or four sections for a poster 6 feet wide.[21] Use Arabic numerals, arrows, or bullets to create a path for viewers to follow.
- Stand on a table to visualize the poster layout on the floor below. This idea occurred to me while watching a scene in the movie "Dead Poets' Society." When the lead character instructs his students to stand on their desks to view the world from a different perspective, I realized that standing on a desk or table gives a poster designer the distance of three to five feet from which most

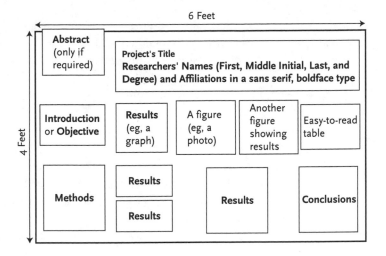

Figure 6.1 Sample layout for a scientific poster display.

will observe the poster. Size your text and illustrations so that they are readable from three feet away, and design your layout to be effective from this distance.

- Highlight the important portions by size, position, and color; the most critical information (usually elements of the Results section) belongs at eye level, usually the space directly below the title section. Do not place the most important graphs and charts or the Conclusions below eye level.
- Explore alternative arrangements to find the most effective layout. For assistance, consider using the page-design templates included with popular desktop publishing software.
- Study posters you admire for additional organizing ideas. A sample poster layout (4 feet by 6 feet) is shown in Figure 6.1.

Using Typeface and Color

Aim for the following:[22]

- Sans serif, boldface type for the main title and subtitle (eg, Avant Garde, Helvetica, or Arial)

- Serif type for the remainder of the text (eg, New Century School-book, Palatino, Times Roman, or Garamond)
- Justified left margins and ragged right margins (that is, uneven line lengths)
- Uppercase and lowercase letters throughout
- Muted colors for backgrounds (for example, blue-gray). Resist the temptation to use bright background colors because they will over-whelm your illustrations.
- Recommendations for type size vary from 1 inch to 3 inches tall for the subtitle and main title characters, and 1/4 inch to 1 inch for the remainder of the text. Woolsey suggests a consistent scale for all parts of the poster, with a type size 30–45 mm tall for the main characters; 25–30 mm for authors' names and institutional affilia-tions; 10 mm for main text headings; and 5 mm for supporting text.[23] Another suggestion is to make subtitle characters twice the size of text characters and the main title characters four to six times the size of text characters. The goal is to choose a type size that is readable from several feet away.

FINAL THOUGHTS

Changes in computer technology will continue to create changes in sci-entific poster production and perhaps in how we view posters at our conferences and meetings. Perhaps poster sessions as we now know them will become a thing of the past, replaced by interactive video dis-plays. Whatever the future holds, the principles guiding presentation of complex scientific information in a visual manner will still apply. Your efforts to learn and implement appropriate uses of color, typeface, layout, and graphic elements will be worthwhile, as will increasing your knowledge of the best methods to communicate your research findings.

NOTES

1. Day, R. A. How to prepare a poster. In *How to Write and Publish a Scientific Paper*. 5th ed. Phoenix, Ariz.: Oryx Press, 1994, pp. 189–192.

2. Briscoe, M. H. Posters. In *Preparing Scientific Illustrations: A Guide to Better Posters, Presentations, and Publications.* 2nd ed. New York: Springer-Verlag, 1996, pp. 131–149.

3. Maugh, T. H. II. Poster sessions: A new look at scientific meetings. *Science* (1974) 184:1361.

4. Tulsky, A. A., and Kouides, R. W. Abstract presentations: What do SGIM presenters prefer? *J. Gen. Intern. Med.* (1998) 13(6):417–418.

5. Coulston, A. M., and Stivers, M. A poster worth a thousand words: How to design effective poster session displays. *J. Am. Diet. Assoc.* (1993) 93(8):865–866.

6. Zeiger, M. The abstract. In *Essentials of Writing Biomedical Research Papers.* New York: McGraw-Hill, 1991, pp. 257–283.

7. Day, How to prepare a poster.

8. Hanna, M. C., and Iles, R. L. *Preparing Scientific Poster Exhibits.* Kansas City, Mo.: Marion Merrell Dow, 1992.

9. Woolsey, J. D. Combating poster fatigue: How to use visual grammar and analysis to effect better visual communications. *Trends Neurosci.* (1989) 12(9):325–332.

10. Hanna and Iles, *Preparing Scientific Poster Exhibits.*

11. Woolsey, Combating poster fatigue.

12. Coulston and Stivers, A poster worth a thousand words; and Block, S. M. Do's and don'ts of poster presentation. *Biophysical J.* (1996) 71:3527–29.

13. Coulston and Stivers, A poster worth a thousand words.

14. Hanna and Iles, *Preparing Scientific Poster Exhibits.*

15. Ibid.

16. Day, How to prepare a poster.

17. St. James, D. Other writing projects. In *Writing and Speaking for Excellence: A Guide for Physicians.* Boston: Jones and Bartlett, 1996, pp. 113–129.

18. Woolsey, Combating poster fatigue.

19. Davis, M. Poster presentations. In *Scientific Papers and Presentations.* San Diego: Academic Press, 1997, pp. 173–185.

20. Woolsey, Combating poster fatigue.

21. Woolsey, Combating poster fatigue; and Briscoe, Posters.

22. Woolsey, Combating poster fatigue.

23. Ibid.

Additional Resources

Browner, W. S. Posters. In *Publishing and Presenting Clinical Research.* Baltimore: Williams & Wilkins, 1999, pp. 133–139.

Johns, M. Planning and producing scientific posters. *J. Audiov. Media Med.* (1998): 21(1):13–17.

McCann, S. A., Sramac, R. S., and Rudy, S. J. The poster exhibit: Guidelines for planning, development, and presentation. *Dermatol. Nurs.* (1993) 5(3):197–199, 201–205.

Penrose, A. M., and Katz, S. B. Preparing conference presentations. In *Writing in the Sciences: Exploring Conventions of Scientific Discourse.* New York: St. Martin's Press, 1998, pp. 92–115.

Simmonds, D. Standards for medical graphics. *J. Audiovis. Media Med.* (1993) 16(2):56–61.

Simmonds, D., and Reynolds, L. *Data Presentation and Visual Literacy in Medicine and Science.* Oxford: Butterworth-Heinemann Medical, 1994.

Tufte, E. R. *The Visual Display of Quantitative Information.* Cheshire, Conn.: Graphics Press, 1983.

Tufte, E. R. *Envisioning Information.* Cheshire, Conn.: Graphics Press, 1990.

7

Dynamic Job-search Materials

Catherine Coffin

As health care and medical careers continue to change, excellent writing skills are no longer optional for your career success. How you present yourself in a curriculum vitae (CV), personal statement, or job search letter—plays a more important role than most professionals realize. In other words, how you write these documents may determine whether you get the position or promotion you desire. A well-prepared CV creates a positive impression of your professional abilities; a carefully composed cover letter demonstrates your grasp of correct business communication; and a thoughtfully written personal statement accurately depicts your personality. Conversely, a poorly written CV, letter, or statement (one containing faulty grammar, spelling, or punctuation; typographical errors; or incorrect word usage) reflects an inability to communicate clearly. An admissions officer, department chair, or search committee member may wonder if that inability to communicate well applies to other areas, such as your skills in research and patient care. Others may question your willingness to pay attention to details or the degree of your interest in a specific institution.

Although almost everyone in a medical profession eventually will have to prepare a CV, few comprehensive guides exist—and no absolute preparation and formatting rules. What follows are suggestions for effective ways to present your professional interests and aspirations, education, training, and experience.

THE CURRICULUM VITAE

Of all types of professional writing, the CV is arguably the most imitated and the most misunderstood. Moreover, putting together a CV can be a frustrating exercise in writing, design, and marketing—skills that may not come easily to a health care provider. The various medical specialties have different expectations about how these documents should look and what they should contain. Literally hundreds of books have been published about preparing résumés, but few on preparing CVs. In the final analysis, an effective CV is an accurate reflection of you that highlights your abilities, accomplishments, and personality in a concise, professional way.

Résumé or CV?

Although the two terms are often used interchangeably, a résumé and a curriculum vitae (CV; the plural is curricula vitae) are distinct documents with different functions and purposes. A résumé is a one- or two-page condensed summary of your education and work experience that usually includes a professional career objective stating what type of position you are seeking. The sole purpose of a résumé is "to persuade a prospective employer to give you a job interview, so it emphasizes the background and experience that qualify you for the job."[1] A résumé may also include information about your nonacademic, extracurricular interests.[2]

A curriculum vitae (Latin for "course or outline of life") is a detailed overview and summary of your professional life and development.[3] Unlike a résumé, a CV emphasizes your professional publications and presentations. It may also be used as a screening tool for hiring, although "traditionally it is used to evaluate applicants for teaching positions, residencies, and fellowships, and to consider nominees for awards, honors, grants, and committee appointments."[4] CVs are used to introduce speakers at professional meetings and are required for faculty involved in continuing medical education activities. Since a CV should be comprehensive, there is no specific limit on the number of pages, but you should avoid any padding or redundancy.

The American Medical Association (AMA) recommends submitting a CV if you are applying for an academic position (or some government positions), and a résumé for all other types of positions, especially those that involve a career change.[5] In either document, your goal should be to organize and highlight your relevant experience, skills, and education to demonstrate progression of your career. The AMA suggests that you think of your CV or résumé as a personal sales brochure that "contains a description of the product [you], identifies why it is better than other products that are available, and makes the reader want to find out more."[6] Although the concept of a CV as a personal sales and marketing tool can be difficult to accept, the competition for jobs in medicine indicates the need to focus on the best possible presentation.

Although there are various CV formats to emulate, yours may be unique, that is, tailored to fit your experience and the specific reason for creating or revising the document. Try not to think of your CV as a historical document that merely records your accomplishments; rather, its content and organization should be flexible and dynamic. For example, you may wish to create a different CV for each program to which you apply, modifying it to fit the needs and requirements of the specific institution. Table 7.1 lists some of the frequently mentioned characteristics of an effective CV and the problems commonly associated with less effective ones.

Importance of the Reader/Evaluator

Most medical CVs are read in three minutes or less.[7] One nursing study determined that the initial review lasts only fifteen to twenty seconds![8] It is disappointing to realize that you may have spent thousands

Table 7.1 Characteristics of an effective curriculum vitae, and potential problems of presentation.

Desirable qualities	Negative characteristics
Easy to read	Poor organization, layout, and design
Informative	"Filled-in-the-blanks" appearance
Honest	Incorrect grammar
Comprehensive but concise	Unreadable or unusual typeface
Consolidated	Inconsistent headings and language
Correct	Poor copy quality
Current	Misspellings or typographical errors
Complete	Little white space
Well organized	Unexplained time periods
Stylish	Exaggerations
	Insufficient information
	Odd-colored paper
	Excessive length

of dollars and dedicated years to your education and training, and you get only a brief moment to present yourself. Consider the initial reader (the selection committee chair, the department head, or the hospital administrator) who sits down at the end of an exhausting day of work with a tall stack of CVs, letters, and other job applications or faculty promotion materials. Will that person give the benefit of the doubt to every unclear, poorly formatted, or questionably accurate CV, or is the reader trying to diminish the pile of work by weeding out CVs that are difficult to decipher or contain errors? This process may not seem fair, but the reality is that your CV often has only one chance to make a good impression, and too often negative information is weighted more heavily than positive information.

Content and Organization

An effective CV is organized into sections to make the information more accessible for the reader. Although you should tailor your CV to each job or program to which you apply, the following is the usual content and one organizational sequence of a CV. A sample CV format appears in Figure 7.1.

Main Heading contains certain personal data, including your full name (as it appears on legal documents); abbreviations for professional degrees usually listed in the order in which they were received, although "MD" usually precedes all others; home address and telephone number; and your fax number, e-mail address, and any Internet personal home page or Web address.[9] (Opinions differ on whether to include your social security and medical licensure numbers because of the potential for misuse. When unsure, do not provide these numbers.) If you are a student or medical or pharmacy resident, you may include temporary and permanent address information. If you are currently employed, you may want to include your work address, position title, and telephone and fax numbers. Think twice before including any cellular phone or pager numbers, because each number you include on your CV should be answered promptly, in a professional manner, by an individual or a machine.

Unless specifically requested, do not include your age, sex, race, height, weight, marital status, names of children, health status, religious or political affiliation, photograph, or citizenship. The AMA suggests that you include a statement such as "Dual _____ (list applicable country)/U.S. citizenship with permanent residence in U.S." if you believe this information would be viewed favorably.[10]

The purpose of this first section is to provide enough information so that the reader can contact you easily. If your CV is to be submitted for an introduction at a medical or scientific meeting or for you to be considered for an award, you may want to include personal data that would not be appropriate for a document used to obtain employment. Finally, there is no need to include the words "Curriculum Vitae" at the top of the first page—you would not type the word "letter" at the top of a letter!

Education and Training should be provided in reverse chronological order (although some specialties and institutions prefer chronological order). Inclusive dates (months and years) are important. If there are time lapses, be prepared to explain them in an interview. Do not include information about education earlier than college unless specifically requested or if it represents an outstanding achievement

Name, MD, RN, DO, PharmD, etc.

Home street address	Work/office street address
City, state, zip code	City, state, zip code
Telephone, fax, e-mail address	Telephone, fax
Website or URL/home page address	

Education and Training

Fellowship	Specialty Medical center or hospital City and state	July 1998– June 1999
Residency	Specialty Medical center or hospital City and state	July 1996– June 1998
Internship	Any special name Medical center or hospital City and state	July 1995– June 1996
Medical school (or other pro- fessional school)	Doctor of Medicine Medical school name City and state	May 1995
College	Undergraduate degree (eg, Bachelor of Arts) College or university name City and state	May 1991

Specialty Board Status

Board Eligible (or Board Certified), governing body of specialty

Licensure and Certifications

List each state of medical or other licensure	Expiration date(s)
Name of each certification (eg, Advanced Cardiac Life Support Provider)	Certification date(s)

Professional Experience (If applicable can separate into sections such as Teaching Experience, Academic Appointments, Hospital Appointments)

Title, Name of organization/institution, city and state	June 1998–present
Title, Name of organization/institution, city and state	August 1997–June 1998

Military or Public Health Service

Title, branch of military if applicable, and where served	Dates

Honors and Awards

Name of each honor, award, honorary degree, etc.	Date awarded

Membership in Professional Organizations

Name of each organization, office(s) held	Dates

Research Projects

Name of each project; include grant funding received and name of director, names of colleagues, institution, address, and dates

Publications

Authors' names in order listed on each publication. Title of each paper. Abbreviated journal name, volume and page numbers, and year of publication formatted using standard bibliographic style. (This section can be separated into Books, Chapters, Journal Articles, and Abstracts, when applicable.)

Presentations

Title of each talk *you* presented, Meeting name, location, date

Community Service (or Community Activities or Special Skills or Special Expertise)

Brief description of each activity or skill; location and dates, if applicable.

References

Available (or supplied) on request.

(Revised_____[Month, year])

Figure 7.1 Sample format for your curriculum vitae.

(for instance, National Merit Scholarship as a high school student).[11] If you wish, you may list your undergraduate major and minor areas of study. If you are currently enrolled in courses toward an additional degree, include that information. Be sure to spell out all school and hospital names and addresses; however, two-letter state name abbreviations are acceptable.

For this and other subsequent similar sections, consider including any dates in a column on the right-hand side of the page (see Figure 7.1). Because English is read from left to right, what appears on the left side of a page gets the most attention; for skimming purposes, your titles and training categories are more meaningful than the corresponding dates.[12]

Specialty Board Status indicates whether you are board certified or board eligible in one or more specialties.

Licensure and Certifications should include the names of the states in which you are licensed but not the specific numbers because of the potential for misuse. Professional certifications, including expiration dates, should be listed with the most advanced certifications first.[13] Language skills may be described here or elsewhere (see Community Service).

Professional Experience should list job titles, name and address of each organization or institution, and beginning and ending dates. (The Education and Training section usually precedes this section on a CV because that information is more valuable for appointment and promotion consideration. However, the Professional Experience section would be listed first on a *résumé*, because it is more important for getting other types of jobs (such as a medical management position). You may also include a subsection containing your teaching experience, if applicable, or separate your academic and hospital (staff) appointments into different subsections with appropriate subheadings.

If you are a medical resident or a nursing, pharmacy, or medical student, this section is where you can list any clerkships, externships, or clinical rotations, including beginning and ending dates, locations, and preceptors.[14] Often the names of your supervisors will be of most importance to the reader. For paid work experience, list your supervisor and his or her title, and use action verbs to describe your responsibilities and accomplishments (for example, developed new staff scheduling software later adopted by the department).[15] As a result, parts of this section may resemble a résumé.

As you progress in your academic career, you may omit details about early experiences by listing the position's title without describing your responsibilities. If, prior to attending graduate or medical school, you held jobs that are irrelevant to the position you are now seeking, you may refer to these experiences with a statement such as "Employment 1992–1994 included office and restaurant work."[16]

Military or Public Health Service should include your titles; branch of the military or public health service; name and location of the military bases, hospitals, or clinics; and dates.

Honors and Awards should include the name of each honor or award and the date received. This section is for relevant special recognition you have received, usually no earlier than your undergraduate college years. If the award's title is eponymous (as in The Joan Doe Award), include a brief explanation of the honor. You may include any academic honors (such as Phi Beta Kappa) here or in the Education and Training section. Omit this section's title on your CV if you have no honors or awards to list!

Membership in Professional Organizations or societies or associations should include the organization name, any offices held, and the dates. If you serve as a board member or reviewer for a scientific journal, include that information in a section with an appropriate heading.

Research Projects should give project name, source and amount of any funding received, name of the director, names of colleagues, and institution, address, and dates. This is also the section in which to list any consultantships, grants, and contracts.

You may include research experience in this section even if you have yet to publish or present the results. Be specific about your role in the research ("Principal Investigator") or include a brief statement of your duties ("Surveyed patients in dermatology clinic" or "Analyzed cost-benefit analysis in a five-hospital system").[17]

Publications should be listed in a consistent, standard bibliographic format. List the most recent publication first, unless instructed to format this section in chronological order (which is the preferred order for some institutions and medical specialties). For each publication, you must include the authors in the order in which they appear in print; you may, however, underline or boldface your name in each list. If you are a student or resident and have a paper in progress or submitted but not yet "in press," consider including such information in the Research Projects section instead. Do not include an abstract as a publication if it only appears in a book compiled for use at a conference. Technically, each abstract listed as a publication on your CV should appear in a professional journal, journal supplement, or book.[18]

As the number of your publications increases, you may use numerals to list them. When you have amassed several different types of publications, you can use subheadings within this section to ease the reader's task (Abstracts, Journal Articles, Book Chapters, and Books). You may also need to create a section for other media such as educational CD-ROMs and videos.

Presentations again should be in a consistent format and include the title of each presentation, the meeting or conference name and location, and the date of the actual talk. Do not include presentations for which you are listed as a coauthor but did not actually give the talk, or presentations delivered as a routine responsibility of your position or as part of a course requirement. This section is usually reserved for professional presentations and does not include presentations given in the community to lay audiences. As you progress through your career, your CV may include a presentations subsection titled Review and Invited Lectures, where you would not need to list your name with each entry.[19]

Community Service (or Community Activities or Special Skills or Special Expertise) may include activities that represent significant involvement and/or demonstrate your expertise in areas outside your professional responsibilities. Teaching first-aid classes at a community center is an example of a volunteer activity that requires professional skill and would be appropriate to mention. If you have knowledge of certain foreign languages, you might write "Fluent in Spanish; can read Portuguese." (Any knowledge of Spanish is especially important if your CV is being used to search for a position in southern California, Florida, Texas, and other southwestern states or large cities.) If you believe that your name or educational background indicates to reviewers that English is not your native language, you may choose to specify your fluency in English, as well as in other languages.[20]

References are always "available on request." A list of personal references with your CV is necessary only when specifically requested, usually when you are contacted for an interview. This list should contain the correct titles, addresses, telephone and fax numbers, and a brief description of your relationship with each individual. *Always ask permission of those you select as references.* Provide them with a copy of your most recent CV, as well as a list of the names, addresses, and phone numbers of the departments and institutions to which you have applied. This list will help if one of your references receives a phone message that contains incomplete contact information. Finally, keep your references apprised of your job search so that they may speak knowledgeably and accurately about you.

Presentation

- Prepare your CV in a professional manner. Use a high-quality laser printer, or spend the money to have the document professionally printed. Use business bond paper that is white or off-white. So many people are now using off-white or ivory-colored paper that white actually stands out in a pile. However, the difference between white and off-white paper color is inconsequential, since most CVs will be photocopied before review. Bright or dark-colored paper does not reproduce well, and these colors will make you stand out for the wrong reason.

- Use a serif typeface (such as Times New Roman, New Century Schoolbook, Palatino, Garamond), boldface, underlining, and different font sizes to create a document that is pleasing to the eye and highlights your accomplishments. Although a 10-point type size is often recommended, 12-point type is easier to read.

- You may want to have two versions of your final CV: one that is scannable and one to be read by human eyes. If your CV is to be optically scanned into a computer database, check whether a sans serif typeface (such as Helvetica or Arial) is recommended; if you need to use white rather than ivory-colored paper; and whether to avoid bullets, underlining, italics or boldface type, parentheses, brackets, and other formatting tools. Unless otherwise instructed, use the tab function of your word-processing program instead of the keyboard space bar to create even columns. Use any résumé template included with your word-processing software to create a first draft of your CV. Consider enlisting the aid of someone with an eye for graphic design to review your final product.

- Section headings and the order in which items are listed should be consistent and parallel. For example, be consistent with all format and design: if your Education and Training main heading is in Times New Roman 12-point boldface, then all other main headings should be formatted in the same way. If the dates for one section are in a column on the right side of the page, then dates in all other sections should appear there. Consolidate your information by placing similar categories of information near each other.

- Allow for top, bottom, left, and right margins of at least 3/4 inch; 1 inch is preferable. Do not decrease or extend margins to get more on a page. Instead, eliminate redundancies and unnecessary words. If necessary after the first page (which should contain the most important information), change the order of your sections to keep the items in each section together on the same page. In general, the categories of your CV are presented in decreasing order of importance (see Figure 7.1), with the exception of Publications, which is conventionally placed near the end.

- Retain plenty of white space; remember that your goal is to create a pleasing, easy-to-read document. Provide a running header or footer (your name and page number at the top or bottom of each page after the first) and a revision date (at the end of the document) so that your reader can accurately interpret a date that states "to present."
- Proofread, proofread, proofread. Then give the CV to at least two other people to proofread.

JOB SEARCH LETTERS

Cover Letters

Because every professional business document requires a covering letter, you should prepare a unique letter to accompany each copy of your CV. Its function is to "introduce the reader to the CV, much [as] a friend introduces you to another person."[21] It provides an opportunity to convey information that does not fit easily into the CV categories and to augment and highlight your special qualifications and accomplishments, not to rehash your CV. A cover letter or letter of interest should convey your knowledge of and enthusiasm for a specific position and show that you can organize your thoughts, communicate well, and pay attention to details.

Guidelines for Writing

- Always write to a specific person (full name and title), never to the unknown "Sir," "Program Director," or "To Whom It May Concern." If necessary, call or search the Web for the appropriate person's name, including the correct spelling, title, and mailing address.
- At the beginning of each letter, identify why you are writing and

demonstrate that you know something about the department and institution to which you are applying. You should mention the name of the person who suggested that you write, if doing so will place you in a favorable light.

- In the body of the letter, refer to your CV to discuss one or two special accomplishments or qualifications that relate to your reason for writing. This is also the place to offer important information that is not on your CV or to explain time lapses in education, training, or employment.
- Avoid overwriting. Your cover letter should present an executive summary or abstract of your CV, not a personal statement or your whole life story.
- Use a standard business format and limit the letter to one page. Any business-writing style manual will give you acceptable letter formatting instructions. Use a serif typeface, preferably the one you chose for your CV.
- Use concise, precise, nonclichéd language. (See sentence 6 in the Common Errors section below for an example of what to avoid.)
- Aim for an appropriate tone. It is important to be businesslike, but the best letter shows your personality and is not a clone of a sample letter from a book. Make your cover letter more like an essay than a memo, but err on the side of showing competence and being clear rather than entertaining.
- For the closing of the letter, opinions vary on whether you should take the initiative and suggest an interview. Reconsider sentences such as "I look forward to discussing a fellowship position with you" if it is clear at the beginning of your letter that this is your reason for writing. If the reader wishes to contact you, he or she will do so regardless of what you write, and your address and telephone number will already be in the letterhead of your stationery or on your CV. If you plan to be visiting the city in which the recipient of the letter is located, or if you plan to attend a scientific meeting at which the reader may be present, you might suggest a

possible meeting at that time and location. You can also offer to send additional materials or information, if needed.[22]

- If you are currently employed, check with your department manager or program director before using any office equipment or postage. Remember that you are applying as an individual and that it is always more appropriate to use your own office supplies, especially your own stationery, and to fax and mail documents from outside the workplace. However, it is customary to use your department or institution's letterhead if your CV is being used to apply for an award, scholarship, or research grant funding.

- Do not fold or staple your CV and cover letter. Instead, send them in a 9 × 12 envelope. This aids the recipient with photocopying and scanning.

- Finally, remember that sample cover letters in books are only samples. Although several books have well-written before-and-after examples to review for general ideas on organization and content (for example, Tysinger's or the AMA's; see Notes), the best letter is the one *you* compose.

Thank-You Letters

When your CV results in an interview, you should always send a short typed letter of thanks to each individual who takes the time to speak with you. The function of the thank-you letter is to show your appreciation and your continued interest in the position or program. The best letters include specific comments about discussions held or about other aspects of your visit to the institution. Send these follow-up letters within a few days of the interviews.

Common Errors in Cover and Thank-you Letters

The following sentences are examples of ridiculous redundancy or pompous, outdated business language. If you would never say something in conversation, do not write it!

1. Let me take this opportunity to once again thank you for taking time from what I am sure is a very busy schedule to meet with me last Thursday (November 18, 1999).
2. I am desirous of finding a position in the area of a family practice setting.
3. Pursuant to our telephone conversation on 8 December 1999, I will forward to you the references you requested.

Other types of errors to avoid include the following:

4. Should you be interested in discussing my credentials further, give me a call at (401) 555-1234.
   (The recipient will call you if interested, and your phone number will be shown on your CV.)
5. Irregardless of your committee's decision, it was a pleasure and honor to have had the opportunity to meet and talk with you in person.
   ("Irregardless" is not a word. Also, this sentence is too self-deprecating.)
6. As my CV indicates, I am the type of person who is not only a "team player" but also one who can "take the ball and run with it."
   (Avoid slang and clichés like the plague!)
7. If you're looking for a bright, single, white male surgeon with superior clinical and research skills, who is also affable and athletic, look no further.
   (Unless you are trying to impress a dating service, do not use such a sentence. Would you want to work with this person?)
8. As a leading authority in infectious diseases, I would like the opportunity to work with you at the _____ Clinic.
   (This sentence contains a grammatical error that affects its meaning: the dangling participle "As a leading authority in infectious diseases" here refers to the "I" in the sentence, not the person to whom you are writing. And *you* are most likely not the leading authority!)

The following two sentences illustrate the fact that it is not your place, but rather that of the reader or a reference, to evaluate your abilities:

9. I am hardworking and mature, with excellent academic and clinical skills.
10. In my opinion, I believe I would be an excellent candidate for the fellowship you currently have in your department at the _____ Medical Center.

Finally, do not tell your readers anything they already know:

11. I am in the final months of my fellowship at the _____ Hospital's Clinical Research Center, which is a unit where patients stay for several days or weeks while physicians and others conduct research on a variety of illnesses and therapies. I am studying treatments for muscular dystrophy, a neuromuscular disease.

PERSONAL STATEMENTS

While a CV lists your professional accomplishments—*what* you have done—a personal statement describes *who* you are, including "the experiences and events that shaped your personality, values, and goals."[23] Selection or admissions committees for medical and other health-profession schools, as well as some residencies and fellowships, require a personal statement as a means for obtaining information not found in any of your other application materials. Because many applicants have the same educational background, the personal statement is a way for you to distinguish yourself among the crowd.

Beyond the usual struggle to write any document, why does creating a personal statement cause such anxiety? Most of us do not like to write positively about ourselves and have never thought about our unique characteristics, strengths, or talents. Writing a personal statement is similar to trying to get a book published: you need to market the product. In a personal statement the product is you. You need to know what the market wants; in other words, you need to figure out what the "reviewers" are looking for, analyze your life's experiences in searching for these characteristics, and then write convincingly about them.

Most selection committees look for evidence of "a good attitude, stability, interpersonal skills, superior academic performance, and maturity."[24] In addition, each program differs slightly. An institution or medical center with a diverse patient population will prefer applicants who demonstrate an ability to work with people from various cultural backgrounds. You will want to write about past experiences in schools, jobs, your community and family, travel, sports, and volunteer activities that have provided you with flexibility, tolerance, empathy, and language skills. If you are applying to a program that stresses clinical research and encourages publishing, your personal statement should describe attributes and experiences that are a close match. As a medical faculty member seeking a new appointment or a promotion, you may be required to write a personal statement of 250 to 500 words describing your clinical and research interests, as well as what you believe have been your contributions to medical or scientific knowledge.

Read the personal statements of others to get a sense of how you might structure your own. J W Tysinger's book (see Notes) contains thirty-five personal statements written for positions in various medical fields. Some training programs may provide you with an outline to follow or questions to address (for example, "Why did you choose your specialty, and what are your long-term career goals?"). One method of writing your statement is to divide the document into five or six paragraphs and emphasize one favorable personal attribute in each. Begin each paragraph with a topic sentence containing your main idea and end with a transition that ties this paragraph to the next. As with any important document, ask others, including your faculty advisor, to review your statement for the usual reasons (grammar, spelling, organization, and clarity) and to assess whether it accurately describes you and gives readers a true sense of your personality.

PERSONAL WEBSITES

As more people turn to the Internet to search for new career opportunities, some candidates are constructing their own home pages, which include a CV, copies of publications, and photos, diagrams, and other illustrations of research findings. Some pages include links to the websites of professional associations, journals, medical centers, and graduate schools.[25] A personal home page takes time and experience to create and is not a substitute for written materials. In addition, you should consider the possibility that, unlike a printed CV seen by only those you choose, many others could view your home page and misappropriate research information. Finally, each person accessing your page would see the same information, not customized, and the page would need to be kept current.

FINAL THOUGHTS

Preparation and presentation of CVs will change with advances in computer technology. Currently, specialized software as well as popular word-processing programs include templates for preparing traditional résumés. Curricula vitae have looked the same for decades, and it is possible that what the Internet is doing for nonmedical résumé preparation and job searches will affect the CVs of medical applicants also. Some schools and institutions already require the submission of scannable résumés. Lots of white space, serif type, boldface, underlining, and action verbs are "out"; minimal blank space, plain sans serif type, specialized key words, and nouns are "in."[26] Ultimately, the savvy, up-to-date medical professional will benefit from creating two CV versions: one for the Web and one to hand to an interviewer.

NOTES

1. Bucci, K. K. How to prepare a curriculum vitae. *Am. J. Hosp. Pharm.* (1993) 50:2296, 2299.

2. Anthony, R., and Roe, G. *The Curriculum Vitae Handbook: How to Present and Promote Your Academic Career.* 2nd ed. Iowa City: Rudi Publishing, 1998, p. 2.

3. American Society of Health-System Pharmacists. Preparing a curriculum vitae. In *Opportunities: The Source for Pharmacy Residency Information.* Bethesda: American Society of Health-System Pharmacists, 1998, p. 5.

4. Bucci, How to prepare a curriculum vitae.

5. American Medical Association. Introduction. In *The Physician's Résumé and Cover Letter Workbook: Tips and Techniques for a Dynamic Career Presentation.* Chicago: American Medical Association, 1998, p. vii.

6. Ibid., p. 2.

7. Hornsby, J. S., and Smith, B. N. Résumé content: What should be included and excluded. *SAM Adv. Manage. J.* (1995) 60(1):4–9; and Bender, L. H. Résumé writing and interviewing skills for getting the job you want. *Orthop. Nurs.* (1997) 16(3):9–15.

8. Markey, B. T., and Campbell, R. L. A résumé or curriculum vitae for success. *AORN J.* (1996) 63(1):192–202.

9. Logan, P. M., and Fraser, D. B. Constructing a CV: The radiologist's resume. *AJR* (1998) 171:923–925; and Heiberger, M. M., and Vick, J. M. *The Academic Job Search Handbook.* 2nd ed. Philadelphia: University of Pennsylvania Press, 1996.

10. AMA, *The Physician's Résumé,* p. 4.

11. ASHP, *Opportunities.*

12. AMA, *The Physician's Résumé,* p. 20.

13. Tysinger, J. W. Résumés and Personal Statements for Health Professionals. 2nd ed. Tucson: Galen Press, 1999, p. 44.

14. Bucci, How to prepare a curriculum vitae.

15. Heiberger and Vick, *The Academic Job Search Handbook,* p. 56.

16. Ibid., pp. 56–57.

17. Tysinger, *Résumés and Personal Statements,* p. 28.

18. Logan and Fraser. Constructing a CV.

19. Ibid.

20. Tysinger, *Résumés and Personal Statements,* p. 35.

21. Markey and Campbell, A résumé or curriculum vitae for success.

22. Heiberger and Vick, *The Academic Job Search Handbook,* p. 108.

23. Tysinger, *Résumés and Personal Statements*, p. 98.

24. Ibid., p. 104.

25. Heiberger and Vick, *The Academic Job Search Handbook*, pp. 104–6.

26. Leonhardt, D. Remaking the résumé rules of the road. New York Times, November 3, 1999, Workplace section.

Part Three

Speaking Science

8

Speaking for Success

Paul J Casella

We are all experts at verbal communication when we really want to be. Effective communication one-on-one or in small groups takes little thought because we do it all the time. Put us in front of a large audience, however, and it's a different story. The enthusiastic, energetic resident in the hallway turns into a different person in the seminar room. In this chapter we will examine how you can adapt your interpersonal communications skills so that they are effective for larger audiences.[1]

REASONS FOR FAILURE

Complaints about presentations usually fall into one or more of the following categories:

1. *Not meeting the needs of the audience.* Know your audience. If there is one factor that can help you prepare to deliver an important message to a group, it is knowing your audience. This rapport will

help you speak to their level of understanding and convey the information that is most valuable to them.

2. *Lack of clear organization.* Heed the old adage: "Tell them what you're going to tell them, tell them, then tell them again." The more organized you are, the better the listeners will remember your information. Audience-based speakers present the organization of their talk up front, to prepare the group for the message.

3. *Unclear purpose.* Be sure to decide your purpose as a speaker before organizing your talk. That way your information will serve your purpose. Be sure also to tell your *audience* the purpose at the beginning of the talk, so that they understand the reason for remembering the information.

4. *Too much information.* Don't hide the crucial information in the midst of information that is irrelevant. An audience can only retain so much information in a finite period of time—they reach a saturation point. Your goal as a speaker is not to prove how smart you are; it is to convey information that will serve your listeners' needs.

5. *Poor delivery.* You may have the best, most relevant information in the world, but if your audience can't understand your voice, or if they are distracted by your ums and ahs, your message will not get through. "The medium is the message." *How* you present your information has a great deal to do with *what* the audience understands.

6. *Bad visual aids ineffectively used.* If a slide is illegible or distracting, it does not serve the speaker or the message. If the speaker uses a visual aid not as a way to reinforce the point but as a means to prompt himself, it is not in the service of the message. The overuse of visual aids as "prompts" is one of the leading manifestations of poor delivery skills.

HOW ADULTS LEARN

As you prepare to be an audience-based speaker, it is helpful to know not only *what* your audience needs to know, but also *how* the members will get to know that information. An understanding of how adults learn can help you prepare to make your points in ways that will be understood and remembered.

Praxis is the process by which adults receive new information, apply it, and refine the learning to suit their needs. Learning is a process; it does not just happen in one fell swoop. For speakers, this highlights the importance of repetition, of applying the information to real-life examples, of allowing information to be learned in a variety of ways.

People learn differently and they learn at different rates. The type of learner you are on a Tuesday morning is probably different from the type of learner you are on a Friday night. What does this mean for you as a speaker? Given that in any audience different learners are learning at different rates, you will need to vary your presentation style to accommodate the different learners. In an hourlong talk, an audience-based speaker will approach the information in at least three different ways.

Types of Adult Learners

In his book *Mastering the Teaching of Adults,* Jerold Apps discusses the different learning styles of adults.[2]

Sequential learners learn best when the information is presented in sequence, with a clear outline and development of the information from one step to the next. For sequential learners, responsible speakers will be sure to give an overview of the topic, maintain a sense of organization, and be sure that each point moves to the next in a logical fashion.

Practical learners need to know the purpose or application of the talk in order to recall the information readily. Practical learners are better able to understand and apply the information if they are given a reason for remembering it. For practical learners, be sure to provide a clear and straightforward purpose statement at the beginning of your talk. By explaining the purpose of the talk, you provide each member of the audience with a bucket, a context in which to carry the information. The information itself is the liquid in the bucket. If you want to give people a volume of liquid, you had better first give them a vessel in which to carry it. The same is true for carrying ideas in our heads. So prepare the audience for the information by first giving them a way to categorize and remember it.

What can you give your audience to help them carry around the information in its context? The handle on the bucket is analogous to the significance of your points, the relevance of your message, its importance, what you want the audience to do with the information. Listening is a passive activity. You have no guarantee that your listeners are asking after your every statement, "Why is this important to me? What am I going to do as a result of knowing this information?" Effective, audience-based speakers will suggest the purpose of their points and why they are important.

Intuitive learners like to figure things out for themselves. They are more likely to remember the information if they had a role in obtaining it. When you allow room for intuition, audience members will be more likely to believe your information because they are literally invested in it: they have put their time and energy into discovering it. To provide for intuitive learners, speakers should encourage interaction.

One of the best ways to promote interaction is to ask questions. Even in situations when answers to your questions are inappropriate, you can still involve the audience. Ask a question, wait a few seconds, then answer it yourself. Be sure to pause long enough to give your listeners time to consider their answers. Many speakers jump right into their answer without a pause, and the interactive process gets lost.

A majority—if not all—of the learners in medical and scientific audiences will be intuitive learners, smart people who are used to making up their own minds. They are not in the audience to be persuaded or convinced by your points. Instead, they will listen to what you have to say, try to follow your line of reasoning, and objectively figure out for themselves the verity and value of the information.

I was working once with a surgeon to prepare his plenary talk before a national meeting. Overall he was a polished speaker. After carefully examining the tape of his dry run, I made only one minor suggestion: instead of saying, "It's my goal to convince you that . . ." I suggested that he say, "I would *ask you to consider* that . . ."

DELIVERY SKILLS

Strong delivery skills are essential to the effective exchange of information and allow the audience to concentrate on the content of your message. Inadequate delivery skills distract the listener and make you appear less knowledgeable.

In a perfect world, *how* you speak would have no influence on the content of your message. However, in this world, your audience cannot help but judge the content of what you say by examining its delivery. It is basic human nature to "read into" a presentation by analyzing the delivery of the information. The more work audience members have to do to understand your message, the less energy they will have to remember it.

One of the best things you can do to be assured that you take advantage of your delivery skills is to prepare your talk well beforehand so that you have time to practice and refine the delivery. Too many speakers wait until the last minute to organize their information, or they try to "wing it," and as a result their delivery suffers. You cannot do two things at once, and if you are trying to organize your ideas at the same time as you deliver them, you will have no energy left for the delivery. So prepare your ideas, and budget time to practice.

Then practice, practice, practice. Practice in the car on the way to and from work, practice as you exercise, practice in front of your partner or a friend, practice in front of both friendly and unfriendly colleagues.

There is no *one* right way to communicate. I work with all kinds of speakers, and I see a wide variety of effective styles. So while there is not any one best way, it is the variation—and exaggeration—of delivery skills that maintain the audience's interest and attention. The all-encompassing concept for effective communication is "Form follows function." That is, the way in which you communicate—the form—should follow or serve the function, the purpose of the communication. Another way to express it is, "Style reinforces content." *How* you speak promotes understanding of *what* you are speaking about.

Presentation

For starters, don't read your talk! And don't read your slides! Reading from the lectern is the major cause of monotonous delivery. When doctors and scientists read, they forget that they are actors and forget that they must exaggerate their delivery. Make note cards with five to eight words per card to cue yourself on the points you want to make. This way you are forced to formulate sentences and then deliver them. If you make yourself go through the process of formulating your sentences in real time, you almost cannot help inflecting your voice.

When you make your note cards, use a magic marker. You will be forced to write large letters that you can see, not 12-point size that will cause you to squint. I prefer note cards over an outline because you see only one point at a time; you can put your energy into each statement and speak deliberately. With an outline you can see whole sections of the talk, and your tendency is to rush through.

But now suppose you have a short, important talk to give at a national meeting, and you do not want to trust yourself to formulate sentences in real time. In this instance you can write out your talk beforehand. When you do, though, remember the difference between the written language and the spoken language. We use shorter sentences when speaking than we do when writing. We use repetition to emphasize our points. We use the active voice more often, as opposed to the passive voice ("We conclude . . ." as opposed to "It is concluded that . . .").

When it is time to prepare your script, be sure to use 24- or 36-point type, big enough so you can read it easily, and format it in a way that emphasizes your delivery. Start a new line of text after each subtle pause in the sentence, usually every three to five words. For instance, you would format the line "We conclude that this method is the best way to detect variations in blood pressure over a 24-hour period" like this (in 36-point type):

We conclude that
this method is the best way
to detect variations
in blood pressure
over a 24-hour period.

Think about the difference between film acting and stage acting to picture the level of emphasis you as a speaker should add to your delivery. To convey an emotion in film, actors in a medium shot (upper half of the body) make what we consider to be natural gestures—those a friend would make when talking to you in the hallway. In a play, stage actors exaggerate their movements. They inhabit less area in the audience's vision than do film actors, whose images are projected on a giant screen. When you speak in front of a group, you become a stage actor. You have to compensate for the distance between yourself and the audience. Talk with enough inflection so that your voice carries to the person in the very rear of the auditorium.

This emphasis should not be at the expense of your objectivity. You can still be objective in your reasoning and take advantage of good public speaking skills.

Inflection

Varying your inflection is the best way to maintain your listeners' interest. By changing the force and pitch and pace of your words, you vary the inflection, the up-and-down quality of your voice. The opposite is speaking in the deadly monotone, a droning sound that lulls the audience to sleep and conveys a lack of interest in the topic. Your listeners are looking to see how interested *you* are in the topic to get a sense of how interested *they* should be. A monotonous delivery conveys boredom. A lively delivery with plenty of inflection conveys interest and excitement. For the benefit of the topic, and for the benefit of those in the audience who might be interested in it, be sure to emphasize your inflection.

You should feel as if you are overdoing it—exaggerating your inflection more than you do one-on-one. With such emphasis the energy in your voice carries to every member of the audience.

Be sure that you finish each of your sentences crisply. A "bang" at the end will prevent your voice from trailing off. Also, be sure that you do not inflect your sentences *up* at the end, as if you were asking a question. This tendency has been called "up-speak" or "valley-talk," and it is interpreted by U.S. audiences as an indication that the speaker is not secure or confident.

Gestures

One of the best ways to maintain a lively inflection is to allow yourself to make hand gestures when speaking. My goal when working with speakers is to have them gesture 100 percent of the time to give emphasis to their words.

If your hands are moving, your voice will follow. Gestures add variation to your inflections. They lengthen your vowel sounds and add punch to your consonants. They emphasize the pauses between your sentences. When speakers gesture, they cannot help but speak with inflection.

Let's imagine you are speaking with slides in a darkened room. You can't see the audience and they can't see you. What kind of actor do you become then? A radio actor. If the audience can't see you, is it then no longer necessary to gesture? No—it is even more important to gesture, because the main reason for doing so is to add inflection to your voice.

Well, how do you gesture? The key to graceful gestures is to have your hands "at the ready" at all times—not in your pockets, not clinging to the lectern. Hold one or both hands in front of your body at belly level. You won't be comfortable just holding them there, so you will naturally want to move them. Even a simple "put the hands together then take them apart, together-apart" strategy will be enough to help add inflection to your voice.

Of course, you can overdo gesturing. Waving your arms around wildly will divert the audience from your message. Pacing back and forth (the professorial march) will be distracting. Keep your feet fairly still (take a few steps now and then) but keep your hands moving at all times. You will find that with practice your gestures will re-enact the content of your words. When describing a procedure or parts of the body, feel free to recreate the steps or point to the parts of your body.

Pauses

In addition to gesturing, the other effective way to emphasize your inflection is to allow yourself to *pause* and say nothing at all. By pausing, you reestablish the baseline quiet tone in the room, and, as a result, your inflections stand out. If instead of pausing you say "ah" or "um," you raise the baseline quiet tone of the room and the strength of your inflections is lessened. Pauses direct the audience's attention to the speaker. They add a little mystery to the information: the audience wonders "What is the speaker going to say next?" Pauses are an important way to vary the sound of your words.

Be sure also that you leave an adequate pause between your sentences. Many speakers run separate sentences together with "and" or, worse, "and-ah." The rule for a sentence is "one idea per sentence." If you put two or three or four separate ideas in one long string of words held together by "and-ahs," then the overall effect is to lessen the impact of each idea. So be sure to allow a two-second pause between your sentences.

Dress

Dress like your audience. If they will be wearing formal clothes, wear formal clothes yourself. If you are at a less formal event, relax your standards. If you are unsure, dress a half-step more conservatively than you expect your audience to do. You will want to save the Mickey

Mouse tie or the sparkly jewelry for the clinic, where fun clothes might lighten a one-on-one interaction. In front of a group, dress conservatively and simply.

Stance and Movement

Do we stand in the hallway with our weight equally distributed on our feet, hands at our sides? No. We tend to put our weight on one foot and slightly bend the other knee. So stand comfortably in front of your audience. Do not pace back and forth, but try to face your listeners at all times. Do not turn to the screen; glance at it when necessary, gesture toward it, but keep your body facing forward.

Although you want to seem relaxed, you do not want to appear *too* comfortable. If you sit down, for instance, you rob the audience of the respect it deserves. Leaning on the lectern or a table also makes a speaker appear rather sloppy. Stand and face the audience, and let your hands do the moving to emphasize your inflection.

You have no doubt seen the speaker who gives an hourlong lecture, all the while jingling the change in his pockets. Remove any change or noisy items, anything that might distract the audience from your message. Turn off your beeper, or give it to a colleague to monitor.

Whenever possible, move around from behind the lectern. It acts as a barrier between you and the audience. By moving away from the lectern, you show the audience the respect of talking to them directly.

You should realize that in some situations it is inappropriate to move from behind the lectern: the podium presentation at a national meeting, for example. In this instance, stand a half-step back from the lectern and allow your hands to gesture as you would without a lectern there. This procedure will maintain the inflection in your voice, and the slight distance from the microphone will remind you to project your voice and add more force to it.

Do not play with the ring on your finger, or with the cap to the marker, or with your glasses or hair. And be very stingy with your use of the laser pointer. Do not punctuate your entire talk with the red dot. You do not need the pointer to direct attention to words, numbers, items in a table, or coordinates on a graph. Limit its use to images, and even then, only when necessary. Tell the audience what you want to show, use the red dot, put the pointer down, and then continue.

Despite what the airline magazines would have you believe, no two-hundred-dollar laser pointer, or two-thousand-dollar projector, will make your audience trust your information. No one will leave your talk thinking, "Well, I didn't really follow the reasoning, but that speaker's laser pointer had a great underlining feature. I think I'll follow the advice."

Speech, Slow and Simple

When you get in front of an audience, remember to speak more slowly than you do one-on-one. In fact, speak *deliberately*. A deliberate speaker appears more thoughtful about and careful with the information. When you speak deliberately, you are assured that everyone in the audience can understand your words.

When I tell people to slow down, they sometimes lose some of their inflection. Conversely, when I tell people to speak with more inflection, they end up speaking more quickly. You can speak slowly and still have lots of inflection.

Often speakers use fillers when they are thinking about what to say next. Do not clutter your points with unnecessary sounds (ah, um, er, and the like). The audience interprets your use of these fillers as insecurity about the information and lack of knowledge. Instead, allow yourself to pause.

To eliminate your use of fillers, practice speaking with this strategy: at any given time you can either think or speak—but you cannot do both at once. Pause and think of the whole idea, then deliver it with emphasis. A friend can help you by raising her hand between your sentences, counting out a long two seconds. When the hand is in the air, you must pause.

When Thomas Jefferson agreed to pen the Declaration of Independence, he said that he sought to put it in "terms so plain and firm as to command their consent." The simpler you can make your argument, the easier it will be for the audience to understand it. If audience members can follow your train of thought, they are more likely to trust it.

Nervousness

Audiences can sense when a speaker wants to be at the lectern; they can also sense when he or she does not. If you appear nervous, the audience will be nervous for you and will be uncomfortable; listeners will remember less of what you have to say. I am constantly reminding speakers that even though they may in fact be nervous, they need not let the audience know it. Studies have shown that audience members detect far fewer signs of nervousness than speakers think they can.

How do you combat nervousness? *Do not* do the following:

- Take beta-blockers.
- Drink alcohol.
- Drink beverages containing caffeine.

The following exercises before your presentation will make you less nervous:

- Envision the talk as going well.
- Do deep breathing and other relaxation exercises beforehand.
- Exercise a full two hours before the talk; your body will be relaxed and your mind will be energized.
- Sit in a hot tub.
- Practice, practice, practice.

Eye Contact

Be sure to look directly at different members of the audience. When you make eye contact with people, you make a contract with them: I see you, you see me, we recognize each other, now we are ready to communicate. Eye contact lays the foundation for communication. I have seen speakers give whole presentations to the screen, or to the rear corner of the auditorium, and the effect is alienating. It is very difficult to trust someone who refuses to look at you.

If you are not comfortable randomly glancing at different people in the audience, you might pick three friendly faces, seated in separate sections of the audience, and alternate your eye contact among them. In a large auditorium, if you look at one person there will be a 6-diopter circle of people around that person who think you are looking at them.

You don't necessarily to have to look directly into people's eyes, either. You can look at their foreheads, their mouths, their cheeks—it will *appear* that you are looking at their eyes. Be careful not to look exclusively at the chief of the department or the boss, because this practice will surely alienate the other members of the audience.

If you are going to choose only a few people to look at, be sure to pick those who are giving you positive feedback, so that your delivery skills are reinforced. By concentrating on the person falling asleep or the person talking to his neighbor, you will get negative feedback, be distracted yourself, and do poorly.

The truth is that medical audiences in general spend far too much time seated and listening to speakers. They sit in auditoriums before the workday begins, they listen to speakers during the lunch hour while eating, they go back to those auditoriums after putting in eight or ten or twelve hours in the hospital. They listen to speakers after being on call, awake, for twenty-four or forty-eight hours. Medical audiences are often tired audiences.

In addition, important things in their lives often take precedence over your presentation—for one, the care of patients. Medical audiences will naturally have distractions from your talk. As a speaker, you cannot let these distractions inhibit your delivery skills. You must block out the people falling asleep, the individuals jumping out of their seats to answer their pagers, those reviewing charts and writing clinical notes during your talk, the two persons in the back (or front) of the room having a private discussion.

You never get the positive feedback you deserve to maintain your delivery skills. The energy to keep your enthusiasm high must come from inside yourself. To this extent, you become an actor whenever you address a group. You must look at the sea of blank faces and see a mass of heads nodding in agreement.

Repetition

Unlike a paper, in which the writer uses repetition only in an abstract or summary, repetition is a speaker's way of emphasizing crucial points. Repetition is not necessarily redundancy. You can stress important information by telling it in a few different ways or by using different examples to emphasize the same point. Remember the different types of adult learners? Why not emphasize your main point by making it first for the intuitive learner, then for the practical learner, and then for the sequential learner? Use repetition to reach out to the different types of audience members.

Repetition is also effective when used as a stylistic device. A speaker I heard in Atlanta said, "If you follow these steps when repotting plants, they will live. *They will not die.*" Other speakers use a form of repetition called parallelism. Remember the famous "I have a dream" speech by Dr Martin Luther King, Jr? His point was not that he had a dream; his point was what that dream was about. But it was his repetition of the words "I have a dream today" that drew in the audience and gave emphasis to his point.

Humor

Humor can be helpful only if it is, in fact, funny, and if it is related to the topic. If it is not funny, then it is not humor. If it is not related to the topic, it will distract the audience from your message. Be sure that you are using humor as a "handle on the bucket," as a means to help your listeners carry around the information.

If you are not a naturally funny person in the hallway, don't try to make your first joke in front of 150 people. If you *are* a naturally funny person, then you can let that aspect of yourself come through by using humor as it relates to your topic, in the service of the topic.

Don't feel a need to break the ice by telling a joke at the beginning of your talk. If you want to engage the audience, start by telling a story related to the topic to "paint the picture," to put the audience in the situation. And don't go searching through the Gary Larson anthology every time you have to give a talk; although Gary Larson cartoons are very funny, they are so overused in medical speaking that they have become trite.

Let's say now that you have the perfect cartoon: it is not only related to the topic but actually reveals a truth about it. And it will absolutely help the audience remember your points. Here's how to use it. When you put it on a slide, mask the caption at the bottom of the cartoon, or white out the words in the bubble. During your talk, show the cartoon and let the audience absorb the image. Then say, "The caption on this cartoon is . . ." or "Here the patient is saying to the doctor, . . ." and read the caption so that the audience gets the joke from you, not from the screen. Let the audience get a burst of endorphins from something *you* said to keep the attention on you and your message.

If you are going to use humor, be judicious with it. Too much joking may detract from the overall seriousness of the topic. Having said that, humor can act as a powerful foil to the serious comments a speaker wants to make. A speaker can radically shift the tone by saying, "Well, we've had a good time here today, had a few laughs, but at this point I need to emphasize that . . ." and in measured, deliberate words convey the seriousness of the situation.

Useful Images

An image that is related to the topic, an image that will help the audience recall the main point is a fine idea. But remember that the rules about humor apply to the vacation slide as well. It is overused, it is trite, and a majority of the time it distracts the audience from the message. Speakers who punctuate their talks with unrelated vacation slides are undermining their own efforts to convey information. A little effort in preparation can go a long way when it comes to images that audiences will remember. A digital camera on hand will allow you to record images that you can transfer into a PowerPoint file. And with most Internet browsers, any image on the Internet is yours in three steps: select the image, copy, then paste.

One study found that 87 percent of what we remember, we recall because we associate it with *images*. Images are the building blocks of memory. Take advantage of them not only in your slides, but in the way you talk. Paint the picture by describing things and events concretely. Put the audience in the examining room by adding all the relevant details. Tell the story.

Of course, in a seven-minute talk at a national meeting you have no time to start your formal study with a case presentation. But in an hourlong talk at grand rounds, be certain to involve the audience by starting with a related case or anecdote. In the one-hour talk, spend the first five minutes introducing the topic with a case presentation, move into the historical and theoretical aspects, and end the talk in the last five minutes by returning to the case you began with, letting the audience know the outcome. This is called putting a frame on the talk.

Examples, Stories, Analogies

We live in a tactile world, surrounded by real things and real people. We experience the world through sight and touch and sound and smell and emotion and combinations of these senses. All these forms of perception make their mark on our memory. For speakers *not* to use these senses in their talks is to inhibit their audiences' ability to remember. Conversely, speakers who draw on all the senses in conveying information give their message the best possible chance to burn itself permanently into the listeners' memory.

We are a storytelling people. The majority of the information we convey in everyday life we transmit through stories. Why would we disregard this natural means of connecting just because we are in an auditorium or a seminar room? Use concrete details. Tell stories. And best of all, convey complex ideas with the help of analogies.

The formal scientific study is like the British detective novel. A crime has been committed—there is a problem—and the detective's goal is to solve it. To do this, he has to devise a way of solving the problem—methods. He tracks down some clues and makes some observations—results—and from these he deduces a solution—the conclusions.

In a scientific investigation, whose story is it? Is it the story of the data or the story of the investigators? It is the story of the investigators that counts. The data do not invent themselves, do not organize themselves into neat charts and graphs. It is the investigators who observe that there is a problem with a particular situation, the investigators who narrow the objective, who design the methods and collect the data, the investigators who interpret the data to mean x. Even in a formal presentation, do not leave yourself out of the story.

Interaction

Remember the adult learner who learns best by intuition? Address this feature by promoting interaction. Speakers can facilitate interaction on many different levels.

Ask Questions

The first and most obvious level of interaction is to ask questions outright. In a classroom setting, or in any situation with a clear delineation of who is the boss and who are the subordinates, certainly ask questions and wait for the answers. When no answers are given, or when you receive wrong answers, your job as a teacher is to pose additional questions, the answers to which will lead to the correct answers to the original questions. In teaching at a community college, there were times when I asked four or five questions in a row before I got any answer, and then my job was to ask the previous questions again. Looking back, I realize that with this technique I was addressing both the intuitive learners and the sequential learners.

Singling out any one student to answer a particular question is ill-advised. Speakers who call on specific students to answer questions create a tense environment in the classroom that is unpleasant for the other students. Open up all questions to all members of the class, and reward correct answers (and incorrect answers, for effort). The resulting environment of support is conducive to participation and learning.

If I am a member of a class and the teacher calls on another student to answer a particular question, I am not very likely to try to answer it in my head. However, if the teacher opens up questions to all members of the class, I feel more obligated to try to find answers.

What do you do about the person who dominates the answers? Simple: after the third correct answer in a row, say, "Congratulations, you've earned your gold star for the day; hold back and let's let the others answer for a while."

Subtle Interaction

In a large auditorium or at a formal meeting, you cannot expect answers to your questions. But you can still phrase a comment or introduce a problem in the form of a question, pause a few seconds, and then answer it yourself. An excellent way to move to your results, for instance, is to ask, "What did we find?" By phrasing statements in the form of questions, you will surely add extra inflection to your voice. And remember to pause to allow time for the audience to think.

Another way you can promote interaction is by using your visual aids correctly. Too many speakers flip to a slide, look at it, and start talking about the information. This method quickly becomes tedious. Effective use of visual aids means using the visual to reinforce what was spoken. Asking "What did we find?" *before* flipping to the first results slide allows you and the visual aids to interact with the audience. As the audience wonders "What *did* they find?" the slide drops with the answer.

Interaction to Promote Objectivity

Another type of interaction has to do with scientific objectivity. As a speaker, you want to convey your points and have your audience walk away believing them. But audiences in scientific settings are most likely to believe that which they figure out for themselves. So you promote this last and most subtle type of interaction not by convincing or persuading the audience of your points, but by letting them decide for themselves.

To do this, present your information in a manner that leaves audience members room to figure it out for themselves. Give them the problem as you saw it, tell them the reasoning behind your methods, trace the line of your interpretation so that it is reasonable and logical, acknowledge the limitations and other points of view and provide your responses to them, and be simple and forthright in your conclusions and recommendations. In other words, give your professional audiences the tools they need to come up with the answers to your problems themselves. If they happen to walk out of the talk concluding what you also concluded, then you have done your job in as an objective a manner as possible.

Enthusiasm and Respect

The above aspects of delivery can be summarized by saying that effective speakers have *enthusiasm* and *respect*. Let your enthusiasm for the topic shine through in the energy of your voice and body movements. As an actor, you must remember to emphasize the natural enthusiasm you have for a topic so that it is apparent to members of the audience seated back in the last row.

In an ideal world, you would only stand in front of a hundred people to talk about topics for which you have loads of natural enthusiasm. In the real world, you often are required to discuss things for which you only have a limited amount of natural enthusiasm. And now and again, you are required to address topics for which you have no natural enthusiasm whatsoever. What do you do in these last two situations? *Fake it.* For the benefit of those in the audience who might be interested in the topic, and in the service of the topic itself, you should make yourself appear to be enthusiastic. You do this not at the expense of objectivity, you do it in the service of your message so that your audience understands and remembers it.

I once saw an actor being interviewed about acting. His comment was, "Embrace your audience, and they'll embrace you." For speakers in science and medicine and health care fields, I translate this to "Respect your audience, and they'll respect you." Respect them to the extent that you take advantage of, even exaggerate, your natural delivery skills. Show your audience the respect of conveying your information in the most effective way you know, and they will return that respect by remembering what you have told them.

Have fun, too. If you seem to be getting a charge out of conveying your information, the audience will stay with you and your reasoning. I often say, "If there's going to be only one person in the entire audience who has any fun during my talk, then it might as well be me." If you lead, then the audience will follow.

PREPARATION FOR YOUR TALK

Make a Timeline

To keep yourself organized as you prepare, make a timeline with specific deadlines. This will save your energy and relieve your worry about the talk. At the very least, you won't be running all over trying to find slides at the last minute.

Prepare and Submit an Abstract

For a talk at a formal meeting, your presentation abstract will first have to be accepted by the appropriate committee. The purpose of submitting the abstract is to encourage the committee to allow you to present your work; format your information with this goal in mind.

An abstract for a meeting differs from one that you would prepare to accompany a manuscript for publication. A meeting abstract is not a publication of record; it does not have to conform to the same standards as one published in a peer-reviewed journal. Thus, abstracts for meetings can have what editors call an "informative" title; you can give away your conclusions in the title. You can make your main point right at the top of the page.

In addition, abstracts for meetings can take advantage of tables and graphs, whereas publication abstracts do not. If your results are more easily understood in the form of tables or graphs, by all means present them that way. Consider using flow charts or decision trees to convey processes. Make the committee's job of understanding and accepting your presentation as easy as possible.

Know the Audience

Before you start to put your information together, find out about members of the audience. This knowledge will allow you to direct the information toward their needs. Consider the following questions:

- How many people will be in the audience?
- What is the purpose of the audience in attending?
- How familiar is the audience with the subject?
- What is the educational background of the audience?
- Does the audience have any biases relative to this topic? If so, what are they?
- What do I want the audience to *do* with the information?
- What materials do I want to leave with the audience?
- What reasonable questions might the audience ask? How will I respond?
- What *unreasonable* questions might the audience ask? How will I respond?

Work with the contact person to help answer these questions. You might consider asking the contact person for the name and number of a representative member of the audience who wouldn't mind a ten-minute telephone call about his or her expectations of the talk.

At the very least, plan to arrive at your talk half an hour early, to greet individual audience members and talk to them about what they know about the topic, why they are attending, and what they expect. I am always impressed by the speaker who refers to members of the audience during a talk, and relates their stories to the topic.

Know the Purpose

If they are not the same, differentiate between the audience's purpose in attending the talk and your purpose in giving the talk.

- Why are you giving this talk?
- What is your purpose?
- How does your purpose differ from the audience's purpose?

Be sure to let the audience know your intentions in a purpose statement toward the beginning of the talk, so that they are prepared to receive your message. State it directly: "My purpose today is to . . ."

Know the Setting

The setting plays a significant role in what you can and cannot do in a presentation. The type of interaction you can foster in a room holding ten people is much different from that which you can achieve in front of four hundred. Knowing the setting beforehand will allow you to plan what you can do and how you can do it.

- What is the room size?
- At what time of day is the talk?
- How will the seating be arranged? Can I control it?
- Is the door to the room at the front, side, or rear?
- What audiovisual equipment will be available?
- Where are the light switches, remote control for audiovisuals, microphone, and the like?
- What distractions are apt to be present? How will I handle them?

Try to get this information from the contact person in advance of your presentation, or check out the room a few days before your talk. At the very least, show up early for your talk to adapt your presentation style to the setting. If possible, move tables and chairs around to best involve the audience. To promote an interactive session, try to arrange seating in a semicircle.

Know the Topic

Obviously, you must know your topic. Be sure to review the latest research. It is worthwhile to run a MEDLINE search the week before your presentation. If you are presenting a very timely topic, be sure to review the most recent *paper* editions of the appropriate journals, because MEDLINE runs four to six weeks behind the paper journals.

When presenting to people who already know the topic well, you should have at least *one* piece of information that no one else in the room will know.

Realize that as a teacher, you are not just conveying information, you are teaching the audience *how to think* about the information. Try to come up with novel ways of looking at the problem that will help audience members understand and remember and approach the topic in their professional work. Conjure up analogies and strategies to help them recall the way you approached the topic.

Consider the following questions:

- What is your subject?
- What is your title?
- How long is your talk?
- How long will you allow for the question-and-answer session?
- Which information is absolutely crucial to convey? Which is less important?
- What is my overall take-home message?
- If the audience will remember only one thing about my talk, what should it be?

For each main point:

- What is the simplest, most straightforward way to state it?
- What examples do I have to support it?
- What stories can I relate to help the audience remember it?
- What is the significance of this point?

- What do I want listeners to do with this information?
- How will they change their practice after knowing this information?
- How does this information fit into the overall scheme of medical knowledge?
- Knowing this, what will future researchers or practitioners be able to find out next?

Narrow your Focus

Remember not to include too much information if it will distract the audience from your main points. Take a lesson from the poets: "Less is more."

Narrow your focus according to the needs of the audience and the breadth of the information. If you are worried that audience members might think that you have missed whole aspects of the topic, acknowledge at the beginning that you are focusing on a certain aspect of what is a large topic, and tell them why you decided to concentrate on that aspect.

Make an Outline and Write the Talk

Once you have determined the audience, topic, purpose, and setting, you can begin to outline the content of your talk. Do you want to write it out? Well, if someday you would like to submit it for publication, that would be a reasonable exercise. But again, remember the difference between the spoken language and the written language. Write out your talk as you would say it: simply and to the point. Then transfer the ideas to index cards, one idea per card, using the tips given earlier in this chapter.

Get Feedback and Revise

No responsible scholar would let his or her work be published without a professional review; likewise, no responsible speaker should address an audience of peers without first soliciting professional feedback. Ask your colleague or mentor for thoughts on both the content and delivery of the talk. Give a few colleagues pads and pens and ask them to write down everything they think about during a dry run of your talk. Ask them to write any questions they have about the content, and use this information to revise your presentation. Ask them to think of possible pitfalls in the talk, possible questions you might receive, unfair questions or statements that might be thrown your way. If you decide not to revise your presentation accordingly, at least you can prepare responses in case these issues arise.

Consider using the following checklist when soliciting feedback: Did the speaker—

- have an arresting opening?
- tell the audience the purpose and agenda of the talk?
- make eye contact?
- use hand gestures?
- use appropriate body position and movement?
- inflect his or her voice?
- maintain the audience's interest?
- pause for emphasis?
- speak in complete sentences?
- repeat important points?
- use concrete and specific examples?
- give at least one example for each main point?
- convey enthusiasm?
- interact with the audience when appropriate?
- have a well-organized presentation?
- tell the significance of the points made?
- summarize the talk?
- tell the audience what they should do with the information?

Make Visual Aids

Only after the content is fixed should you make your visual aids. That way you will be assured that the visual aids are there to support you, not the other way around. (See the section on Visual Aids later in this chapter for tips on design and use.)

I suggest that you make visual aids only for information that satisfies one or more of the following conditions:

- It is better understood visually than from words.
- It is important enough to reinforce with visual aids.
- It is designed for the audience's understanding, not to cue the speaker.

Before you have the images transferred to slides, I suggest that you practice a few times with the hard copy of the images to be sure that each visual aid is essential to the audience's understanding of your message. Eliminate any that are unnecessary. Just because you are part of the scientific or health care community, you do not need to have a visual aid for everything you say. The overwhelming abundance of slides and computer presentation programs helps to explain why so many speakers cannot deliver their messages effectively.

Trick question: What is your best visual aid? Answer: You. You are your own best visual aid.

Videotape Yourself

An excellent exercise that you can do in the privacy of your own basement is videotaping yourself to check your presentation. When you set up the camera, be sure not to zoom the lens in, but put it at its widest setting so that you are a stage actor, so that you recreate your image as it will appear in front of an audience.

Try first giving the talk without any visual aids. Often speakers put so much energy into flipping the slides that they forget to maintain their delivery skills. When I work individually with first-time speakers and they are having trouble talking and changing the slides at the same time, I say, "Let's turn off the projector. First, tell me the story of what you did." Once we are happy with their delivery skills, we integrate the visual aids into the talk.

Here is something else I do with speakers who are not as lively and full of inflection as I know they can be. When reviewing the tape on the television, I turn *down* the sound and look at the silent image.

Then I point to the image and say, "Now, does *that* look like someone who appears to be interested in the topic?" This usually gets a laugh of recognition that the person on the screen actually appears to be bored by the topic.

Before I have a speaker try again, I say, "OK, no one is in this room except for you and me. This time, as you give the talk, become a used-car salesman. Being cheesy is not easy. But this time, *overdo it*. Give me everything you've got. If it's too much—if it impinges on your objectivity in any way—we'll take you back a step or two. But we don't know what you can do unless we see you try." And in more than six years of using this technique, almost without exception speakers have *liked* the way they looked when we reviewed the tape. Only twice did have to I say, "That was too far," and we found a middle ground.

Practice without Visual Aids

After you have practiced with your visual aids, practice again without them—this time to be sure that you can give the presentation even if the bulb in the projector burns out, the electricity fails, the computer can't communicate with the projector, or anything else goes wrong. What do you do when the visual aids fail? Keep talking. Speakers who stop when the slide jams in the projector lose their credibility.

Carry a hard copy of your slides. You can, at the last minute, make copies of them and distribute them as handouts, or you can make acetates of them and use the overhead projector.

THE DAY OF THE TALK

Be sure to get a full night's rest the night before your presentation. Eat healthy foods on the day of the talk. Exercise or do relaxation techniques if you worry about looking nervous. And for your own peace of mind, show up early. Run your slides through the projector once to make sure all of them are oriented correctly. If you plan on using the computer projector, show up at least an hour before the start of your talk to troubleshoot the many things that can go wrong with what is still a new technology. Greet people as they arrive, shake their hands, and ask them about their interest in the topic.

Nobody faults a speaker if he or she finishes a bit ahead of schedule; in fact, most appreciate it. If it is not clearly stated, let the audience know at the beginning of your talk when you plan to end, or when you will take a break. It is only fair to give your audience a break every hour or so. People need to stretch and go to the bathroom.

The Basic Short Presentation at a Formal Meeting

In a seven- to ten-minute talk at a regional or national meeting, you have just enough time to trace the thinking behind—and make the case for—your *one* major conclusion. Too many speakers try to crowd too much information into a limited period. By eliminating the less important information, speakers can be assured that they give proper emphasis to that which is most important.

Furthermore, many speakers get bogged down in the Introduction and Background and are just starting to discuss their Methods when the yellow light on the lectern comes on. With two minutes to go, they hurry through their Results, their delivery skills weaken, and their Conclusions and Recommendations get lost in the rush.

Here is a ten-step outline for presentation of a study at a formal meeting. Notice that for each section of the study, I recommend that the speaker say a few words to make the transition clear.

1. After being introduced, say, "Thank you, Dr _____. Dear Colleagues . . ." You do not have time to thank each and every member of the panel. The "Dear Colleagues" is simple and respectful, and inclusive of all in the room.
2. "I am here to present (title of presentation)." Say the title exactly as it is written on your title slide. Do not paraphrase, as this causes confusion for the audience.
3. "Dr _____, Dr _____ (the other authors), and I first became interested in this issue when . . ." Here you acknowledge the other authors and give a little personal background. You associate

the issue with the authors and give a few details that set up the story of what you did.

4. If you plan to review the literature on the issue, be brief. I like speakers who list on a slide the authors who have addressed the topic and say, "As you can see, a variety of researchers have looked into this problem . . ." and then mention those whose work is most relevant to the presentation.

5. Transition to the Objectives: "So we set out to answer the following questions: Number 1, . . . Number 2, . . ." State your objectives in a clear, direct way, numbering them for precision.

6. Transition to the Methods: "To answer these questions, we designed these methods: . . ."

7. Transition to the Results: "What did we find? Well, . . ." By using a question to introduce a new section, you add a little suspense to the presentation and continue to use the information to tell a story.

8. Transition to the Discussion/Limitations: "As to the limitations, we are obligated to mention . . ." Acknowledge the limitations, then offer your responses to them.

9. Transition to the Conclusions: "In conclusion, then, we find that . . ." Or, "So, given these results, we can conclude that . . ." Be sure to use the word "conclusion" or "conclude" to alert the audience to this crucial section.

10. Transition to the Recommendations: "Given these conclusions, we recommend that . . ." Or, "What does this mean for your practice? It means that . . ."

Be sure to separate Conclusions from Recommendations—and Results from Conclusions, for that matter. Too many speakers say, "In conclusion, 68 percent of patients in our study . . ." which is a confusing and sloppy ending.

Questions and Answers

Be sure to leave adequate time for questions and answers. If the setting allows and if you are comfortable with it, at the start of the talk encourage people to interrupt you to ask questions instead of waiting until the end. If you do offer to entertain questions at any time, be ready to regain control of the audience if it gets too far off the topic.

When asked a question, either repeat it for the benefit of those who did not hear it, or respond in a complete sentence that incorporates the question into the answer. Reward questioners with positive feedback: "Good question."

If you call for questions and nobody asks one—and you know that people have questions and are just being shy—you can get the ball rolling by asking your own question, and then answering it: "People often ask me, . . ."

If you are asked a question to which you do not know the answer, don't try to bluff your way through a response. Sincerity is on your side. Say that you do not know; let the questioner know you will get back to him or her. But don't just leave it at that. Remember that you are not only conveying information, but also teaching the audience how to think about the issue. Trace the first few steps that you will pursue to determine the answer, and give the keywords you will employ in a literature search. You are seeking to empower your listeners to discover the answer on their own.

If you get a question to which you do not know the answer and you are *not* the expert in the room, by all means defer the question to the person who is. Virtually everyone will know who the expert is, anyway. Your role then is as facilitator, so maintain control.

If someone phrases a question in the form of a statement—an implied question—rephrase the statement in the form of a question, then answer it. For example, "I understand your question to be . . ."

Occasionally you will hear a question that begins, "I have just one question; it has fourteen parts. The first part is . . ." Make notes for yourself if someone asks a long or complicated question. Sometimes it becomes necessary to interrupt a questioner. Remember that you are responsible for maintaining control. If things get out of hand, look to your contact person for help.

While it doesn't happen all the time, it happens often enough to warrant mentioning here: a person, during the question-and-answer period, makes a statement with the intent to do battle with you. Remember that this period is the time for you to reply to *valid* concerns about your presentation. It is not the place for a debate about unrelated or tangential material. It is your job to remind the audience of the proper context of the topic and the role your presentation plays in it.

Let's say you have just given your experience with problem A in population B. Someone stands up and says, "Well, *we* found that . . ." and goes on to talk about issues not related or out of context, or frankly contrary to your conclusions. Here are a few ways to regain control. You can say:

- "You bring up an interesting point . . ." and go on to talk about the one aspect of the point that *does* relate to your topic.
- "Well, in the context of the work I am presenting here . . ." In this way you have reminded the audience of the proper context.
- "Allow me to address one aspect of your point," and go on to address the aspect most related, or somewhat related, to your work.
- "Frankly, this isn't the time or place to debate this issue. I will reiterate, however, that . . ." and go on to reinforce your main point.

Here's the trick: when you reply to this sort of question, be sure to turn your eyes *away* from the unfair questioner and look at the rest of the audience.

I'm not saying that you should become a politician. When people raise valid issues, of course you should address them honestly and sincerely. Remember that objectivity, integrity, and scientific rigor are on your side. By acknowledging certain limitations and drawbacks to your ideas during the presentation you can preempt the tough questions and give prepared responses to those issues.

SPEAKING TO THE MEDIA

There may come a time when the local newspaper or television news calls your office and asks to interview you right away. The first thing to remember is that, despite any reporter's urgency, you can still prepare what you will say. If you agree to the interview, be sure to allow yourself enough time to prepare your comments. Make notes on the important things you want to convey, and refer to them during the interview.

Recall the purpose of the popular media: to sell newspapers or airtime. Their standards of objectivity are far lower than yours. You should demand to review the article or video before it is finalized, to check for inaccuracies or any of your comments that are taken out of context. Make such approval a condition of your participation.

Establish some ground rules in advance. Ask about general areas to be covered. Indicate areas where you will not or cannot respond. Do not allow yourself to be intimidated. Ask about the length of the interview.

Select a couple of main points you would like to convey and be ready to emphasize them at each opportunity. Think of possible questions you might be asked. Include in your list antagonistic questions as well as fair ones. Consider providing the interviewer with a list of questions to ask.

During the interview itself, be sure to speak in complete sentences to avoid any of your comments being taken out of context. If there is a camera, pretend that it is not there; look at the interviewer. Remember to maintain eye contact, inflect your voice, and gesture so that you are interesting to listen to. Maintain the level of enthusiasm, intensity, seriousness, or levity that the topic deserves. Remember to smile.

Don't let the interviewer or reporter bully you into speaking before you are ready. Take your time and answer as clearly and concisely as possible. If you get off track when you are speaking, stop, reorganize, and start over. Correct the interviewer immediately if he or she says something that is incorrect or out of context.

Remember the power of images, examples, stories, and analogies. You are speaking for a mass audience; be sure to take advantage of concrete details.

VISUAL AIDS

Keep in mind that the purpose of visual aids is not to prompt the speaker; they are to aid the audience's understanding and retention of the message. To cue yourself on what you want to say, make note cards. Or print out hard copies of the slides, three to a page. Or make a list of the titles of all your slides and refer to that. Introduce the topic first, *then* show the audience images that will help them remember.

Do not feel obliged to incorporate every single one of your points into a visual aid. You will end up making far too many of them, and your most important points are apt to get lost.

The most effective use of visual aids occurs when speakers know the subject of the next visual aid and say a few words about that topic *before* they flip to it. This strategy enables speakers to use their visual aids as a means to interact with the audience. Even if the speaker merely asks, "Well, what are the limitations of our study?" before the "Limitations" slide, the audience is involved. If using a slide of an X-ray to point out something, let the audience try to find the spot before you point it out yourself. Even though the lights may be out, you can still promote interaction and make the experience of learning a more involved one.

Graphic Visual Aids

In the last two years I have been challenging presenters to limit their visual aids to purely graphic ones, or at least to strongly limit their text-based visual aids. Words on the screen compete with the speaker, who is also using words. Images better complement a speaker's points. So if you must choose between a table and a graph of the same data, be sure to choose the graph. You can combine text and illustration to make your points clearer, too: consider the flow chart, the decision tree, and other elements that take advantage of both graphic and textual information in the same image.

The popular slide-making programs, and the computer presentation programs, were designed for business applications. Therefore, they do not maintain the same standards of objectivity that you and your listeners do. There is no scientific reason, for example, for a pie chart to be shown in three dimensions. The only scientific reason to show a chart or graph in three dimensions is if you have three variables. Using three-dimensional graphics without a valid reason undermines the objectivity of your data. Some might think that you are using optical illusions to alter the audience's perception of your data, and this will undermine your credibility.

Text Slides

When you are forced to make a text-only slide, be sure to put it in outline form. No sentences on slides; no paragraphs on slides. Speakers can read a paragraph at about 150 words per minute; audiences can read it at 400 words per minute. Audiences will have finished reading the paragraph before the speaker is halfway through it. They are then forced to sit through the rest of the narration, which is doubtless in a monotone because the speaker is reading, and they get bored.

One exception might be a Conclusion that a group of authors have decided that they want to word in a certain, specific way. In that case, one sentence per slide is reasonable. Having said that, allow me to report a trend I have noticed at meetings in the last year: a few speakers have actually asked for the lights to be *raised* during the presentation of their Conclusions and Recommendations, which reinforces that those sections emanate from a live person, not a screen or monitor.

Be careful to avoid using an entire set of text-only visual aids. That kind of organization can put a speaker in a verbal rut and rob him or her of the natural sense of rhetoric and flexibility that characterizes much of our interpersonal communication.

When putting together outlines for your text slides, follow the 7×7 rule: have no more than seven lines of text per slide, and no more than seven words per line. This rule will prevent your text slides from getting too busy and illegible.

Use bullet points to make clean outlines. Start each bulleted entry with the same type of word (for example, all nouns or all verbs) so that the information is parallel and consistent. A reader should be able to append each bulleted entry to the title and receive a single idea.

If you are using numbers instead of bullets, be aware of what numbers imply that bullet points do not: a sequence, an order, a hierarchy of importance. If you do not mean to imply any of these, stick to bullets.

Avoid using red or any shade of red in your visual aids. Although red looks fine on a computer screen, it does not project well in the auditorium or seminar room. When used for words or numbers, it bleeds into the background; when used as a background, it is assaultive. In addition, some people are color blind and color deficient and cannot see red.

Dual Projection

In the last ten years the use of dual projection has become popular, especially at meetings. If you plan to use dual projection, do so only if you need to show two images at once in order for the audience to understand the message. Dual projection is often employed to show twice as much information, which can only result in confusion.

When using dual projection, the images must be complementary. For example—

- table and graph of the same data
- before and after
- photograph and diagram
- English and another language
- textual and graphic

Format for Slides and Computer Images

When designing your own slides, remember to be consistent. Choose a template for your slides and stick to it. Maintain the same template for all your presentations, so that you can use the slides in the future in different combinations and they will still be uniform.

If possible, consult with an audiovisual department. You should be able to enlist the help or advice of an expert there.

The ideal text slide will have the following characteristics:

- Horizontal with 2:3 ratio
- Content limited to main point
- Black or dark blue background
- Title in yellow, all capitals
- Outline format in white, lowercase
- Maximum of seven lines of text
- No more than seven words per line
- Sans serif type, such as Helvetica or Arial
- Use of capitals and italics limited

The ideal graphic slide will have:

- No more than five to seven bars, columns, or pieces of a pie chart
- Title in capitals, all yellow
- Clear labels or legends in corresponding colors.

NOTES

1. St. James, D. *Writing and Speaking for Excellence.* 2nd ed. Sudbury, Mass.: Jones and Bartlett, 1998.

2. Apps, J. *Mastering the Teaching of Adults.* Malabar, Fla.: Krieger, 1991.

9

Techniques for Teachers

Kirk T Hughes

With the vast proliferation of scientific knowledge, increasing specialization, and the ongoing pressure to "responsibly cover the basics," teaching graduate and professional school courses in the life sciences is more challenging than ever. Thoughtfully attending to course logistics and lecturing techniques saves time and sharpens the focus of medical teaching.

TOWARD AN EFFECTIVE SYLLABUS

Part calling card, part lecture schedule, part grading contract and marketing tool, a strong syllabus maps the territory to be covered in a course. While a basic syllabus provides logistical information, the best syllabi organize that information into a teaching tool. A strong syllabus outlines the purpose of a course and explains its value.

Given the benefits of a complete course syllabus for today's students, it is worth understanding some of the objections to them raised by teaching faculty.

Objection: "Smart, well-prepared students like ours don't need to be spoon fed."

Fact: Regardless of how or where your students were prepared, odds are that their backgrounds are extremely varied. The rightfully celebrated diversity of today's students guarantees they will arrive at your class with different expectations about the kind of material that will be taught, how it will be taught, and how students will be evaluated. A complete syllabus makes the rules clear to everybody.

Objection: "Some classes go faster than others, and my class schedules always change. Why map it out, when it's all going to change anyway?"

Fact: Although teaching schedules often change during a term, having a plan encourages people to stick close to it. Listing times, dates, assignments, and exam schedules from the outset gives students the freedom to schedule their own efforts accordingly. On-line syllabi have the added advantage of allowing instructors to update or adjust schedules as needed; the revised syllabus is available with a couple of key strokes.

Objection: "The best lecturer I ever had showed up with a textbook and a piece of chalk. I learned more from him than from anybody else."

Fact: Many of the most charismatic teachers of yesteryear were undisputedly low-tech in their teaching approach. Few teachers today, however, have their classical rhetorical training, and all of us work in a technologically more complex scientific environment. We have more information to wade through than our predecessors did, and our students have far more complex systems to comprehend. Anything today's teachers can do to facilitate the organization of information makes us more effective.

Objection: "Lectures are what matter; who has time for this silly administrative stuff?"

Fact: Class time that is focused on training students *does indeed* matter most. Think for a minute about how often schedule changes, assignment updates, and exam instructions have eaten up chunks of class time that could have been much better spent explaining difficult material. Time spent preparing your syllabus saves time for teaching tasks far more important than communicating logistics.

Furthermore, given the fact that professional review and promotion committees increasingly focus on the effectiveness of teaching faculty, stronger course syllabi can be a professional plus. Many review committees consider such syllabi a measure of teaching effectiveness, just as they consider publications a measure of research productivity.

Consider the two syllabi in Figures 9.1 and 9.2. Which looks more familiar? Which course would you rather take? Both syllabi refer to the same course material, but the second one articulates the purpose of the study. It provides students with complete schooling and "how much does it count" information they can use throughout the term. Notice that the first syllabus is teacher focused. It reads like a speakers' schedule, clearly listing which faculty member is responsible for which primary text. Syllabus 2, by contrast, is more student focused. The lecture titles give some idea of how the speakers will be approaching the material, and the bulleted course description promotes the course as an opportunity to develop three kinds of awareness: historical background (a "survey" of influences), critical method (use and misuse of "empirical facts"), and professional application ("ongoing consideration" of history's influence on professional medicine).

While there are no hard and fast rules about syllabus design, the following is a helpful list of what to include:

- Course Logistics
  Include meeting time, place, duration, and any laboratory or discussion sections. Identify lead instructors and include a way for students to contact them (e-mail, phone, office hours). List the names and contact information of teaching assistants as well.

```
HISTORY OF MEDICINE 755
PDQ SCHOOL OF MEDICINE
FALL 2000

Week Topic                                           Instructor

9/8    Introduction                                  SCHMIDT
9/15   Job and Thucydides                            SCHMIDT
9/22   Hippocrates and Galen                         SCHMIDT
9/29   Aristotle                                     SCHMIDT
10/6   Renaissance anatomy                           SCHMIDT
10/13  Reaumur's physiology                          BRITTAN
10/20  Lavoisier's respiration                       BRITTAN
10/27  Schwann and cell theory; midterm              BRITTAN
11/3   Koch's bacteriology                           BRITTAN
11/10  Pasteur and germ theory                       BRITTAN
11/17  Mendel and genetics                           WRIGHT
11/24  Break
12/1   Krebs's metabolism                            WRIGHT
12/8   Watson's double helix and genetic             WRIGHT
       engineering
12/15  Final examination

Lectures: Tuesdays and Thursdays, 1:00–2:30, Smartly
203

Texts: A reading packet will be available at the campus
copy center.
```

Figure 9.1 Sample syllabus 1.

- Course Description and Goals

  A strong course description is like a paper abstract; it is brief but accurate about what is inside. In addition to the description of the course, consider including a list of course goals that states what you expect students to be able to do as a result of the course. One sure way to ascertain the effectiveness of your teaching and your students' learning is to see the goals set forth in the syllabus are met at the end of the term.

- Course Requirements and Grades

  Explicitly state your attendance policy, exam dates, project due dates, and instructions for any other graded assignments. While instructors should expect responsibly completed and timely work on the part of their students, students deserve clear information about when their work is due and how it will be weighted.

- Readings

  List authors, titles, and editions of all required readings as well as where students may acquire them. In the coming years, course textbooks will increasingly be made available on-line. MIT's experimental hypertext biology text at ⟨http://esg-www.mit.edu:8001/esgbio/7001main.html⟩ is an example of things to come.

- Schedule

  Along with the general topic or the more specific title of a class lecture, include the textbook chapters, or the authors and titles of work to be discussed that day. Incorporate exam dates and vacation breaks to help keep everyone on track.

- Graphics and Syllabi On-line

  Keep the graphics simple, but use bold headings, bullets, and spacing to facilitate quick reference to the material. Given the frequency of change over the course of a semester, teaching faculty report that on-line syllabi and course Web pages have several major advantages. Many teaching faculty use an on-line syllabus to—

  1. Post and immediately distribute schedule changes, saving precious class time.

HistMed 755:
Historical Perspectives on the Life Sciences
PDQ School of Medicine, Fall 2000
Instructor: Al B Wright, MD, PhD
E-mail: alwright@PDQ.edu
Office: Finde Lab 234
Office Hours: Thurs 3:00–4:00 & by appointment
Class meetings: Tues/Thurs 1:00–2:30, Smartly 203

Historical Perspectives on the Life Sciences: From Affliction to Disease

Course Description

This course reviews original writings by major thinkers from antiquity to the present, whose inquiries developed into what we now call life science. Selected historical texts illustrate major trends in thought, observation, and experimentation that have defined Western thinking in the life sciences. The goals of this course are as follows:

- To survey some of the major historical events and debates that so often influence current topics of medical research and interest.
- To develop an understanding of the way empirical facts are used and misused in the development of historical arguments.
- To develop self-education skills that will facilitate ongoing consideration of historical trends as they affect contemporary medical science and practice.

Course Requirements and Grades

Attendance at all class meetings is required, and students will be responsible for the following:

1. Reading the primary texts
2. Leading one class discussion
3. Preparing written questions for guest lecturers
4. Writing one research paper of 2,000–2,500 words (8–10 pages) reviewing a historical monograph on one major thinker.

Written exams and grading will be as follows:

Midterm examination	(27 October 2000)	25%
Final examination	(15 December 2000)	25%
Research paper	(due 20 December 2000)	25%
Class participation/presentation		25%

Readings

A class reading packet is available for purchase at the campus bookstore, and selected readings will be available on-line. Research monographs are on reserve in the medical school library under Wright, HistMed 755.

Schedule

1. Premodern Thinkers from Antiquity to the Renaissance (Dr Schmidt)

8 Sept: Introduction: When did medicine begin?
10 Sept: Hippocratic medicine: Hippocratic Corpus, "Tradition in Medicine"
15 Sept: Biblical affliction, The Book of Job
17 Sept: Galen's physiology, "On anatomical procedures" and "The uses of breathing," etc.

Figure 9.2 Sample syllabus 2.

2. Include useful Web-based resources (hypertextbooks, data-bases, journals), as hyperlinks. Pointing and clicking to a syllabus "Resources" section can give students time-saving access to resource and reference materials for the course.

3. Provide quick access to the whole range of course materials previously distributed as handouts. On-line publishing of problem sets, review questions, exam answer keys, lecture outlines, and the like encourages faculty-student communication and can make teaching and learning more efficient.

ADVANCED LECTURE TECHNIQUES

As lecturers, teaching faculty often think of class presentations as a series of speeches. An entire term-length course can be prepared, organized, delivered, and enhanced with visuals in the same way a single conference paper or grand rounds presentation might be; the principles for effective speaking outlined in Chapter 8 certainly apply. Lecturers, however, face the challenge of covering more material in much greater depth. Because they revisit student audiences again and again, teaching faculty have the added responsibility of developing the kind of rapport with students that sparks interest, gets students thinking, and motivates them to make connections with complex material. Besides knowing and loving the material they teach, many of the strongest lecturers make effective use of three important lecture techniques: linking, questions, and blocking.

Linking

When medical students are asked about what makes a lecture boring, they often respond with accusations: "It's irrelevant! How on earth is the etiology of anthrax ever going to help me in the ER?" While the faculty member may usefully deflect the student's objection with a defense of bacteriology as essential for all clinicians, such a rebuttal misses the point. The significance of such complaints is that they indicate a failure of linking. While the lecturer's knowledge is not in question, he or she has failed to explicitly draw the connection between a detailed discussion and the greater clinical perspective of a physician-in-training.

One master lecturer explained the power of linking with a reference to her new automatic sure-shot camera. "It's satisfying, is it not," she argued, "to go from the panorama setting to full zoom? After looking for a moment at a forest horizon ablaze with orange autumn color, I can zoom in and see one red maple there in the middle of some yellow birches." Similarly, it is satisfying for students when a lecturer zooms out from the technical detail of an explanation, problem, or proof to remind them of how the specifics fit in to the larger scope of their class.

Beginnings and endings of class meetings are ideal times for linking the day's material to the greater themes, goals, and objectives of the class, as are transitions between major chunks of material. These tips encourage linking:

- Within the first few minutes of your lecture, include an answer to the question, "Why is today's material important?" Remind students of how the material fits into the subfield, but also remind them of how expertise in the subfield contributes to their training as well.

- Outline three or four main points of the day's lecture on the board. After you cover each section of material, walk back to the board as a reminder to yourself to reiterate where you have been, what you have just covered, and where you are going next.

- Use introductions of guest lecturers (and thank-yous) as opportunities for linking. In addition to telling the class who the lecturer is and what the day's topic is, link the speaker's material to the greater themes of the course by saying *why* the material is meaningful to your particular course of study. Is the lecture important because of its cutting-edge and up-to-the-minute information? Does the work serve as a model for an original and well-written case study? Does the lecture explain the basic science underlying common clinical practice? Giving explicit answers to such questions reminds students how they might usefully contextualize the data to come.

Questions

While teachers and students alike agree that lively bouts of question and answer energize classes, most teachers have experienced question after question being met with excruciating quiet and rows of dead stares. How teachers ask questions, and which questions teachers ask, can make all the difference.

What-questions

Notice where your mind goes as you formulate answers to the following questions:

> What serves as the powerhouse of a cell?
> What systolic pressure indicates hypertension?
> In what year did Lavoisier fully articulate his quantitative method?

What-questions invite listeners to scan their own store of accumulated knowledge to see if they know the right answers (mitochondria, 140+, 1773). What-questions test for specific information. They serve well in examinations, but few students will volunteer speculative answers in the classroom that might get publicly shot down. What-questions are the ones most frequently met with silence.

How-questions

Now notice the kind of thinking these questions invite. What kind of response might you expect from a room full of students?

> How many of you have learned something new from today's article?
> How many of you would appreciate a quick review of last week's problem set?
> How many of you can explain at least one difference between RNA and DNA?

Even the stodgiest audience members find themselves responding to how-questions with nodding heads or a show of hands. After half the class admits to having learned "something new" from the day's article, it is easy for the instructor to follow up by inviting the student— there in the third row—to share what she learned. How-questions invite no-risk response on the part of students. They serve as a dependable primer for a question-and-answer session by establishing a pattern of ask and answer between the lecturer and the listeners. How-questions have the added benefit of quickly surveying the group's immediate understanding. If no one can name one difference between RNA and DNA, the instructor knows that a quick review of nucleic acids is in order before diving into advanced enzymology.

Which-questions

This set of questions invites a still different cognitive strategy. Where does your thinking go to answer these questions?

> Which of the case reports we have reviewed do you think is most significant?
>
> Which of these symptoms do you think is most prevalent in rural settings: high blood pressure, high cholesterol, or diabetes?
>
> Which of the laboratory results do you think clinicians value most?

Which-questions focus listeners on a set of information. To answer which symptom is most prevalent, for example, listeners compare the list with their store of knowledge and choose one. Whether the response is right or wrong, which-questions give opportunities to repeat and emphasize important sets of information. After hearing the three symptoms in the question, reviewing them in their heads, and listening to them discussed in the answer, few students will forget those three prevalent symptoms. Because they are so effective in reviewing material, which-questions are a useful tool to wrap up a section of material before moving on to the next.

One award-winning lecturer in immunology admits to penciling in three which-questions at the end of every section of his outline. "By asking my medical students which-of-whatever do they think most significantly informs clinical practice," he points out, "I presuppose that basic science *always* informs clinical experience. It's a powerful teaching strategy because it encourages my students to constantly make connections between what they encounter in ward rounds and what they study in class."

Blocking

If Shakespeare's right that "all the world's a stage," his dictum goes double for teachers. Yet few lecturers use their stage space at the front of the classroom or lecture hall to full advantage. By tying a specific kind of teaching task to a specific location in the room, teachers can cue students to focus their attention more effectively.

Consider four kinds of tasks students may focus on during a typical lecture, and the very different kinds of attention these tasks require.

Note taking on important course content
Answering questions that link material to course themes
Integrating information through illustrations and anecdotes
Noting assignment changes and laboratory instructions.

To block your class, simply assign a specific location to each teaching task and go there while completing that task. Go to one base to move through course content. Step to a different base to engage your students with questions. Use still a different place to give logistical instructions. One lecturer maps her bases as shown in Figure 9.3.

Which particular space you choose as your question base, your example base, your content base, or your logistics base is immaterial. What matters is training yourself to match each teaching mode to a specific place. With consistency, a pattern develops. The movements of your body visually mark different sections of the lecture, and students' attentions respond accordingly. After one anatomy lecturer noticed her students perk up every time she moved into her place-

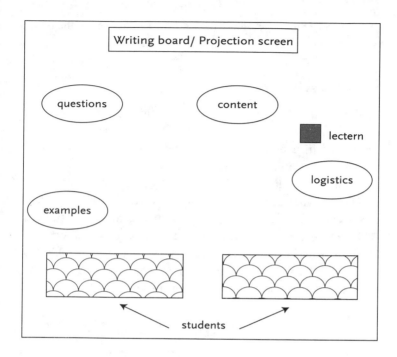

Figure 9.3 An example of blocking.

where-I-tell-stories-to-illustrate-lecture-points space, she realized
how powerfully her once-a-week anecdotes were helping her students remember things. By term's end she had rebalanced her material to include at least two stories per class.

At the simplest level, lecturers who use more of their space add
visual variety to their talks; such diversity is far more interesting than
watching a talking head float on top of a podium for an hour. Many
who incorporate this technique into their teaching note an added
benefit as well: students pay better attention. Within a week or so, one
instructor noticed that without saying a word he could walk toward
his "giving assignments base" and the class would start reaching for
their day planners and syllabi. Blocking uses nonverbal cues to add

variety to a lecture, to reinforce thoughtful organization of the material, and to refresh attention with sensible shifts of focus.

ANNOTATED REFERENCES

As data in the life sciences proliferate faster and faster, students depend more and more on teaching faculty to help them sort through everything. In publications, accurate reference lists verify reliable sources. In teaching contexts, *annotating* a reference list helps readers organize and filter the information based on key categories. Because none of us can possibly read all that is available, annotated lists of references filter the wealth of information into reasonable subsets. Where references simply list, annotated references list and sort.

Compare the two reference lists in Figures 9.4 and 9.5. Which do you think will have more success as a teaching tool? Which do you think does a better job of encouraging further consultation of the sources?

While simply changing the graphics makes the second list more readable, titles, headings, and brief descriptions of the works guide readers quickly to the most valuable information. The annotated list includes fewer references (nine instead of nineteen), but it explains how each work is relevant to the themes of the class. Annotating reference lists develops the very skills that researchers use in advanced literature searches: categorization and evaluation. To help incorporate annotated reference lists into your teaching, here are some tips.

- Develop annotated reference lists of your own for students to use as a model. Your headings in themselves establish the main points of focus of class material.
- Use fifteen or twenty minutes of lecture time to verbally annotate a list of ten or twelve key course references. Printing out reference lists with plenty of blank space encourages students to jot down their annotations as you read through the list. At the end of your review, ask the students to develop three or four headings under which the references might be grouped.

References

1. Aristotle. *The "Art" of Rhetoric.* Loeb Classical Library. Oxford: Oxford University Press, 1926.

2. Banner, J., and Cannon, H. *The Elements of Teaching.* New Haven: Yale University Press, 1997.

3. Bonner, T. *Becoming a Physician: Medical Education in Great Britain, France, Germany and the United States, 1750–1945.* New York: Oxford University Press, 1995.

4. Brendan, R., and Lemon, M. Evidence-based morning report. *Am.J.Med.* (1997) 103:419–426.

5. Cassell, E. J. *Doctoring the Nature of Primary Care Medicine.* New York: Oxford University Press, 1997.

6. Davis, M. *Scientific Papers and Presentations.* San Diego: Academic Press, 1997.

7. Harnack, A., and Kleppinger, E. *On-line: A Reference Guide to Using Internet Sources.* New York: St. Martin's Press, 1998.

8. Hurst, J. W. *Essays from the Heart.* New York: Raven Press, 1995.

9. Kassirer, J. P. Redesigning graduate medical education—location and content. *N.Engl.J.Med.* (1996) 335:507–509.

10. Lanham, R. *The Electronic Word.* Chicago: Chicago University Press, 1993.

11. Lewkonia, R. M., and Murray, F. R. Grand rounds: A paradox in medical education. *Can.Med.Assoc.J.* (1995) 152:371–376.

12. Li, X., and Crane, N. *Electronic Styles: A Handbook for Citing Electronic Information.* Medford, N.J.: Information Today, 1996.

13. Lynch, P., and Horton, S. *Web Style Guide: Basic Design Principles for Creating Web Sites,* 2nd ed. New Haven: Yale University Press, 1999.

14. MacLeod, P. J., and Gold, P. Medical grand rounds: Alive and well and living in Canada. *Can.Med.Assoc.J.* (1990) 142:1053–56.

15. Connor, J., and Seymour, J. *Training with Neuro-linguistic Programming.* London: Thorsons, 1994.

16. O'Donnell, J. J. *Avatars of the Word: From Papyrus to Cyberspace.* Cambridge, Mass.: Harvard University Press, 1998.

17. Tufte, E. R. *Visual Explanations.* Cheshire, Conn: Graphics Press, 1997.

18. Tufte, E. R. *The Visual Display of Quantitative Information.* Cheshire, CT: Graphics Press, 1995.

19. Wolff, R. S., and Yeager, L. *Visualization of Natural Phenomena.* Electronic Library of Science, Santa Clara, Calif.: Springer Verlag, 1993.

Figure 9.4 Sample reference list 1.

LECTURE TECHNIQUES

James M. Banner and Harold C. Cannon, *The Elements of Teaching* (New Haven: Yale University Press, 1997).

Like a medieval "book of virtues," this brief essay reviews characteristics such as "authority," "order," "ethics," and "pleasure" with concise explanations and engaging stories of exemplary (and awful!) teachers to illustrate each. Teaching faculty should reread this book every year between semesters as an inspiration, as a reminder of the artfulness of what they do, and as a model of how powerfully anecdotes can teach.

Joseph O'Connor and John Seymour, *Training with Neuro-linguistic Programming* (London: Thorsons, 1994).

A practical counterpoint to Banner and Cannon's *Elements*, this book presents microtechniques for teaching and training developed in the competitive 1980s consulting world. Derived from the linguistics and communications theories of Chomsky, Grinder, Bandler, Bateson, and others, it is a brief and schematic review of useful nonverbal presentation skills. Three brief chapters—"Dealing with Difficult People," "Questions," and "Metaphors"—are worth the price of the book and one's patience with the occasional lapses into pop psychology.

Edward R. Tufte, *Visual Explanations* (Cheshire, Conn.: Graphics Press, 1997).

Along with his 1983 classic on the visual display of quantitative information, this volume gives Yale professor Tufte's rules for design excellence in the display of numbers—everything the PowerPoint help screens don't bother to tell you. A must-read for those using charts, tables, and graphs to present statistical data. See especially the chapter entitled "Visual and Statistical Thinking."

Richard Lanham, *The Electronic Word* (Chicago: University of Chicago Press, 1993).

This already dated, but still useful overview demonstrates how digital technologies are changing the way people think, argue, write, rewrite, format, publish, and teach. Lanham is a scholar of Renaissance literature and the history of rhetoric, turned writing-program director. Includes some prescient thoughts about integrating high technology into the laboratories, libraries, and lecture halls.

Patrick J. Lynch and Sarah Horton, *Web Style Guide: Basic Design Principles for Creating Web Sites* (New Haven: Yale University Press, 1999).

Director of the Yale Center for Advanced Instructional Media, Lynch has collaborated with graphic designer Horton to offer a clear, sensible, and practical design for teaching websites. A hypertext version of this helpful and reliable guide is available online: ⟨info.med.yale.edu/caim/manual/⟩

James J. O'Donnell, *Avatars of the Word: From Papyrus to Cyberspace* (Cambridge, Mass.: Harvard University Press, 1998).

Here are the "must-read" reflections of a classicist-turned-vice president-for-information-systems at the University of Pennsylvania. O'Donnell offers a pragmatic middle road between enthusiastic technophiles and reactionary, head-in-the-sand curmudgeons. The author is as savvy and computer literate as he is learned. On scholarly journals, for example, he writes:

> [Soon] the journal's peer review and stamp of approval will come after the fact of distribution and will exist as a way of helping identify high-quality work . . . In that world, the journal title will be something like a *Good Housekeeping* seal of approval, applied after the fact . . . and there will be no reason, intellectual or economic, to deny a single article as many different such seals as editorial boards see fit . . . We frown on

[multiple publication] because trees and ink and shelf space are scarce. But if instead of multiple publication it were a matter merely of multiple electronic tags, then the form of indexing and access-enhancement that comes from identifying an article with the approval given it by a specific editorial board could be made more valuable." (p. 61)

GRAND ROUNDS AND PHYSICIAN TRAINING

J. Willis Hurst, *Essays from the Heart* (New York: Raven Press, 1995).

This earnest collection of reflections on teaching and learning twentieth-century medicine was written after the author's thirty-year career as chair of medicine at Emory University. A cardiologist, Hurst helped promote the problem-oriented record as a medical teaching tool.

Jerome P. Kassirer, "Redesigning Graduate Medical Education—Location and Content," *New England Journal of Medicine* (1996) 335: 5–7, 509.

So much for bedside manner and the lecture hall! The author suggests that medical training may need to shift settings in the years ahead to prepare physicians accurately for careers in ambulatory care.

Raymond Lewkonia and Fred R. Murray, "Grand Rounds: A Paradox in Medical Education," *Canadian Medical Association Journal* (1995) 152: 371–376.

This brief article helpfully summarizes the history of grand rounds from Osler's midcentury patient focus to the contemporary slide show. There has to be something more than medical students snoring in the back row, the authors comment, but what?

Figure 9.5 Sample reference list 2.

- Assign annotations as a class requirement. Start by handing out an alphabetically organized reference list (like the one in Figure 9.4), then ask the class to read, annotate, and regroup the sources. This works particularly well as a small-group assignment for three or four people, where students can share the load of reading. Limiting annotations for each entry to one hundred words or less encourages the kind of succinct summary so useful in crafting abstracts. In addition, debate among group members about the choice and phrasing of their headings encourages review and thoughtful comparison of the readings. Posting completed annotated lists on a class website can make each group's work a valuable resource for the rest of the class.

While there may indeed be talent, style, and inspiration in the work of our most masterful teachers, effective teaching is also a matter of well-practiced craft. Well-organized syllabi alone do not a great teacher make. More often than not, however, strong syllabi are signs of the kind of interest, engagement, and organizational acumen that committed instructors demonstrate in many aspects of their teaching. Likewise, designing more thoughtful lectures with techniques of linking, questioning, and blocking help even the most knowledgeable instructors to share this knowledge more effectively with their classes.

Part Four

Teaching Science

10

The True Teacher in Medicine

J Willis Hurst

"Many students graduate having accumulated whatever number of courses is required, but still lacking a coherent body of knowledge or an inkling as to how one sort of information might relate to others. And all too often they graduate without knowing how to think logically, write clearly or speak coherently." So states the well-known Boyer Report. Issued in 1998 by the Carnegie Foundation for the advancement of teaching, the document is a scathing indictment of undergraduate education in American research universities. The report continues, "The university has given [students] too little that will be of real value beyond credentials."[1] Because some of these graduates matriculate in medical schools and some of them become medical teachers, we have clear reason to be concerned about the state of teaching and learning in medical schools and teaching hospitals.

Most of this chapter has been abstracted with permission from J Willis Hurst, *Teaching Medicine: Process, Habits and Actions* (Atlanta: Scholars Press, 1999).

Trainees have much to overcome as they struggle to learn medicine and eventually try their hands at teaching.

Ours is not the first generation to be concerned about the training of physicians. Abraham Flexner's highly influential 1910 report condemned turn-of-the-century medical didactics:

> During the ascendancy of the didactic school, it was indeed essential to good results that lecturers and quizmasters should be able to gauge the general level of their huge classes; but this level might well be low, and in the common absence of conscientiousness usually fell far below the allowable minimum. In any event, the student's part was, parrot-like, to absorb. His medical education consisted largely in getting by heart a prearranged system of correspondences, an array of symptoms so set off against a parallel array of doses that, if he noticed the one, he had only to write down the other: a coated tongue—a course of calomel; a shivery back—a round of quinine. What the student did not readily apprehend could be drilled into him—towards examination time—by those who had themselves recently passed through the ordeal which he was now approaching; and an efficient apparatus that spared his senses and his intellect as entirely as the drillmaster spared his industry was readily accessible at temptingly low prices in the shape of "essentials" and "quiz-compends." Thus he got, and in places still gets, his materia medica, anatomy, obstetrics, and surgery. The medical schools accepted the situation with so little reluctance that these compends were—and occasionally still are—written by the professors and sold on the premises.[2]

Flexner urged the closing of many small medical schools, and he strongly recommended that the better medical schools associate themselves with universities. Through the leadership of legendary medical educators such as Sir William Osler, chief of medicine at the University of Pennsylvania and at the Johns Hopkins University School of Medicine, Flexner's recommendations took hold. Osler wrote, "In what may be called the natural method of teaching, the student begins with the patient, continues with the patient, and ends his studies with the patient, using books and lectures as tools as means to an end."[3] Osler's concept of beginning with the patient, continuing with the patient, and ending with the patient is being ignored today more than it was a few years ago. A didactic approach to teaching clinical medicine is returning, a trend that should concern the teachers of today. Surely Flexner is watching.

Too few teachers understand what "true teaching" is about. Fewer still adequately distinguish between medical information (found in books, journals, computers, digitalized databases, reference materials, lectures, and conversations) and medical thinking (the use and rearrangement of medical information). After teaching several generations of medical students and chairing the department of medicine at Emory University for thirty years, I argue that clear thinking and true teaching are needed now more than ever before. What follows are some of my observations about teaching medicine, learning medicine, and the challenges that face a new century of teachers and physicians.

THE DIFFERENCE BETWEEN TEACHERS AND TRUE TEACHERS

Imagine a physician faced with these facts.[4] A patient is short of breath on effort. His heart is large. Pulsus alternans is present. Auscultation reveals aortic valve regurgitation and a left ventricular gallop sound. The deduction that the heart has failed to maintain its normal function because of diastolic overload of the left ventricle cannot be determined from the individual facts. Rather, the thinking physician "clusters" the bits of information. He or she interrelates the pieces of information and determines that heart failure is present. The thinking physician would also wonder what caused the aortic valve regurgitation and would pursue the answer to that question. Critical thinking skills that rearrange and cluster the facts are as essential as the skills required for the collection of the facts in the first place. A teacher is usually interested only in information. The true teacher is interested in whether or not the trainee rearranges the information into a new perception.

The comprehension of medical data is a necessary but not sufficient part of medical education. There must be more to medical teaching than information-dispensing conversations or lectures, and multiple-choice examinations in which the information is regurgitated. Of course, physicians need information—lots of it—but they also need thinking skills to classify, reclassify, and categorize information into new perceptions. Because medical knowledge is continually expanding, physicians must also develop lifelong commitments to learning. For this work, true physicians need true teachers.

I distinguish true teachers from teachers who simply dispense information. Teachers simply cram information into the heads of their trainees. True teachers are different: they want those they teach to understand and think for themselves. True teachers enter their trainees' brains and observe, in follow-up, what their trainees do.

Eugene Stead has been my academic mentor for years. He was the first full-time chairman of Emory University's department of medicine. He was, and still is, a true teacher. His influence on generations of practitioners has equaled that of Osler. Stead wrote: "The learning process can be divided into the accumulation of bits of information (memory) and the movement of these bits into patterns which are new to the individual (thinking). . . . The compulsive learner is incapable of thinking. There is always another bit of information to be memorized, and, if they are all learned, there is little time to rearrange the bits in original patterns."[5]

True teachers also distinguish themselves by their attitude. Their curiosity, caring, enthusiasm, interest, wonder, persistence, and concern are far better exemplified than they are explained. True teachers are generous with their time. They take interest in their students because they value the qualities of learning that develop through relationships. True teachers do not hide the fact that they do not know all the answers. They are honest and say, "I will look that up," or "I will ask Dr So-and-so because he knows more about it than I do."

Better still, the true teacher involves the trainee by saying, "Why don't you join me? You look up the answer too, and we will take ten minutes to talk about it tomorrow." Here the true teacher not only instructs, but also models. A true teacher introduces the trainee to the value of focused, problem-based inquiry, and joins the student in collaborative problem solving. Such attitudes take hold as students are forming the mental habits of their profession. In this respect, true teachers never die; their curiosity, enthusiasm, and persistence enter the minds of their trainees as attitudes that they will carry and, in turn, pass on.

To summarize, true teachers distinguish themselves by the qualities of their knowledge and by their attitude. True teachers—

- Know and love the subject they teach but are also interested in many subjects
- Value relevance and recognize the importance of clinical science to clinical medicine
- Respect the data that are collected from patients and insist on clear and accurate medical records
- Communicate (talking and writing) with precision
- Continue to develop their curiosity and wonder, never separating their teaching from their own learning
- Give time to their students, recognizing that no two students are alike and all deserve equal respect
- Study, ask questions, and persistently look for answers
- Are never bored with their work with trainees. In a sense they "never die" because their attitudes are passed on to the trainees who, in turn, pass them on.

THE PROBLEM-ORIENTED RECORD

An enthusiastic young intern once presented me with a patient she confidently described as having "classic pericarditis." I asked, of course, "What data did you use to diagnose pericarditis?" The intern was silent. I immediately moved in with an easier follow-up question.

"Did the patient have chest pain?" "Why yes," she offered. I continued with a few more leading questions, hoping to tease out more of her observations. "Did it hurt the patient to . . . , to . . . , to . . . , to take a deep breath?" The intern was silent. I tried again, asking, "Did you hear a . . . , a . . . , a . . . rub? You know, was there was pericardial friction rub?" Silence again. "Well then, let's move on to the electrocardiogram. Did *it* reveal signs of pericarditis?" More silence. Somewhat disappointed in the young intern at this point, I continued: "We have just mentioned the three common clues needed to diagnose pericarditis. You did not mention any of them. How did you make the diagnosis?" "Well . . . um . . ." the intern stammered, "I knew the patient had pericarditis because the attending physician told me."

I should not have been so startled, because the young intern's response is not unusual. She had simply accepted the attending physician's diagnosis, and he had erroneously assumed that she knew the three cardinal features of pericarditis. This is a frequent error on the part of attending physicians. They commonly believe that medical school graduates are trained observers and skilled thinkers. The fact is that medical school only introduces students to skills. The usual graduate's head is stuffed with a huge amount of information that has not been *used* in a thought process. The true teacher's job is to uncover the lack of thinking by trainees and to emphasize that thinking—the proper use of information—is the ultimate goal.

The skills needed for data collection and cognitive skills (thinking) must be practiced and refined during house staff training and as long as the physician lives. Both the house officer, who accepted the diagnosis of pericarditis without thinking, and the attending, who wrongly assumed that she understood, would profit from the proper use of the problem-oriented record.

This document was first introduced to the profession in the 1970s by L L Weed.[6] The problem-oriented record has helped improve data collection and use of the data in clinical medicine. I strongly supported Weed's views decades ago, and I still do.[7] Having worked with the problem-oriented record approach for twenty-eight years, I am convinced that it improves patient care and facilitates medical teaching. A problem-oriented record has four parts: the Database, the Problem List, Plans (diagnostic, therapeutic, and educational) and Progress Notes. Let us now examine these four elements, and how to use each as a teaching tool.

The Database

The database is an accurate recording of the defined information (data) that has been collected from a patient. It is important to remember that there is no such thing as a "complete" or "thorough" examination. There are always more questions to ask, more physical signs to elicit, and more laboratory tests to run. This is why the elements included in the database must be defined so that an examiner can attain a specified goal. If a general internist's goal is to deliver comprehensive care, his or her data collection must include information about all organs and body systems. An ophthalmologist might limit data collection to the eye. A cardiologist focuses on the cardiovascular system but collects sufficient defined data about other organs to allow sound judgments about the heart.

As a teaching tool, the database provides the supervising true teacher with a focused method to assess a trainee's data-collecting skills. Noticing, for example, that the patient has severe heart failure and a large heart, the true teacher might state, "I am surprised that there was no gallop sound or abnormal V wave in the deep jugular pulse noted in this patient; let's check that out." If a trainee has overlooked physical findings, the true teacher should demonstrate the abnormalities. The trainee should then be urged to review the pathophysiology of the abnormalities and return the next day prepared to discuss the matter. Used as a teaching tool during coexamination of a patient, the database helps true teachers focus attention on the most relevant gaps in the trainee's skill and knowledge. Proper use of the database helps a true teacher determine what the trainee knows, and what the trainee does not know but should know.

An appropriate and defined database form should consider:

- Screening all organs or body systems for disease when the physician intends to render comprehensive care.
- Screening a specific organ or body system for disease when subspecialty care is to be rendered. When this is the goal of the physician, he or she should collect sufficient data about the other organs or body systems to enable sound judgment about the specific organ in which he or she is predominantly interested.
- Diseases that may be prevalent in specific populations. One does not search for Chagas disease in Georgia, but must in Brazil.
- Time and personnel restrictions. With a patient load of fifty per day, it would be ludicrous to design a database form requiring an hour to complete.
- Including items medical students and house officers must learn to elicit.
- Avoiding commercial forms. The chiefs of service and directors of house staff should determine the goals for the patients and trainees they serve. These staff members can best design database forms to serve their specific purposes.

Here are some questions for true teachers to ask trainees about a database:

- Do you have sufficient skill to collect the data listed on the database form? It would be unusual if you did. Let us go over some of the items together. For example, show me how you elicit the story of stable angina pectoris, the pulsations in the deep jugular pulse, and interpret electrocardiograms.
- Do you understand the clinical science that explains the normal and abnormal findings on this patient? For example, explain the mechanisms responsible for heart failure.

Once the type of data to be collected has been defined, the true teacher must help the trainee develop the skill to collect the data and to understand the clinical science that is germane to the data.

The Problem List

Having surveyed the abnormalities recorded in the database that were discovered in the history, physical examination, and laboratory examination of the patient, the examiner then creates a problem list. The problem list itself should be placed at some designated part of the medical record so that it can be found quickly and easily. Problem statements can be of two types: several abnormalities might be clustered together to make a diagnosis; and symptoms, signs, or laboratory results that are poorly understood should be listed separately. Examiners should number each problem statement and date each entry. When the physician discovers a new problem in the long-term follow-up of a patient, it is dated and numbered and added to the problem list. When a problem is poorly resolved, the examiner marks it with an arrow (to note that the problem needs further attention) in the plans section of the medical record. For example, the problem, "#5 chest pain" is poorly resolved, so the examiner shows "#5 chest pain→." As will be discussed later, a protocol is developed for #5 chest pain that includes diagnostic, therapeutic, and educational plans. The differential diagnosis should be listed in the diagnostic plans. As an example, it might include coronary atherosclerotic heart disease with unstable angina pectoris as well as gastroesophageal reflux. A diagnostic plan would then be written to separate the two conditions (see later discussion).

A problem list is the end result of the examiner's thought process in assessing the items in the database. No "guesses," no "probables," or "questions" and no "rule outs" should be listed on a problem list. Rather, there must be evidence in the database to support starting the problem as it is stated. The problem list is objective evidence of the thought process of the individual who examined the patient. It is a true teacher's dream because it gives that teacher the opportunity to enter the trainee's brain; the trainee has annotated his or her views and the true teacher responds.

As a teaching tool, the problem list helps the true teacher assess the diagnostic thinking of the trainee. After reviewing a trainee's problem list, the teacher can ask, "Which data did you use to formulate this problem?" If the trainee proceeds to relate the patient's entire medical history, to review the entire physical examination, and to laboriously restate every laboratory finding, the true teacher should stop him or her. The true teacher, in order to focus the trainee's response, comments: "I'm interested in the few bits of data you selected that led you to formulate the problem as you have stated it. After reviewing the data, which did you use to state the problem?" The true teacher then proceeds to help the trainee refine the answer to the question.

Finally, the problem list provides direction for future study. Developing the discipline to research poorly resolved problems ties reading in reference books and journals to the specific problems trainees identify in their patients. Such a connection energizes inquiry and helps integrate new information into a trainee's store of knowledge.

Here are questions you may ask trainees about items on the problem list:

- Are all of the abnormalities you recorded in the database accounted for in the problem list, as attributes of a diagnosis or as poorly resolved statements?
- Are there adequate data in the database to formulate the problems as you have stated them?
- Can you enumerate the criteria needed to make a specific diagnosis? Are such criteria present in your patient?
- Have you updated the problem list as newly acquired data became available?

Plans

The third section of the problem-oriented record consists of Plans that address and respond to each of the listed and numbered active problems on the problem list. Plans may be diagnostic, therapeutic, or educational.

When the diagnosis is definite, *diagnostic* plans include further steps to clarify certain aspects of the diagnosis. For example, the physician may order an echocardiogram to determine if a stenotic mitral valve due to rheumatic heart disease may be treated with balloon valvuloplasty or if surgery will be needed. The echocardiogram was not ordered to diagnose mitral stenosis; the examiner should diagnose that with a stethoscope. The test was ordered to answer a different question. If a diagnosis is not clear (as in the chest pain example), a differential diagnosis is developed. The examiner should list each possible diagnosis on the left, and the diagnostic procedure needed to prove its presence or absence on the right. The sequence of performance of the procedures should be specified as well.

Therapeutic plans are also written according to problem number. Diagnostic and therapeutic *orders* are written on the order sheet; they are identified with the problem number that was assigned to the problem on the problem list. This procedure ensures that numbers stay consistent throughout the entire record. For example, #5 refers to "chest pain" in the problem list, and it will refer to chest pain in the plans, in the orders, and in the progress notes. While this approach does not require high intellect, it does make for efficiency, which saves time—and that is precious.

While they are often neglected, *educational* plans are extremely important. Here, the physician records what has been explained to the patient. The note should indicate that the physician has instructed the patient about diagnostic and therapeutic plans, the side effect of drugs, risks of surgery, and so on. This entry also communicates the physician's statements to others who are involved with the patient's care.

Clear, pertinent discussions between the trainee and the true teacher develop over whether the proposed plans are acceptable or not, and differences in opinion bring opportunities for research of the literature.

Here are a few questions true teachers might ask trainees about the plans:

- Do the numbers of your plans correspond to those on the problem list?
- Where in the plans have you included the differential diagnosis of the poorly understood problems that are listed on the patient's problem list?
- Which therapeutic plans were prescribed at the time the problem statement was written?
- Were the orders numbered and titled to match the numbers and titles of the problem statements given in the problem list?
- Do you believe it wise to propose this treatment plan for problem #1 when it will undoubtedly make problem #4 much worse?
- Which patient education plans did you write for the problem?

Progress Notes

When I ask trainees what they do during follow-up visits to a patient, they typically discuss a generic approach to the activity. They walk in. They ask the patient, "How are you feeling today?" and then they perform a cursory examination of the relevant body parts. On the chart they often write, "Doing well." Specific, numbered and dated Progress Notes responding to each active problem are the best solution to the generic statement that has been scribbled on far too many charts. Although it may be accurate, "Doing well" is too vague and general to be of clinical use; it says nothing about whether a specific problem has been followed up or not. This causes one to wonder if the trainee knows what he or she should follow up for a problem, or if the trainee knows what to follow up but forgets to write down the observations.

As the fourth section of the problem-oriented record, progress notes are titled, numbered, and dated. The numbers must match those on the problem list and in the plans. Examiners list *Subjective* complaints related to teach problem, and then include *Objective* observations. After Assessing these data, new Plans are written to address the problem in its new stage. The plans should always consider the need for updated diagnosis, new therapies, and further patient education. (Note that when the first letters of the four parts of the Progress Notes are all listed, the word SOAP is created.) Consistent numbering and careful dating of progress notes enables anyone studying the patient record to identify the orderly work and treatment of the patient's problems. When a poorly resolved problem is solved, the data used in the solution are clearly recorded in the progress notes. The date of the progress note is placed above the arrow adjacent to the problem statement on the problem list. Accordingly, "#5 chest pain →" becomes "#5 chest pain <u>Jan. 6, 1999</u> → unstable angina due to coronary atherosclerosis." This is the way the problem list is updated.

Here are questions that a true teacher may ask a trainee about the progress notes:

- Which subjective data did you record as being germane to the problem?
- Which objective data did you include as being relevant to the problem?
- How have you assessed the new subjective and objective data?
- What new plans have you written for the problem, given its current stage?
- Have you updated the problem statement on the problem list? Did you add the date of the progress note above the arrow, to help track how you have arrived at your new understanding of the problem?

The problem-oriented record is a useful teaching tool because its format requires that the examiner stop and ask:

- Do I have the skill to collect the data required of me in the database?
- Have I formulated the numbered problem list with statements that are supported by the data?
- Are my numbered plans and orders for each active problem clearly stated?
- Are my numbered progress notes specific and complete?

These four stoplights are clear and easy to see. They represent ideal junctures during the work-up of a patient where the trainee and the true teacher can pause, assess, think independently, and then think together.

The best problem-oriented records are as brief as they are clearly defined and complete. The goal is to create a record that encourages the practice of focused clinical thinking—the kind of thinking that results in excellent patient care. The first step in solving a problem is to state the problem accurately. This requires thinking. The next step is to develop the self-discipline to seek a solution appropriate to the problem. This requires self-discipline and perseverance.

The four parts of the problem-oriented record are interdependent. An excellent problem list cannot be created without a defined, accurate database, and medical care cannot be delivered without proper plans, and progress notes that are germane to each problem. My years of experience have taught me that the value of such an approach is highlighted best by initially emphasizing the problem list, because everyone can recognize its value in patient care and teaching.

Space does not permit the presentation of a completed problem-oriented record of a specific patient. Space does permit the presentation of two different problem lists on the same patient (Figures 10.1 and 10.2); one is poorly done and one is excellent.

The first example is undated, and the reason the patient was admitted to the hospital is not shown. The signature of the trainee is illegible. The problem statements are inadequate. Heart failure is not a diagnosis. It is a physiologic complication of heart disease, which is not stated. The type of diabetes is not indicated. Hypertension is a physical finding rather than a diagnosis. A true teacher can instantly perceive the level of thinking used to create this problem list. Obviously, the trainee does not realize that he or she has failed to establish the causes of any of the problems listed. The true teacher should discuss the necessity of establishing the etiology of physiological or biochemical abnormalities.

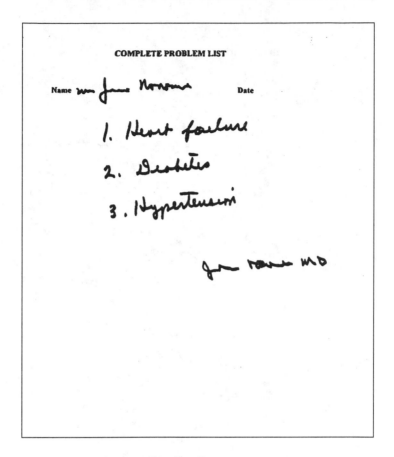

Figure 10.1 A poorly executed problem list.

In the second example, the date of the record is shown and the trainee's signature is legible. Note that the heart disease is characterized according to the format suggested by the New York Heart Association. The type of diabetes and the type of hypertension are given, as is the reason for admission to the hospital. This problem list reveals considerable understanding on the part of the trainee. Here the

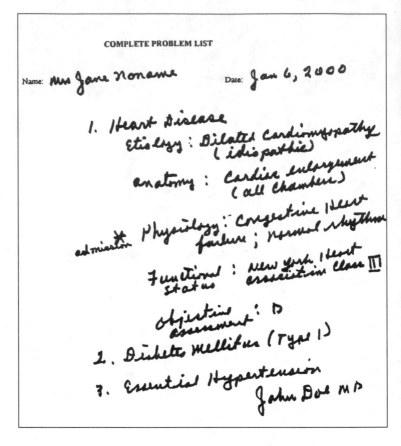

Figure 10.2 An excellent problem list on the same patient as in Figure 10.1.

true teacher might discuss some of the finer details of the physiology of heart failure and its treatment.

Any perceptive true teacher, medical student, house officer, physician assistant, nurse, or patient can determine which of the two problem lists indicates excellent work on the part of the examiner. Also, you the reader might ask, "Which physician would I choose to take care of me if I needed medical attention?"

The true teacher should teach the examiner who created Figure 10.1 how to create Figure 10.2. Having learned that, the examiner who created the first problem list will gradually improve. He or she will begin to understand that heart failure is a physiologic consequence of heart disease and must never be listed outside the context of heart disease. The importance of establishing the etiology of disease will also be appreciated gradually by the trainee. That individual will also appreciate the importance of determining the degree of functional improvement and the objective assessment of the seriousness of the problem but, as a rule, it takes a true teacher to lead the way.

The true teacher, recognizing that the examiner who prepared the second problem list is undoubtedly an excellent observer and thinker, may ask, "What data did you use to diagnose dilated cardiomyopathy?" or might ask, "Why is the patient having more heart failure now than she was having last week?" The true teacher might then inquire about the plans and follow-up (progress notes) on each problem. The trainee has made a commitment to his or her diagnosis and the true teacher analyzes the trainee's logic and thinking. *All of the discussions are relevant to the patient's problems. No mini lectures are given.*

TEACHING ENCOUNTERS

Gene Stead taught me that a teaching hospital is a place where *everyone* teaches. The problem-oriented record, when used properly by a true teacher, focuses on the patient's problems. It follows Osler's admonition about beginning with the patient, continuing with the patient, and ending with the patient. The teaching of clinical medicine with its relevant clinical science by true teachers is best accomplished when it is tied to a patient. Every medical educator eventually appreciates the value of linkage: the fact that trainees and seasoned physicians learn best when they observe, read about, and discuss their patients' problems.

Ward Rounds

I believe that ward rounds, when performed properly, give the true teacher the best of all opportunities to teach. Medical schools only introduce students to clinical skills. It is the responsibility of the attending physician, who should be a true teacher, to help trainees practice and refine their clinical skills during the house staff training period. This effort should include refinement of the trainee's thinking skills as well as data-collection skills. Ward rounds provide an opportunity for the true teacher to ask questions about certain skills and to assess a trainee's clinical thinking. They provide an opportunity to discuss the clinical science that is related to the clinical findings. During auscultation of the heart, for example, the attending can ask questions that develop the habit of connecting anatomy and physiology with the auscultatory findings. The true teacher might ask, "What anatomic and physiologic variables determine the intensity of the first heart sound? Why does the patient have polyuria?" Formulating answers to these questions helps trainees develop the habit of linking scientific knowledge to clinical observations.

Should a true teacher discover on ward rounds that a trainee does not know the pathophysiology of heart failure or some other clinical problem, he or she should ask the trainee to read about the problem and discuss it with the trainee the next day.

The attending, acting as a true teacher, demonstrates the value of interrelating information by correlating the data found via high-tech procedures with the data discovered on routine examination of the patient. The true teacher should emphasize the technique of correlation as a method of learning.

Diagramming is an excellent low-tech teaching tool that enables true teachers quickly to assess a trainee's perception, knowledge, and understanding. For example, Figure 10.3 depicts auscultatory findings at the cardiac apex. Figure 10.3A illustrates the normal findings, Figure 10.3B illustrates the abnormal heart sounds and the murmur produced by mitral stenosis, and Figure 10.3C illustrates the aus-

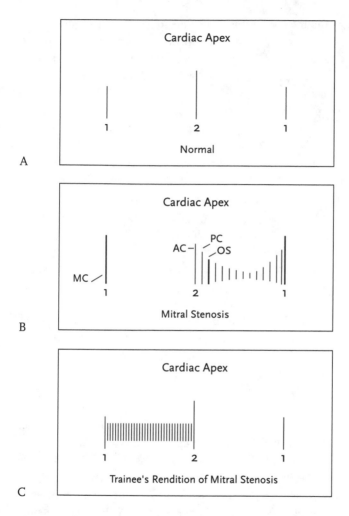

Figure 10.3 A. Auscultatory findings at the cardiac apex: normal heart sounds. B. Diagram created by a trainee who understands that auscultation of the heart is far more than simply hearing the sounds. C. Diagram created by an unskilled trainee.

cultatory findings of a trainee. Note the loud first heart sound (MC), the loud pulmonary closure sound (PC), the opening snap (OS), the short interval of time between the aortic valve closure sound (AC), the opening snap (OS), and the low-pitched, diastolic rumble with presystolic accentuation in Figure 10.3B. Should a trainee produce such a diagram, the true teacher can conclude that the individual has learned to listen to the cardiac apex, and it is likely that the trainee understands how to learn auscultation.

On the other hand, should the trainee create Figure 10.3C after listening to the same patient, the attending can immediately deduce that help is needed. The trainee placed the murmur of mitral stenosis in systole rather than diastole, a common error. The shape of the murmur is incorrect. The abnormally loud first heart sound, opening snap, and loud pulmonary valve closure sound are all missing from the trainee's rendition of the auscultatory events. Questioning the trainee about the diagram immediately determines whether the problem derives from an inaccurate knowledge base (perhaps the trainee does not know about the opening snap of mitral stenosis) or from poor sensory perception (the trainee's hearing has yet to be fine-tuned enough to hear the sounds). Either way, the diagram (like those in other specialties illustrating skin lesions, masses, areas of tenderness, and so on) helps the attending to instruct the trainee on how to further refine her or his skills.

On ward rounds, teaching attendings can demonstrate, observe, assess, and refine the clinical and thinking skills of the trainee. They can teach the linkage of clinical science to the abnormalities that are discovered. Teaching attendings can demonstrate effective communication with patients. Done properly, ward rounds teach trainees to respect their patients and the data they collect from them, thereby inspiring an ongoing refinement of clinical skills, clinical thinking, and patient care.

The attending physician must always decide how much should be discussed at the bedside of the patient and how much away from the bedside. Remember that ward rounds should be instructive and therapeutic for the patient as well as a teaching experience for the trainee. Remember too that when the attending physician and trainees are clustered around the patient's bed, all discussions and actions are focused on the patient. It is wise to listen, listen, listen.

Morning Report and the Problem List

Properly organized, morning report can be an excellent place for trainees to develop the clinical thinking required to formulate clear problem statements. It is not the place where a true teacher checks the accuracy of a database; that is done on ward rounds. A one-hour 7:00 A.M. ritual at most teaching hospitals, morning report collects house officers, fellows, and students in the same place at the same time to review medical, administrative, and social issues of the previous twenty-four hours. Trainees are expected to bring with them the work-up they have performed on each of their patients including the database and problem list. They should also bring with them the electrocardiograms and X ray films on their patients.

Trainees are asked to write on a blackboard their problem lists for patients they have seen during the last twenty-four hours. When convenient, a transparency can be made of the problem list and it can be shown on a screen using an overhead projector. The entire group of trainees is asked to study each problem list.

Reviewing a problem list, the true teacher may ask: "You say that this patient has had a myocardial infarction. You listed it as problem 1. What data did you use to state the problem?" If the trainee gives a long dissertation, he or she should be stopped. The teacher restates the question: "Although I am interested in all of the information you collected from the patient, my question was, What specific data did you select from all you collected that enabled you to state that the patient had a myocardial infarction?" The true teacher should then add that formulation of the heart problems should follow the format suggested by the New York Heart Association. When appropriate, a similar approach should be used for all problem statements. At all times the trainee should make an effort to give the etiology of a problem.

The next question is, "Are there any data in the database that are not accounted for on the problem list, either as a problem of the attribute or a diagnosis?"

When the problem statement indicates that the problem is poorly understood, the true teacher asks the trainee to list the differential diagnosis created in the plan. Should the trainee place the differential diagnosis on the problem list, the true teacher must again define what a problem list is. Or should the trainee place the phrase "rule out disease so and so" on the problem list, or put guesses or probable diagnoses on the problem list, the true teacher must reemphasize the definition.

Electrocardiograms and X ray films that are germane to a patient's problem can be reviewed at morning report.

As the days pass, the true teacher should ask the trainees themselves to review and discuss the problem lists of their peers. The point should be made that in practice, partners in a group do that every day. Partners in practice who cross-cover depend on one another to create medical records that communicate accurately.

Focusing morning report on the problem list and plans prevents trainees from reciting, in junior student fashion, every detail of the database. When a trainee presents to a true teacher all of the data collected on a patient, he or she shifts the thinking to the teacher. This is not the purpose of morning report. Instead, all those in attendance give their attention to the way the trainees discriminate, analyze, and reorganize data to formulate problems. Done properly, this exercise teaches the trainees to think.

Grand Rounds

The shift from patient-centered grand rounds to lectures in many institutions has been much noted and much bemoaned. While easier to organize, lecture-format grand rounds are rarely effective at true teaching. The purpose of the lectures is often ambiguous, and their clinical relevance is often slight or nil. All one has to do to prove the ineffectiveness of most lectures is to ask members of the audience one week later what information they remember. Their silence is a clear indictment. Most lecturers present information that can be found in textbooks or journals, and most people who are trying to learn can read faster than a lecturer can speak.

A much more effective format for grand rounds focuses the attention of trainees and seasoned physicians on patients and their problems. The presence of a patient always brightens what might otherwise be a dull lecture. For patients frequently have something to tell that is not in the textbook. The following format involves a patient and four or more physicians in a tight, productive sixty-minute time frame.

Welcome and Introduction (5 minutes), Organizer

The session organizer announces the title of the session, welcomes the audience and thanks the patient for coming. He or she introduces the residents involved and the various specialists and clinicians who are to participate in the session. Reviewing the agenda orally, with an outline on the board or with a handout, helps audience members to focus their attention and helps the discussants to control their time.

Patient Presentation (10 minutes), Resident

A well-prepared and practiced resident should use simple slides to present briefly the patient's problem list. He then presents the data used to formulate the problem that will be the subject of grand rounds.

Comments and Demonstration (10 minutes), Organizer

The organizer should talk with the patient in order to highlight the symptoms related to the problem. The moderator may also demonstrate certain physical findings. Abnormal heart sounds and murmurs should be transmitted by special equipment to the entire audience. The organizer might ask the radiologist to review the X ray films that are relevant to the case. Alternatively, a cardiologist might discuss the electrocardiogram.

Clinical Review (10 minutes), Clinician

At this point the organizer invites a previously designated clinician to discuss the clinical aspects of the patient's problem. He or she should cover what is in the textbooks, but must also add the unique findings in the patient. This is very important. Textbooks teach a generic approach to problems; an expert always knows something that is not in the textbooks.

Clinical Science Review (15 minutes), Clinician

The organizer then calls on another previously designated clinician to present the clinical science that underlies the patient's problem. Successful integration of clinical science into medical training has been a vexatious question. Teachers of anatomy, pathology, biochemistry, epidemiology, and physiology, for example, are rarely clinicians themselves, and they may have little interest or experience in drawing connections between underlying scientific principles and clinical conditions.

I submit that there are two types of basic science. *Clinical science* explains how the parts of the body work harmoniously together, enabling us to breathe, circulate our blood, digest our food, walk, talk, and think. All clinicians need a solid understanding of this type of science. The more *elemental science* considers the molecular biology of cells that make up parts of the body. Although essential to the development of long-term solutions to diseases, it is rarely immediately useful to the clinician trying to understand and solve the problem of a patient in front of him or her. Framing the presentation of clinical science within this grand rounds format helps to ensure clinical relevance. It shows the immeasurable value of understanding the scientific bases for problems and their solutions, and it directs trainees to areas of further study to improve their clinical work.

Questions and Discussions (10 minutes), Moderator

With the resident, specialists, and clinicians gathered as a panel, the session concludes with ten minutes of questions from the audience. The moderator may direct questions to the appropriate respondent. The moderator may also come prepared with questions to help stimulate audience participation. The students and house officers must be encouraged to ask questions; when they do not, the session has failed.

By involving several people, this grand rounds format offers a model for collaboration that makes the most of people's different areas of expertise. Focusing on a current patient brings the clinical manifestations of disease to life and prevents presenters from trotting out canned lectures. The approach also links the appropriate clinical science to the clinical problem. Trainees and seasoned physicians remember best when information is linked to patients. Abstract material that is not linked to a patient is much more difficult to absorb.

JOURNAL CLUBS AND DEBATES

Use of the problem-oriented approach can improve two other popular educational exercises: the journal club and the debate.

On the premise that trainees should know the most recent literature, *journal clubs* usually consist of a series of informal gatherings (often over a meal). Two or three members of the group have the responsibility of presenting a review, questions, and critique of a recent article they have read. Many journal clubs have short lives. Presenters prepare less and less. Cursory summary takes the place of analysis and critique. Often meetings devolve into social gatherings until they are abandoned as "not particularly productive."

Journal clubs fail in part because the educational premise described above is flawed: the most recent literature may not be the best on a subject, and trainees rarely remember abstract medical information that is gleaned from articles until it is linked to their experience with patients.

Instead of reviewing an article that was chosen because the journal arrived only a few days earlier, another approach may be more successful. The organizer of the group should at least determine the patient problems that members of the group have encountered during the recent past. Suppose they have all seen patients with coronary atherosclerotic heart disease. The organizer should then ask two members of the group to discuss the prevention of coronary atherosclerosis. Furthermore, the organizer should not limit the choice of articles to those that have become available during the last month, but should ask the discussants to select from journals that have arrived during the last few years. This approach underscores the fact that the most recent article on a subject may not be the best one, and attempts to make the discussion relevant to the experience of those in attendance.

Despite this effort, most journal clubs fail because the hassle is greater than the reward. After all, self-disciplined trainees should read about the problems they find in their patients. They should not need any other emotional reason to investigate.

Organizing *debates* among trainees encourages reading, review, and critique of relevant scientific literature. Medical knowledge changes day by day. Trainees must be constantly reminded that many of the views they are exposed to are not set in concrete and that not everyone is in agreement about what doctors do. I remind my trainees that we formerly used quinidine a great deal. We thought it was highly effective in treating certain arrhythmias. Now experts tell us that in fact it is often harmful. Years ago we taught that the systolic hypertension of the elderly was not harmful. Now we know that it is. I have always taught that it takes about five years to determine whether a new procedure, a new drug, or a new concept is as valuable as it was initially hyped to be. That is why the aphorism "Hurry up and use a drug while it is still working and has no side effects" has stood the test of time.

One particularly effective format for debate is the following. The training director selects a controversial topic commonly encountered among the patients admitted to the hospital or outpatient department. For example, "Should all menopausal women be treated with estrogens in an effort to prevent coronary atherosclerotic heart disease?" Four trainees are selected to be the debaters. These four (two teams of two) collect and review the literature, preparing arguments for and against. On the day of the debate, the toss of a coin determines which team will argue which side. Thus, each debater is prepared to argue either side of the question. The debate begins with—

- 10 minutes on the pro side
- 10 minutes on the con side
- 5 minutes pro rebuttal
- 5 minutes con rebuttal

More senior physicians can judge the debate, but it obviously does not matter who wins. The purpose of the exercise is evident: it teaches the debaters and the audience that there are two sides to many issues and one must learn to assess data in order to have an opinion.

EVALUATION OF MEDICAL TEACHERS

Those who teach clinical medicine—even true teachers—may not be promoted, as are their colleagues who work almost exclusively in research. The reason usually given is that it is difficult to evaluate the quality of teaching rendered by a member of the faculty, whereas publication in a peer review journal of the research performed by a faculty member is evidence of excellent work.

I disagree. I believe teachers can be evaluated. The questionnaire shown in Figure 10.4, when filled out by a trainee, gives considerable information about the teaching ability of a faculty member. In addition, it informs the teacher and trainee on some of the aspects of true teaching.

Name of teacher: _____

Date: _____

Type of teaching exercise (*Circle one or more of the following*):

Ward rounds   Patient conference   Lecture

Circle the appropriate response for each question.

1. Was the teacher always on time?   Yes   No

WARD ROUNDS

2. Did the teacher include you as a member of the team?

       Yes   No

3. Did the teacher check the database (history, physical exam, laboratory data, chest X ray, electrocardiogram) you prepared and compare it to his or her own examination of the patient?

Excellent   1   2   3   4   5   Poor

4. Did the teacher determine whether you utilized all the abnormalities found in the database to create the problem list?

Excellent   1   2   3   4   5   Poor

5. Did the teacher review the problem list you created and ask what data you used to create the problem statements?

Excellent   1   2   3   4   5   Poor

6. Did the teacher encourage you to look up information about the problems you found in your patients and then, at a different time, review with you the information you found?

Excellent   1   2   3   4   5   Poor

7. Did the teacher discuss the clinical science background of the abnormalities found in the patient?

Excellent   1   2   3   4   5   Poor

8. Did the teacher seem to be concerned about accurate recording of the abnormalities that were found in the patient?

Excellent   1   2   3   4   5   Poor

9. Did the teacher establish an appropriate relationship with the patient?   Excellent   1   2   3   4   5   Poor

10. Did the teacher transmit his or her concern for the patient's welfare to the patient?   Excellent   1   2   3   4   5   Poor

11. Did the teacher provide constructive feedback on your performance?   Excellent   1   2   3   4   5   Poor

12. Was the teacher enthusiastic about teaching?
                    Excellent   1   2   3   4   5   Poor

13. The learning process involves information (data), thinking, and usage. Did the teacher lead you through this process?
                    Excellent   1   2   3   4   5   Poor

PATIENT-CARE CONFERENCES

14. Did the teacher organize and run a patient-care conference with skill and enthusiasm?
        Yes   No   Not applicable

15. Did your teacher include you in the discussion?
        Yes   No

16. Did the teacher lecture or develop an interactive session?
        Lectured   Interactive

LECTURES

17. Did your teacher seem to know the subject being discussed?
                    Excellent   1   2   3   4   5   Poor

18. Did your teacher realize that he or she must make the contents of the lecture relevant to the needs and interests of the audience?
                    Excellent   1   2   3   4   5   Poor

19. Did your teacher show complex slides and discuss other matters while the slide was shown on the screen?
        Yes   No

20. Did the lecturer use slides as cue cards?

> Yes   No

21. Did the lecturer emphasize a few focused points, or were too many points discussed without emphasizing which mattered most?

> Few   Too many

22. Did you remember some of the points made by the lecturer and use them?

> Yes   No

23. Would you like to be assigned to the teacher again for ward rounds or attend a conference he or she organized?

> Yes   No

24. Would you like to hear the teacher lecture again?

> Yes   No

Figure 10.4 Teacher evaluation form.

SELF-TEACHING

While much needs to be done to improve the quality of teaching in teaching hospitals, true teachers are only half of the equation. Trainees, too, must take responsibility for the quality, depth, and refinement of their own knowledge and skill. During their clinical rotations, trainees can consider the problem-oriented record as a tool that directs their own learning. When they become practicing physicians or true teachers (or both), they will have the following characteristics. They will—

- Create excellent databases, problem lists, plans, and progress notes.
- Develop a customized library that gives immediate access to information useful in their daily work.
- Look up the answers to questions they themselves raise about their patients, realizing that is the best way to learn.

- Study the clinical science that is relevant to the clinical problems discovered in their patients.
- Remember that memorization is not the same as thinking, and thinking is not the same as learning.

NOTES

1. Carnegie Foundation, Boyer Commission on Educating Undergraduates in the Research University. *Reinventing Undergraduate Education: A Blueprint for America's Research Universities.* Stony Brook, N.Y.: SUNY, 1998, pp. 5–6.

2. Flexner, A. *Medical Education in the United States and Canada: A Report to the Carnegie Foundation for the Advancement of Teaching.* Bulletin No. 4. Boston: Merrymount Press, 1910, pp. 20–27.

3. Osler, W. *Aphorisms: From His Bedside Teachings and Writings.* Collected by Bennett, R., and Bean, W. B. New York: Henry Schuman, 1950, p. 46.

4. Material in this section is taken from Hurst, J. W. *The Bench and Me: Teaching and Learning Medicine.* New York: Igaku-Shoin, 1992.

5. Stead, E. A., Jr. Thinking ward rounds. *Medical Times* (1967) 95: 706–708.

6. Weed, L. L. *Medical Records, Medical Education, and Patient Care.* Chicago: Press of Case Western Reserve University, 1970.

7. Hurst, J. W., and Walker, H. K., eds. *The Problem-Oriented System.* New York: Medcom, 1972.

Part Five

The Business Aspects of Health Care

11

Communication in Health Care

Stephanie Barnard

Often health care professionals tell me: "I'm a physician (pharmacist, nurse), not a stockbroker. I'm not in business; I'm in health care." What these professionals do not acknowledge is that *health care is business*. While health care professionals are trained in scientific methods and patient care, they also supervise others, coordinate care plans, oversee facilities, and collect payments. Since health care professionals earn a living in health care, the setting *is* a business.

In this business of health care, adapting to the changing environment creates the need for more effective communication. The old days of running a practice or clinic with hand-written charts are being replaced with the new days of applying for acceptance by a health maintenance organization, defending your practice techniques to Medicare, and collaborating with attorneys over litigation. And this is only the beginning. As new scientific research and computer technology continue to improve, health care professionals will rely even more on their communication skills to interpret the complex changes for their patients and colleagues.

From patient counseling to speaking up at meetings to writing to an insurance company, your skills as a communicator directly affect your success as a health care professional. You will see in Part V of this book that improving these skills will help you to gain better results in your career.

WHY SHOULD MEDICAL PROFESSIONALS BECOME BETTER COMMUNICATORS?

People judge others based on their skills as communicators. We often think an articulate person has greater knowledge simply because that person is able to express ideas easily. Likewise, patients rarely refer friends or relatives to health care providers because the staff consists of "the most talented medical professionals," but they do refer patients to providers where the staff is "helpful and friendly." In addition, better communication is simply more efficient. Physicians frequently say, "But we have only fifteen minutes to spend with each patient." All the more reason to make those fifteen minutes count! Sometimes, in an effort at efficiency, providers rush through their "canned" consults, forgetting to see the patient as an individual. The patient, uncertain about the diagnosis, treatment, and outcome, leaves confused and may never return.

I have worked with a variety of health care professionals who are excellent physicians, dentists, administrators, and pharmacists. Yet many of them have hired me to repair situations they could have handled themselves, or even prevented, if they were more effective communicators. For example, patient satisfaction surveys I have conducted show that the most frequent patient complaint has little to do with quality of care. Rather, most patients and their families want better service: a shorter wait in the reception area; a polite and friendly lab technician; a competent, informative charge nurse; a caring, compassionate physician; and a professional receptionist. What do these requests have to do with communication? Everything. Each is a call for clearer communication. You may not be able to control the daily fluctuations in your scheduling, but you *can* train your staff to communicate them effectively to your patients.

Satisfactory communication relies not on the newest innovations of technology, but rather listening to what others are saying, preparing before you speak or write, and offering positive, concrete feedback. This chapter presents techniques for better oral and written communication.

INTERPERSONAL COMMUNICATION AND HEALTH CARE CAREERS

The best way to sharpen your skills as a communicator is by changing your behavior. I issue certain challenges to those who attend my seminars as a catalyst for them to alter their communication styles. Monitoring your behavior will help you to change it. Even small changes accumulate over time. My challenges are scattered throughout this chapter, accompanying each related topic. Try a new communication challenge every few weeks and watch the positive results.

Building Professional Relationships

Whether you work for a hospital, private practice, health maintenance organization, or other health care institution, you interact with colleagues throughout your day. Why not make each interaction the best possible? Instead of feeling uncomfortable about calling an unknown colleague with a question or a request, try to meet that person *before* you call. Build relationships with other health care professionals by using the following techniques:

1. *Take the initiative.* The best time to solve a problem is before it starts. Don't wait for your colleagues to introduce themselves to you. Start meeting them now. Many pharmacists tell me that their first contact with a new physician is a phone call to request a therapeutic interchange. The doctor's first greeting from the pharmacist is not "Hello, welcome to County General Hospital. I'm your pharmacist." Instead, it is "Hello, this is the pharmacist. I'm calling about Mrs.

The Public Speaking Challenge

One of the biggest fears people have is public speaking. Perhaps this is why we are so impressed with those who do it well. Professionals who can stand up in front of a crowd and deliver an organized, clear message will always rise to the top. Start small: speak up at a professional society meeting or offer to do an in-service at a local nursing facility. Then move on to more challenging audiences, such as a group of nurses, pharmacists, or physicians.

Smith's prescription. Are you sure you want to give her 500 mg?" Build relationships early. Then when you call others for a favor, you will have increased your chances of getting an affirmative reply.

Use good manners and judgment to build relationships. Here are a few techniques you might employ.

- Speak to everyone you see at work. You do not have to stop working or have long conversations; a smile and a "Hello" on the elevator will do.
- Spend at least one hour a week meeting new colleagues. In a community practice, take lunch to the referring physicians and their office personnel. In a hospital setting, share a coffee break with the charge nurses, pharmacists, and other coworkers. In a teaching hospital, make an effort to welcome new residents and other new colleagues to the hospital.
- Offer to present new information at staff meetings, in-services, or rounds for other specialties. Not only will you sharpen your skills as a presenter; you will impress your colleagues with your expertise. (See Chapter 8 for tips on preparing a presentation.)

2. *See yourself as an educator.* An excellent way to persuade others is to become a resource. Share journal articles, recent studies, and case reports with colleagues. Ask others what kind of scientific informa-

tion they need and provide it for them. Imagine how satisfying it would be if a colleague handed you an article that helped with a presentation or diagnosis. All professionals want the latest well-chosen, well-written information. With continuing advances in the Internet and the ease of e-mail attachments, becoming a resource has never been so easy. Sharing your knowledge, reading, and browsing are fine ways to build relationships that may help you later.

3. *Establish a rapport.* Let's say that two children appear on your doorstep one afternoon selling wrapping paper for soccer uniforms. One is a neighbor who plays with your children and whose parents are your friends. The other is a complete stranger. You can only buy from one of them. Which one would it be? Surely, the child you know. People do business with those they like and trust. You do not have to socialize with your colleagues outside work, but you can build mutually beneficial business relationships while at work.

Speaking Positively

Sometimes in an effort to be succinct, we become abrupt and unintentionally abrasive. While waiting in the reception area of a physician's office, I heard a patient inquire about the wait to see the doctor. The receptionist snapped, "We're running behind; you'll just have to wait your turn." What a condescending answer! Yes, the receptionist gave the patient accurate information, but did she really need to issue a reprimand? Even if the other party is mean or rude, you should rise above the temptation to respond with a witty or sarcastic answer. Instead, be positive. Choose an upbeat, specific answer such as "We are running about ten minutes behind."

I have found that the most successful health care specialists, from nephrologists to pharmacists to skilled nursing facility administrators, do not spend time and money on lavish facilities or big advertising budgets. Instead, they capitalize on the cheapest resource they have, speaking positively. Your office could be modern, well equipped, and beautifully decorated, but if you or your staff behave in a negative way toward your patients and their families, all your

spending is futile. Become a more effective communicator by selecting more influential words.

1. *Select positive words.* Negative words and phrases carry connota-
tions or meanings that we associate with those words in spite of their
textbook definitions. Choosing positive words may be difficult at first,
but they can save you a lengthy explanation and/or apology later.

Example

Instead of saying
"You shouldn't be getting so *fat.*"
Try
"I'd like to see you weigh about 20 pounds *less.*"

2. *Speak in specific terms.* When you are specific, you decrease
misinterpretation. Many patient problems and colleague misunder-
standings can be avoided by clear communication. For example, what
does "soon" mean to you? Ten minutes, three hours, two days?
"Soon" is not a very concrete answer, yet we use it often in an effort to
placate others. If you tell a colleague or patient, "I'll be finished
soon," you create the opportunity for misinterpretation. The other
party may interrupt you and your staff by calling back every ten
minutes for an answer. By contrast, the specific answer "I'll be finished at 2:30" should placate the clock-watching colleague or patient
so that you can get on with the business at hand.

3. *Make yourself aware of tone.* Sometimes *what* we say is misunderstood because of *how* we say it. Be aware of a rise in your voice,
added emphasis on certain words, or any other verbal technique that
distorts your tone. If you find yourself becoming impatient, take a
deep breath and focus on lowering your voice before you speak.

Listening to Understand

One of the most important components of effective communication
is the one we ignore most. Listening requires us not only to hear what
the other person is saying but to comprehend it as well. Unfortunately, when we are supposed to be listening, most of us are thinking

The Eye-Contact Challenge

What is your impression of a person who does not make eye contact during a conversation? We tend to believe that the individual is embarrassed, nonconfident, and deceitful. When we are talking, the person listening to us but not looking at us seems not to be paying attention. Similarly, we think the person speaking to us but not looking at us is hiding something. Eye contact is the most powerful nonverbal tool you have. Master it. For at least two weeks, practice sustaining eye contact in casual conversation. At the grocery store, practice looking at the clerk. When you meet someone new, try to make eye contact. Rotate where you look on the other person's face, and that person will think you are making eye contact during the entire conversation. Patients will be impressed if you pause to look at them while making a diagnosis or recommending a treatment. You will be a more persuasive, effective communicator if you master eye contact while both speaking and listening.

of a clever response rather than paying attention to the speaker. How do we tell if others are listening? We watch for verbal and nonverbal feedback. A person who is looking away, fidgeting, or not responding gives the appearance of *not* listening. Talking to someone who does not appear to be listening is frustrating. Become a better listener by trying the following techniques:

- Make eye contact: focus on the other person's face throughout the conversation.
- Smile, nod, and acknowledge; offer reassuring comments such as "I understand," "yes," "okay, right."
- Echo what others have said to show you are paying attention.

Example

"It sounds as if you are concerned about . . ."

Persuading Others to Change Their Behavior

No matter what you do for a living, if you interact with others on a daily basis, eventually you will need to persuade someone to change a behavior. As a pharmacist, you may want to persuade a colleague to make a therapeutic interchange; as a physician, you may want to persuade the pharmacy and therapeutics committee to add a product to the hospital's formulary; as a certified diabetes educator, you may want to persuade a patient to adhere to a sugar-free diet. In all of these scenarios, the key word is "persuade." Developing your skills as a persuasive communicator will enhance your career, your job satisfaction, and even your relationships. In the past you have probably used persuasion techniques without even realizing it. The following steps will help you to effectively persuade others.

1. *Ask questions to establish rapport.* As soon as we realize that we need to persuade someone, we usually launch into a sales pitch. The problem with this enthusiastic style is that the person we are trying to persuade is probably not listening. When counseling a patient, many health care professionals have a set agenda for each diagnosis. Rather than listening to the patient's concerns, the professional often jumps in with the "top-ten-reasons-procedure-X-is-a-good-idea" pitch. Meanwhile, the patient does not listen to the provider because all she really wants to know is "Will it hurt?" Instead of pulling out the top-ten list, ask the patient what concerns her and focus on that *one* item. You will save time and increase patient satisfaction.

Example

Instead of saying

"Ms Campbell, you really need to check your blood sugar every day; that is the only way we are going to be able to tell if you need insulin."

(Ms Campbell probably already has that information. Why not find out why she will not check her blood sugar daily?)

Try

"Ms Campbell, I would really like to get your blood sugar under control. Is there a reason why you do not check your blood sugar every day?"

(Be sure to give the patient time to think and speak. You may think you are too busy to allow the patient extra time, but you will save time and effort if the patient resolves the problem now instead of in a phone call or repeat visit later.)

2. *Establish a need.* Most people will support ideas that affect them. Sometimes in order to persuade others to adopt your idea, you have to help them establish a need. For example, patients with hypertension may not experience any symptoms and therefore will not adhere to the recommended medication, diet, and exercise. They do not see a *need* to comply. How can you establish a need for them? Counsel these patients with a verbal consult combined with educational literature.

Example

"Mr Burns, I am concerned because your blood pressure is 145 over 92 and I want to encourage you to take steps toward preventing a heart attack."

Consider timing when you are persuading others. After you and a colleague have had a grueling week at the hospital, approaching that individual in the parking lot on a Friday is a bad time to pitch a new hospital policy.

3. *Focus on the benefits.* Consider what motivates you. Most people respond to ideas that benefit them. If you want to persuade a colleague to adopt your idea or a patient to take your advice, add a benefit. Benefits are the motivators that persuade. For example, you might persuade a patient to try a new allergy medicine by pointing out, "This medicine is very effective; it lasts up to twenty-four hours." But what is the *benefit?* "The new twenty-four-hour dosing conveniently allows you to take the pill only *once a day.*" How do you know that once-a-day dosing is important? Ask the patient, "When is a convenient time of day to take this medicine?"

Example

One of the most frequent opportunities to persuade others is the recommendation of a therapeutic interchange. While your colleague may have experienced fine results with a certain drug or therapy and may not want to change, you may be implementing a new formulary decision. When you feel that your recommendation is a better choice, focus on the *benefits:*

- Stronger mechanism of action
- Greater patient compliance
- Less expensive drug with same outcome.

To strengthen your argument, always support your benefit with the facts: package inserts, recent journal articles and case studies, and patient charts and lab reports.

4. *Close the conversation.* You can close a telephone call, a meeting, or any conversation by creating a call to action. The pharmacist advocating therapeutic interchange might close a phone call to a nurse with, "If you'll double-check the chart for allergies, I'll call the doctor to check on this antibiotic." At the end of a counseling session, a physician might say to a patient, "Let's set some reasonable weight-loss goals . . ." The call to action at the close of a conversation can help the other party buy into the idea simply by putting the idea into action.

IMPROVING VERBAL COMMUNICATION

Think of a person whom you believe to be an outstanding communicator, perhaps a colleague, a mentor, or even a politician. What makes this individual a great communicator? In addition to using the delivery techniques mentioned in Chapter 8, the best public speakers tell stories. These tales supply a mental visual aid to accompany the main points. A good story does not have to be lengthy. You can tell a brief anecdote or even offer an analogy to illustrate your point. Remember meeting someone for the first time but not being able to remember her name later? You probably exchanged names, talked about your personal lives, and even told a few stories. A few days later, you recall every detail of a funny anecdote this person told you, but somehow you cannot remember her name. People remember stories. Use them to illustrate your ideas.

Practice Before You Speak

Once you have planned your persuasive idea with specific stories for each point, you need to practice. There are many reasons why you should practice: to overcome anxiety, to time your conversation, and to try out delivery techniques. The most important reason, however, is to tighten up your ideas. When we tell a joke for the first time, we stumble over it and sometimes even start over. By about the third time, we have mastered it. Practice allows you to work out any delivery problems *before* presenting. It also helps you simplify your ideas and make your persuasive conversation interesting. No one wants to adopt something that sounds difficult, and nobody listens to a dull speaker. I often hear health care professionals comment on how a colleague has a "natural talent" for public speaking and communication. I suspect that colleague has probably given many talks and, more important, has prepared and practiced them. Practice bits of your talk or conversation while taking a shower, driving to work, or mowing the grass. Before you know it, you will feel comfortable with your material.

Communicating by Telephone

In this age of digital technology, it is imperative for health care professionals to master communication over the telephone. Although voice mail, cellular telephones, and long-distance calling cards make calling others more convenient, they also make calling others more complicated. Just a few years ago, when you called a colleague or an insurance company, you talked to an actual person. This person wrote down your name and number correctly, clarified why you called, and even reminded the person you phoned to return your call. When you call someone today, you usually have to just leave a message, and the voice-mail system is often an easy excuse for others not to return your calls promptly.

How do we choose which call to return? Usually we take the path of least resistance. If someone's number is handy, the question is clear, and the caller is pleasant, we do not mind returning the call. Have you ever received a call from someone who lacks focus, rambles, and simply wastes your time? Do you eventually just avoid that caller? If you want others to respond to your calls, sharpen your telephone skills. Most of the techniques below apply to both live conversations and voice-mail messages.

1. *Strive to be a better telephone communicator.*

   Develop your listening skills. Avoid interrupting, working on other projects, and speaking to others while on the phone. To foster conversation, ask open-ended questions such as "What solution works best for you?" and then acknowledge what the other person has said.

   Use telephone time efficiently. Be prepared before making a call by organizing questions and issues. During the call, take notes to help you remember important points and concentrate on what the caller is saying by closing your eyes. Most people have voice mail, so always contemplate what message you will leave.

2. *Divide calls into three sections and include the following:*

   Introduction

   Introduce yourself and state your intentions. Include the patient's name and other relevant information, to allow the other health care professional to prepare mentally and to retrieve the proper charts and materials. Offer the other person a brief agenda. If someone calls you and says, "I have three things to tell you," wouldn't you automatically grab a pen and prepare to write down those three things? Offering an agenda keeps both parties on task and makes calling more efficient.

   Example: "Hello, Dr Payne, this is Dr Burkhead. How are you? (Wait for response.) Great. I have three things to ask you about . . ."

The "Um" Challenge

Have you ever listened to someone who said "um" or "ah" after every breath? Without realizing it, most people say "um" several times in a conversation. Unfortunately, it has no meaning. Using "um," "you know," "okay," "sort of," "if you will," and other fillers may actually distract the listener from your message. Practice pausing instead; your listener will appreciate the brief silence.

Body
Get to the point of the call. If the other party tends to chat about irrelevant issues, bring the conversation back in focus by saying, "Let's get back to number two."
Example: "First, did you receive my fax? Second, . . ."
Conclusion
Summarize the call with directives for you and the other party. A pharmacist once told me that she called a colleague to suggest a therapeutic interchange. She and the physician discussed the new therapy in detail and the physician sounded uncertain. At the end of the call, the pharmacist said, "Let me summarize. You do *not* want to change Mr Knorr's prescription to drug Z." The physician responded, "No, I *do* want to try drug Z." A simple clarification at the end of the call can save time, money, and error.
Example: "Let's see, I'll talk with Mrs Frank about the biopsy if you'll check your calendar for a surgery appointment next week."

While these steps may seem elementary, few people actually perform them. By organizing your points with numbers, you prioritize the information before you call and give the listener a verbal cue that the information is coming.

3. *Train your telephone voice.*
   Replace vocal garbage. Replace such expressions as "you know," "um," and other fillers with a pause.

Smile when speaking over the phone. Many telemarketing callers have mirrors at their desks to remind them to smile when they use the phone.

Speak slowly and clearly. Choose the fewest words needed to state your message and allow time for others to make notes while you speak. Since you do not have to repeat information, speaking slowly prevents miscommunication and shortens the call.

Using Voice Mail

Voice mail can be a useful tool for busy professionals. Since most hospitals and offices have some system of voice mail, be sure you are prepared to leave a specific, detailed message *every* time you call. This system can be your best ally. Another advantage of tightening up your voice-mail messages is the carryover to other conversations. If you develop the skill of making your point in thirty seconds or less on the telephone, you will probably fine-tune the same skill in person-to-person conversations. In a busy clinic, hospital, or surgical suite, this skill can be as critical as your medical training.

When *recording your own voice-mail answer message:*

- Leave dates and times you will be available to speak in person, information the caller may want to know (such as your fax number), and how to transfer to someone else in your office for immediate assistance.
- Respond to all messages promptly.

When *leaving a message* on a colleague's voice mail:

- Plan your message *before* you call and be prepared to record. Many health care professionals tell me that they are surprised to receive a voice mailbox when they call someone, and they are unprepared to leave a voice-mail message. If you are prepared for a voice mailbox but get a person, you will sound more articulate.
- Leave your phone number or fax number in the message. Speak slowly, spell names, and repeat numbers.

The Listen-To-Yourself-On-Voice-Mail Challenge

Have you ever heard yourself on voice mail? Few people relish the sound of their recorded voices. Yet they could learn a lot about their communication style by listening to their own messages. At least once a month, listen to yourself on voice mail. Once you get over the shock of hearing your own voice, you can assess whether your messages are clear, concise, well organized, and positive. You will also hear the unnecessary "ums."

- Get to the point immediately and save small talk for face-to-face communication.
- Practice before you call.
- Be specific with the information you want, the best way to reach you, and when you will call back.
- If possible, listen to your message after you record it and rerecord if necessary.
- Leave instructions on how to reach you by pager or cellular phone.

OFFERING CONSTRUCTIVE FEEDBACK

If you run your own practice, get promoted into a supervisory position, or just want to communicate more effectively with your peers, sharpening the way you offer feedback will yield many positive results. After all, feedback should improve performance, not strain your relationship. Take a minute to recall your favorite boss. Why is that person your favorite? Next, remember your least favorite boss. What does that person need to improve? Lots of excellent books are available on how to motivate and supervise others. The most successful supervisors, however, use common sense. If you did not like having a boss who reprimanded you in front of others, your own employees probably will not care for it either. The following list offers some basic communication techniques that apply to almost any feedback situation.

1. *Recognize and encourage colleagues.* By recognizing the efforts of others, you will foster a better relationship and improve performance. Most of us are motivated as much by praise as by paycheck. Even if you do not supervise others officially, acknowledge and praise their efforts. Another time they will be apt to work harder for you.

2. *Ease criticism with assertive phrases and "I statements."* I statements are sentences that move the blame from the other party to you. They can help introduce a sensitive or negative subject without eliciting a defensive response. When I was first married, my husband—a six-foot-four man with size 14 shoes—used to leave his shoes all over the house. One day I tripped over a pair of tennis shoes that he had left in the middle of the kitchen floor. I was getting tired of putting his shoes away for him and was tempted to tell him, "You keep leaving your shoes all over the house for me to pick up. I am not your maid or your mother!" I knew that kind of statement would only make matters worse, so when I decided to approach him about this annoyance, I chose an "I statement" to ease the criticism. I said, "When you leave your shoes around the house, *I feel* as if you are leaving them for me to pick up." I was able to initiate a conversation rather than a confrontation. Ultimately, I got the result I wanted.

   Instead of saying
   "*You* really should not worry about this test."
   Try
   "*I understand* your concern about this test. I may not have given you all of the information that you need. Let's review . . ."
   Instead of saying
   "Mrs Weatherby, *you* have been late for the last three days."
   Try
   "Mrs Weatherby, *I notice* that you have arrived at work late for the past three days. Our patients are coming to the office with no one to greet them."

3. *Remember there is a time and place for everything.* Some things will

take care of themselves over time. While our instincts tell us to reprimand immediately, doing so is not always the most effective technique. If necessary, allow yourself time to reflect before you speak (wait twenty-four hours), and plan what you are going to say before you approach your peer or subordinate. Avoid discussing the matter with coworkers, and choose a private, neutral location (a conference room) at a convenient time (the end of shift) for a talk.

4. *Offer feedback that motivates.* "You catch more flies with sugar than with vinegar" applies to colleagues and staff as well as patients. Using persuasive communication techniques, focus your feedback on the *benefits* of changing behavior. The easiest way is by phrasing the request in "if, then" or "when, then" terms. For example, you may persuade a colleague to take on a new daily responsibility by saying: "If you gather these files before we open the office, *then* our patients will not have to wait while we frantically search for a chart. Would you start organizing the files each day before we open the office?" Offering a benefit of *why* helps to motivate others.

5. *Turn criticism into feedback.* While criticism often is hard to accept, it can be even harder to give out. Delivered appropriately, criticism can be feedback. Think of how you prefer to receive criticism and adapt your style accordingly. Consider also the recipient of the criticism: What motivates the employee? How can you help that person to achieve the new goal? Try these steps in offering feedback:

a. The Problem

In private, ask employees to offer their side of the story first and give them a chance to offer their views *without interruption.*

Example: "Susan and Betty, I overheard you discussing Mrs Smith's diagnosis and I think Mrs Frank overheard also. Did you realize that Mrs Frank was standing at the counter when you started talking?" In this scenario, Susan and Betty will probably apologize and make excuses for their behavior.

b. Specific Solutions

After the employees explain their behavior, acknowledge the comments and ask them to modify the behavior with specific actions. Correct work performance rather than employee personalities.

Example: "I understand that you are upset by Mrs Smith's diagnosis; I am too. (Pause instead of saying 'but.') We still need to recognize patient confidentiality by not discussing patients where others may overhear. I recommend that we avoid discussing patients in the reception area."

c. Call to Action

Reassure employees by ending the conversation with a call to action and by thanking the employees for responding to your suggestions. Try to comment on both good and bad work.

Example: "Do you have any other suggestions for ways we can ensure patient confidentiality?" (Wait for answers.) "Great thought, Betty. Thanks for your time and ideas."

The old adage "Praise in public and criticize in private" still applies. Criticism stings more when there is an audience; always take employees aside to offer criticism. If you use your personal office for privacy, be sure also to call employees into your office with good news occasionally.

DEALING WITH UPSET PEOPLE

Most health care professionals deal regularly with upset people. Patients and their families can be under tremendous pressure about a potentially negative diagnosis, a frightening surgical procedure, or a large medical bill. Colleagues may be stressed because of a formulary decision, a peer's opinion, and a desire for status. Both groups may experience personal problems that feed their anxiety (marriage, family, financial stress). These situations can trigger upset behavior in even the calmest person. Thus, the best way to understand what an upset person wants is to recall the last time you were the upset person. What did you want the other party to do? Listen. Avoid making excuses. Fix the problem quickly. The following checklist offers concrete techniques on how to deal with an upset person. These steps chip away at the upset person's anger while allowing you to maintain control of your emotions and the situation.

1. *Remain silent.* Wait for the other person to "vent" before you comment. Most people who are upset realize that you may not be able to change the situation. Their goal is to let you know how they feel. They usually just want to be heard. Be sure to show you are listening by making eye contact, nodding your head, and responding with words such as "yes," "I understand," and "okay."

2. *Echo what has been said.* When you repeat back to someone what has been said, you focus on listening rather than responding. By reflecting or rephrasing what upset people have said, you will illustrate that you are listening, clarify the problem, and show them how they sound. Often people who tend to exaggerate will modify their complaints after hearing their words coming from your mouth.

   Example

   Patient: "Every time I come to this clinic I have to wait at least two hours!"

   Staff member: "You have to wait at least two hours every time you visit our clinic."

   Patient: "Well, maybe not every single time."

3. *Make an intention statement.* After echoing what the other person has said, the next words you speak should express intent.

   Example

   "It's not our intent to upset you, Mr Grayson. Our goal is to give you the best care possible." Be sure you make this statement with sincerity. Patients and colleagues can detect a patronizing tone or sarcasm in your voice.

4. *Offer a solution while giving the upset person a choice.* Giving the upset person a choice puts him or her in control—which is what most of us want.

Example: "I am sorry we are running behind. Would you like to come back for your prescription after lunch or on your way home from work?" This technique not only gives the upset person control; it also shifts the focus away from the problem and places it on the solution.

COMMUNICATING WITH PATIENTS

Sharpening the Patient Consult

The following tips are a collection of techniques gathered from physicians, pharmacists, assorted health care professionals, and patients. Listed in chronological order, they offer specific ways to increase patient compliance and satisfaction and therefore lead to positive outcomes.

1. *Greet patients* with a handshake or pat on the shoulder, eye contact, and a smile. Eye contact and appropriate physical contact allow you to appear more attentive and sincere. The first time I saw my new obstetrician/gynecologist, he met with me in his personal office prior to the exam. This technique put me on equal turf so that I could speak freely about my health. Because he was seated, I felt he had plenty of time to listen to my concerns. Because I was fully clothed, I felt comfortable. The doctor's personal office was located out of earshot, so he left his door open to maintain the appearance of propriety without compromising privacy.

This technique works well on hospital rounds also. A client of mine who is a surgeon told me he did not have time to chitchat with patients while on rounds. He said he was afraid of getting trapped in a lengthy conversation. I asked him to try three quick and easy techniques during rounds. First, I suggested that he sit in a chair or on the edge of the bed during the consult. Sitting down put him at eye level with the patient and gave the impression that the patient with whom he was talking was his primary concern. As a bonus, when the surgeon stood up, he gave the nonverbal cue "time to go," which helped bring the conversation to a close. Second, I recommended that the surgeon read the chart notes aloud to the patient, allowing him to share important information while checking for any new developments. For example, "Mrs James, I see your blood pressure is . . ." The third technique I offered was that the surgeon summarize the conversation. Thus, toward the end of the consult, the surgeon said, "It looks as though you are doing well, Mrs James; I think we may be able to send you home by Friday." All three of these techniques incorporated the patient into the exam, gave the impression that the surgeon had plenty of time to share, and offered verbal and nonverbal signals of when he needed to leave.

2. *Introduce yourself*, explain who you are, and use the patient's name. Taking the time to introduce yourself will foster your relationship and increase patient compliance. Explain what you do. Many people do not realize the amount of training that goes into being a surgeon, or that podiatrists write prescriptions and perform surgery, or that pharmacists read lab reports and consult with physicians on treatment. Also, using a patient's name will make that individual feel more comfortable and will help you to remember the name later.

3. *Start patient counseling* with brief but specific questions such as "What is the main reason you are here today, Mrs Dorn?" This technique breaks the ice and allows the patient to ease into the conversation with a focused answer. Avoid the open-ended "How are you today?" You may get trapped into hearing irrelevant stories.

4. *Invite questions* and respond appropriately. *Resist the desire to interrupt the patient.* According to the *Journal of the American Medical Association*, the average clinician interrupts the patient after only twenty-three seconds.[1] Time yourself as you explain something new. Doesn't it usually take more than twenty-three seconds?

Many health care providers tell me that they sometimes feel trapped with their patient during the interview. The patient does not focus on the problem and the medical professional has to interrupt to get the person on track. To help the patient focus on the problem, try these suggestions:

- In a large clinic where your budget will allow, hire a "greeter" to circulate around the reception area to help patients complete forms, answer questions, and keep things moving. This added expense could save you time and money in the long run by keeping highly paid and skilled nurses, therapists, and physicians from spending time on these issues. Your insurance clerk will appreciate the accurately completed forms.
- Design and print cards that say "My top three concerns are . . ." at the top with blank lines below. Offer a card to each patient to fill out at check-in, then go over the responses during the exam. Your patient can prepare to talk to you while waiting to see you.

5. _Strive to maintain eye contact_ throughout the conversation. If you have trouble focusing on a patient's eyes, rotate your gaze on the person's face. Eye contact can be the key to patient satisfaction and compliance, yet many health care providers forget to look at their patients when talking to them. I have noticed topnotch physicians explaining a prescription while writing it. Instead of writing the prescription and pausing to explain it to the patient, these doctors assume that the patient is listening while they write. Meanwhile, the patient sees a busy physician who does not have time for questions and does not ask any. The ramifications of this poor communication scenario are numerous: misunderstanding, low compliance, and dissatisfaction, which may ultimately lead to a negligence lawsuit. By contrast, physicians who strive to make eye contact are able to gauge patient comprehension, foster a relationship, and increase compliance, leading to positive outcomes. Patients with positive outcomes rarely sue for negligence.

6. During the consult, _demonstrate genuine interest in_ and concern for the patient. Patients respond to health care providers who appear to care about their health. After all, why do they go to the doctor? They want to get better. Most people dread going to the doctor because it means waiting to be seen; having to undress, weigh, and undergo an exam; and then paying to leave. Even well patients who are having an

annual examination experience the stress of the visit and the possibility of having a negative test result. Make them comfortable by listening and responding appropriately.

7. *Strive to reassure* the patient about the diagnosis, treatment, or outcome. Most patients need reassurance in order to deal with their situation. While you do not want to offer false hope or incorrect information, you should make it clear that you will help them cope with the problem.

8. During the consult, *inquire about personal issues* such as work and family, then make notes in your files on areas you need to remember for the next visit. Patients are impressed with health care providers who seem to care about their personal lives. You may also learn key information about their care. Even though I know my physician reads my chart ahead of time, I still light up when he enters the room asking about my work: "So what big medical meetings have you spoken at lately?"

9. If you have trouble responding to a comment or question (especially a negative remark), *repeat the question* or comment back to the patient. This shows the patient you are listening, gives you time to formulate an answer, and clarifies the individual's concern.

Example

Mr Bennett: "I really don't understand why I should have surgery for this. Why can't I just have more chemotherapy?"

Dr Roberson: "I understand that you are concerned about the surgery." (Pause here and the patient will usually fill the silence.)

Mr Bennett: "You're darned right. My brother died on the table last year and I do not want any part of that."

If Dr Roberson had said "You don't need to be afraid of surgery" instead of reflecting Mr Bennett's response, he might not ever have found out why Mr Bennett did not want surgery and might have lost him to a more "compassionate" doctor.

10. *Take patient concerns seriously,* no matter how trivial. Give the patients brochures, videos, and other information to help them understand a treatment or prescription. Offer your business card with

an invitation to call you later with questions. Patients take their health seriously and expect you to do the same.

11. *Explain the disease state,* the prescription information, and other instructions in detail and in layman's terms. If possible, draw diagrams for the patient and give out brochures. Most people are visual learners. Offering visual aids will increase comprehension, retention, and compliance while decreasing telephone calls with questions. Visual aids also allow the patient to review a procedure or diagnosis after the visit.

12. *Speak to a patient in the same tone as you speak to a colleague.* Most people appreciate advice from a peer rather than a "parent." Of all the tips in this section, I believe that treating your patient as a peer is one of the most influential. Many times I have heard friends, family, and strangers complain about how their physician, pharmacist, or therapist spoke to them with a condescending tone. Even though your patients and peers may not have your specialized training, they can learn enough to understand a complex diagnosis and make important medical decisions. As an effective medical communicator, you should develop the skills needed to explain complex information in comprehensible terms.

I organized a patient satisfaction survey for a small medical practice in a rural southern town. One of the doctors received some negative feedback from the survey, so he asked me to coach him on interpersonal communication skills. I asked him to describe a typical annual exam from start to finish. When he described his steps in examining a patient, he referred to the breast exam as an opportunity for the "breast self-examination lecture." At this point, I knew exactly why his patients rated him so poorly. Does anybody go to the doctor for a lecture? Fortunately, this physician was willing to make behavior changes to prevent future problems.

After I injured my ankle playing tennis, my doctor recommended physical therapy. I made an appointment but had to cancel because of a work-related schedule change. When I called the physical therapist for a new appointment, she launched into a condescending lecture on why my physician had sent me to physical therapy and why I should not cancel habitually. She treated me as if I were an inconvenience to her. Avoid the "bad patient" lecture. Instead, foster a positive relationship by thanking the patient for calling and changing the appointment to a more convenient time.

13. *Allow patients to voice concerns* before giving them additional information. Patients will listen better after they have absorbed the diagnosis. As soon as patients hear words like "test," "lump," "abnormal," and "follow-up," the rest of what a doctor says often goes unheard.

14. *Explain why to patients:* why a certain procedure will work, why patients should take their medication, and so on. This technique increases patient compliance and satisfaction because it offers *benefits* to the patient.

Example: "Mrs Gray, if you use these drops three times a day, we should be able to clear up this eye infection by the end of the week."

15. *Offer patients written instructions* for taking medications and following your recommendations. Patients are more likely to comply with easy-to-understand instructions that come in the form of a chart, calendar, or list. Written instructions are a particular benefit to elderly patients, who may experience dementia, usually take multiple medications, and could have various caregivers administering medicine. If you have listened to the patient's comments from the beginning of the consult, you may be able to tie them into your recommendations.

Example: "Mrs Rumley, you'll need to take this pill with a big meal. Since you eat a substantial lunch every day, I recommend you take it with lunch."

16. *Do not be afraid of physical contact:* sit down beside patients and touch their hands when you speak to them or give patients a handshake when they are leaving. Patients are used to being poked and prodded in the doctor's office. Most people view nonsexual physical contact as reassuring and comforting. Many health care professionals

have asked me, "What is appropriate nonsexual physical contact?" to which I respond, "From the elbows down." You can usually touch another person's hand or arm without misinterpretation. But if in doubt, avoid physical contact.

Increasing Patient Compliance

Patients and their families often endure a lot of stress when they visit a clinic or hospital. They may not be as focused as usual. Communicate with them as you would if they were your relatives. Give patients and family a chance to explain their concerns and you will save time, build trust, and improve compliance.

1. *Offer multiple modes of instruction:* give patients videotapes with additional instructions and tape recordings of your counseling sessions. One of the primary reasons for malpractice suits is poor communication. Tape-recording your counseling session can prevent the "nobody-told-me-about-complications" lawsuit. You may also set up a small video-viewing room for patients. If you perform lots of surgical procedures, collect a video library of them. Ask your patients to watch the appropriate tape, then review any questions or concerns with them afterward. Your video library can also be a great source of continuing education information for you and your staff.

2. *Use adult learning strategies in your counseling sessions.* When you are listening to something new, what kind of explanation appeals to you? What kinds of teaching techniques help you to remember information? Most people have difficulty paying attention to a boring speaker, so strive to be enthusiastic and interesting. Most of us learn by listening to an explanation, processing the information, and using the new knowledge immediately. One way to achieve these three steps is by asking the patient and family some assessment questions throughout the session.

Example: "Let's review, Mrs Waters; how often are you going to take the fluid pill?"

Another learning strategy is to divide complex information into more than one session. I once heard a pharmacy director say that she understood a speaker's explanation because the instructor "cut it into bite-sized pieces."

Example: "Mr Jones, I know you have heard a lot of information on diabetes today. We have fifteen minutes in this session and I'd like to talk to you about what kinds of foods you eat. Is that okay with you?"

You can also help the patient organize a system for taking prescriptions. Lack of compliance may be due to lack of convenience. Try setting up a system to maximize convenience. For example, suggest that a patient keep prescriptions in the kitchen as a reminder to take the medicine at mealtime.

3. *Speaking at the same pace as your audience.* Matching the pace of the person with whom you are speaking will put that person at ease. Slow down also when you say something important. Most people state their names, telephone numbers, and other familiar items too fast to be understood. If English is your second language, ask a colleague to help you with pronunciation.

4. *Keep it simple.* Here is perhaps the best advice on communication in teaching adults, writing documents, delivering speeches, and counseling patients. Choose the fewest number of simple words to convey your message. If you are concerned about talking down to well-educated patients, ask them to tell you about their jobs. You will quickly be able to assess their educational levels and possibly make correlations between their diagnoses and their education and training.

Examples

Use laymen's terms to describe medications, diagnoses, and treatments: choose "flu shot" instead of "vaccination."

Use the fewest words possible to illustrate a point: choose "one" instead of "a limited number."

Select words that have fewer syllables: use "some" instead of "proportion."

5. *Use visual aids.* Gestures, drawings, brochures, and other visual aids increase comprehension and retention. In today's busy clinic, a

picture is indeed worth a thousand words. Preparing an informational brochure about a specific disease that you treat often will save you time and confusion in counseling while simultaneously serving as a marketing piece for your practice.

6. *Let them talk without interruption.* Allow the patient and family to vent frustrations, ask questions, and voice concerns. People who are absorbed with their concerns and questions cannot focus on your counseling advice.

Responding Positively to Patient Complaints

Sometimes it can be hard to take criticism about your practice or clinic, especially if you are in charge. Your initial reaction might be to defend yourself. If you go with that instinct, you may give your patients the impression that you do not take them seriously.

Most people who complain think they are helping you. They are. Patients who think your receptionist is snippy but do not complain may leave and never come back. After these patients leave, they tell their friends and neighbors who tell *their* friends and neighbors. One angry patient may not seem like much until you factor in all the people who hear the complaint later.

When I consulted for a long-term-care nursing facility, the administrator asked me to conduct a customer satisfaction survey of the residents' families by telephone. My staff and I spent about fifteen minutes per call. We asked the family members if they were satisfied with their loved one's care, if we could do anything to make the resident more comfortable, and if we needed to have the administrator or director of nursing call them to discuss a care plan. Most families were satisfied with their loved one's care, but a few had concerns that needed to be addressed. We responded by faxing the family member's comments to the appropriate person at the nursing facility. For example, we sent meal comments to the dietary manager. If the complaint was serious, we called the director of nursing or the administrator with the news, and one of them responded to the family by phone within twenty-four hours and in writing within seven days. What a brilliant idea! For a nominal amount of money, this administrator not only met the needs of his residents, he also prepared an impressive patient satisfaction binder for the state survey team, and encouraged his employees to improve patient care.

Many patients who complain have good intentions. Accept the information with a smile and move quickly to correct it. Barlow and Maul suggest eight steps for responding to customer complaints.[2] The six steps below are an adaptation of their list.

1. Thank patients and explain why you are glad they complained. You will probably surprise them if you thank them instead of launching into a litany of excuses.
2. Apologize for the problem. Even if you are not to blame, you must apologize for the organization. If the patient is complaining to you, then to that patient you represent the organization.
3. Promise to deal with the problem right away.
4. Collect all the information you need. Make sure you know specifics about the problem or incident.
5. Correct the mistake as quickly as possible. The patient will never trust you again if he or she returns and sees no change.
6. Follow up to make sure your patients are satisfied with your actions. Help prevent similar situations by letting everyone in your organization know about the problem.

Remember that dealing with a complaining patient is not your opportunity to lecture or to win an argument. It is your opportunity to improve service and build trust.

Communicating with Older Adults

As medical technology advances and people live longer, the average patient becomes the elderly patient. The tips previously described in this chapter apply to communicating with all patients and their families. Add the following considerations for older adults:

1. *Review their senses.* Most elderly adults wear glasses or suffer from some kind of visual impairment and experience some kind of hearing loss. Chronic illnesses compromise the senses: diabetes

affects vision, hearing, and touch. Elderly adults often focus on basic needs: food, water, bathroom visits, and sleep. Compromised physical conditions make these basic needs difficult to attain.

2. *Try to imagine what elderly patients are thinking and feeling.* Many health care professionals tell me that older adults miss the mobility and freedom of their youth and appear lonely. These feelings, combined with multiple illnesses, translate into longer office visits. The reception-area greeter suggested earlier works well in practices and clinics that have large populations of older patients. A busy retail or outpatient pharmacy that services many older patients might incorporate a similar greeting system for sorting patient prescriptions, answering nonmedical questions, and collecting payments.

3. *Remember that aging affects people differently.* Cognitive abilities may be compromised. Lack of understanding does not always mean you should talk louder. Examples of what elderly patients might be thinking:
   - "This kid (a fifty-year-old pharmacist) is wet behind the ears. Why, he's young enough to be my grandson."
   - "Boy, I hope this doesn't last long. I need to use the bathroom."
   - "I can't hear a thing he's saying. What's he got in his hand?"

4. *Note barriers to medication compliance.* Gerontologists note many obstacles to compliance by elderly patients:[3]
   - Multiple prescriptions (polypharmacy) make it difficult to remember which pills have been taken.
   - Complex dosage schedules can be hard to follow if caregivers rotate shifts or if physicians rely on patients to take their own medicines.
   - Drug side effects that compromise mental alertness and cognitive function may cause patients to forget to take medications or to administer them improperly.
   - Lack of appropriate information or poor communication from the physician, nurse, or pharmacist may lead the patient to believe that the drug is not important enough to take.

- Patients on fixed incomes may not be able to afford the cost of medications.
- Patients with compromised physical conditions or limited incomes may not be able to pick up prescriptions.

NOTES

1. Marvel, M. K., Epstein, R. M., Flowers, K., and Beckman, H. B. Soliciting the patient's agenda. *JAMA* (1999) 281:283–287.

2. Barlow, J., and Maul, D. *Emotional Value: Creating Strong Bonds with Your Customers.* San Francisco: Barrot-Koehler, 2000.

3. Ennis, K., and Reichard, R. Maximizing drug compliance in the elderly. *Postgrad. Med.* (1997) 3:211–224.

12

Building Your Practice

Stephanie Barnard

You may think that in order to start your practice all you have to do is hang up a sign or join a thriving medical facility. Yes, joining an established office will help you jump-start your practice, but you need to keep the patients you have while working to recruit more. If you are joining a large practice, health maintenance organization, or hospital, the community relations and human resources departments can help you phase into the community. In addition, the following inexpensive and ethical steps can help you get started.

1. *Have a professional picture taken.* Buy about six black-and-white prints to use in news releases, hospital newsletters, brochures, and other marketing materials. Men should wear a dark suit without a lab coat, a solid light-colored shirt, and a plain tie. Women should wear a dark suit without a lab coat, simple jewelry, and modest makeup.
2. *Draft a news release* about your new position including your education, specialty areas, and so on. For a nominal fee, a local college

student may be willing to help you. (A sample release is given in Chapter 14.) Send the news release with your professional picture to the newspapers in your area, the alumni/ae magazines at the schools you attended, and the professional periodicals in your specialty. Notify your church or synagogue of your new practice.

3. *Send out professionally printed announcements* about your position in the practice to local medical offices, hospitals, health agencies, and other referral sources. Any commercial printer can typeset and print these for you. (See the sample announcement in Chapter 14.)

4. Encourage your facility or hospital to *host a reception* to introduce you to the community. Invite anyone who may refer patients to you. For example, many patients with minor back problems may see a chiropractor first. If you are an orthopedic surgeon, a relationship with a chiropractor can lead to many referrals.

5. Set aside *one lunch per week to meet and greet* other medical officers and physicians in your area. Since people do business with those they like and trust, establish rapport early in your career by meeting your peers.

6. Ask another physician (of a different specialty) to *introduce you around the community and hospital.* Aligning yourself with an established, respected peer will help you gain patient referrals and business contacts.

7. Send out a *memo to local civic and church organizations* asking for an opportunity to give a fifteen-minute talk on health issues. (See the sample memo in this chapter and reread Chapter 8 on giving a community-based presentation.)

ALIGNING YOURSELF WITH NEW PATIENTS AND COLLEAGUES

Even if you are an established and reputable physician, physical therapist, dentist, or pharmacist, you will lose patients as they move, change health maintenance organizations, die, or decide to use another health care professional. For these reasons you should continue to market your practice to recruit new patients and retain existing ones.

1. *Gather new business.* Spend at least an hour a week gathering new business by calling colleagues on the telephone or visiting their offices. Some of your best referral sources may be from another specialty or even another field:

   Referring physicians—general practitioners, podiatrists, and dentists

   Medical professionals—nurses, physical therapists, office personnel

   Local professionals—attorneys, bankers, and real estate agents.

   After having nose surgery for a deviated septum, I asked my otolaryngologist to refer me to a pulmonologist for an asthma checkup. He asked his assistant to call to make an appointment for me at a local office. As she was dialing, she turned to me and said, "Which doctor do you want?" I said I wasn't sure, so she responded, "Dr Brown is not very nice. Dr Evans is okay, but I really like Dr Adams." I picked Dr Adams.

   One of the best ways to develop relationships with referring practices is for you and your staff to take lunch to them. Offer an opportunity to meet, eat, and exchange ideas. Your staff will appreciate the contacts later if they have insurance, billing, or patient questions, and you will appreciate the referrals of new patients.

2. *Get involved in the local community.* The beauty of community involvement is that you get to help others while bolstering your practice. Volunteer for a local charity's board of directors, a public school fundraiser, or your local soup kitchen. For example, a pulmonologist who serves on the board of directors for the local cystic fibrosis foundation will likely be asked to represent the organization in a media interview during a special event or fundraiser.

   Organize a fundraiser for a local charity that relates to your practice, and you will receive lots of goodwill and good press for your efforts. For example, a family medicine practice might organize a five-kilometer walk for diabetes. The time and resources you use for this event will be offset by the ethical, inexpensive promotion your practice will potentially receive from television and radio interviews, newspaper stories, flyers, T-shirts, and other promotional items. Or organize a health awareness event at your office. For example, a urology practice organizing a free prostate cancer screening will attract both media attention and community response.

Join the local chamber of commerce; you will keep up with community news, make excellent business contacts, and give back to your community. In many small towns the local chamber of commerce has substantial influence with regard to city ordinances and business dealings. It publishes a newcomer's guide that includes only members' businesses and usually refers only within its organization. If you want your occupational therapy practice to have a chance at that big corporation's contract, you should join the chamber.

If all of this community involvement leads you to speak to reporters for television, radio, or newspaper, follow these tips on looking good and sounding articulate.

Since radio and newspaper audiences will not see you, the next suggestions apply to television interviews only. Wear flattering, simple clothing in subtle colors. Avoid stripes because they appear to move on the screen, and bright hues as they look much brighter on television. Leave the lab coat at the office and opt for a suit jacket instead. Avoid large jewelry, short skirts, and ill-fitting clothing. For a radio, telephone, or newspaper interview, wear something professional and comfortable.

In a television interview, look at the interviewer. The camera crew and reporter will make sure you are facing the camera when they shoot. I have seen many novices trying to figure out where to look and ending up with an unflattering interview. In a radio, telephone, or newspaper interview, look at your notes.

In both television and radio interviews, ask for a set of questions in advance so that you can prepare and practice your answers. Most reporters want a quote, so speak in sound bites. Have you ever seen a local citizen interviewed on the television news after a big event? The reporter will ask for a comment on the event and the unprepared citizen, not knowing how to stop talking, will get cut off in the middle of a sentence when the newscast airs. Reporters only have a few seconds for quotes, so make yours short, specific, and upbeat. If you are taping an interview and are not pleased with something you said, ask the reporter to reshoot your comment. Always give the reporter your business card, so that your name will be spelled correctly on the television screen. Fortunately for radio, you can refer to cheat notes; take them with you when you go to the station. In the telephone newspaper interview, do not be afraid to put the reporter on hold or even call back once you have found your notes and are prepared to answer difficult questions.

A seasoned physician who is chairman of a family practice department told me that one of the easiest interviews to flunk is the deposition. At some point in your career, you may be called to answer questions that may affect your practice or the career of a colleague. As with any other public-speaking opportunity, the best advice is to prepare before you speak. Try to find out what questions you will be asked and think through your answers before you arrive. Avoid rambling, disorganized answers. Once you have given a sufficient answer, be quiet.

3. *Hire employees who are a reflection of your philosophy, and implement a training program.* Time and again I hear horror stories about office managers who have embezzled from medical practices. Screen your employees thoroughly and check their references. It is worth the extra time and effort.

Train your staff to be professional at all times by implementing a dress code and specifying how you want employees to answer the phone, greet patients, screen calls, and handle upset patients. Your employees may come with excellent experience and references but you still need to specify how they should communicate in various situations. Most of us have observed a receptionist asking a patient delicate financial or health questions in front of an audience of patients in the reception area. Modify your reception area and, more important, train your staff to handle delicate questions appropriately. Reward employees who go beyond the call of duty; everyone appreciates recognition for a fine performance. If you praise and thank your employees and colleagues regularly, they will respect and protect you.

Lead by example. Lots of physicians, nurse managers, and pharmacists believe that because of their status in the organization, they can bend the rules. Your employees are always watching. Show how you expect them to behave by your own actions.

Discourage employees from discussing patient issues within earshot of others and outside the office. A local physician in the small town where I grew up stopped to speak to my mother one afternoon. Mom asked about a neighbor who was under his care in the hospital. The doctor offered a general answer, but added very specific, very personal information. All health care professionals learn about patient confidentiality in their training. This doctor ignored the privacy of the patient and compromised his practice. I suspect his staff follows his lead.

4. *Strive for professionalism in everything.* On your next vacation or road trip, notice the billboards along the major highways. Those promoting gas stations advertise "Clean Restrooms" along with directions to the gas station. When you take the exit, note which gas station you choose and why. If gas prices are comparable, you will probably choose the station that has the best appearance: new pumps, a large minimart with snacks and restrooms, and even a new fast-food restaurant. Your patients are doing the same thing when they approach your facility. You may be one of the best surgeons in the area, but if your office is decorated in 1970s-style furniture your patients may think you are not on the cutting edge. Similarly, if you have a lavish facility your patients may resent

your fees. Use common sense and heed advice from patients and colleagues:

- Keep your office and grounds neat and orderly. Put a cigarette-butt disposal container outside the front door and garbage cans in the reception area.
- Redecorate to help your office appear up-to-date.
- Keep the grounds lighted and professionally landscaped.
- Check the restrooms regularly during the day to make sure they are clean and well stocked.
- Dress for success. Consider logo shirts or uniforms for your employees.

MAINTAINING YOUR PATIENTS

Most patients choose their physician based on nonscientific data. Rather than look up background information on a doctor, they rely on the opinions of others. There are many opportunities in your community to maintain patient relationships and gain new patients. Earlier I mentioned developing relationships with local professionals by getting involved in the local community. My physician benefited from this technique. When I moved to Columbia, South Carolina, in 1998, my husband and I knew only a few people. It was time for my annual exam, so I asked my real estate agent to recommend a physician. She referred me to my new doctor and I was so impressed with him that I in turn referred my new neighbors to him.

1. *Speak to patients personally.* Whenever possible, speak to patients on the phone yourself and always acknowledge them in public. One of my clients, a small-town podiatrist, told me he has a policy of "speak to everyone you see." Both in his office and out in the community, he always smiles and acknowledges people. One time, while entering the local dime store, he smiled and said, "Hello, how are you?" to a woman he saw but did not recognize.

She responded, "I'm so much better since you did surgery on my foot last year." Had the doctor not acknowledged this patient, she probably would have returned home to complain to her friends and neighbors. Also, many people in the community recognize this doctor because he has a thriving practice. His "speak to everyone" policy is a simple behavior modification that helps develop and maintain patient relationships.

2. *Send hand-written notes.* With the evolution of e-mail, word processing, and database computer programs, the hand-written thank-you note has become even more special. One of the easiest and most inexpensive ways to promote your practice or department is by sending hand-written notes to colleagues. Think about how you sort your mail. What do you open first? Usually most people head for the big stuff (brown envelopes and packages) and the small stuff (invitations and hand-written notes). If you want to make an impression, take out a pen and paper.

A rule of thumb for a hand-written note: Write one to thank anyone who spends more than fifteen minutes or five dollars doing something for you. That may mean referring a new patient to you, waiting a long time to see you, or bringing you a tin of cookies during the holiday season. Hand-written notes work well for dropping a line to a colleague with a journal article. Hire a commercial printer to design your cards with your practice or department logo, address, and contact numbers (phone, fax, e-mail) on them. Printing envelopes is costly, so you may choose to stamp your address on the envelopes when you write the notes. Be sure to share the stationery with your staff.

3. *Train your staff in customer service.* If the average patient visit lasts from one to two hours, how much of that time is spent with the doctor? At best, fifteen minutes. Physicians from all over the country are being pushed to see more patients per day and to become more efficient. As you corral your patients from the

reception area to the lab to the treatment room, notice all of the staff members who work with them. You may offer the best care possible, but if your lab technician is rude to your patient, that patient will go somewhere else and you will never know why. Train your staff to be an extension of your philosophy. Teach them how to acknowledge the waiting patient even while helping someone else, and how to handle an upset patient or family member. Well-trained, friendly staff members will *prevent* most customer service problems.

4. *Survey your patients and colleagues to assess your customer service strategies.* When I recommend that my clients ask their patients or customers to evaluate their performance, they sometimes balk at the idea. I understand how hard it can be to take criticism, but the only way to improve service is to ask rather than assume what needs to be improved. A patient satisfaction survey is one of the easiest ways to improve patient service, compliance, and satisfaction. Your patients are your customers and their opinions count. Even patients in a managed-care setting have a choice and a voice on which provider they choose. Unfortunately, most patients share the bad stories more readily than the good. The best way to prevent a bad story from circulating about your practice is to identify and repair the problem early. Your patients or clients will appreciate your attention to customer service, your staff will realize that they are part of customer satisfaction, and your colleagues will improve service.

Here are four effective ways to measure service.

a. Organize informal *focus panels* of key patients and referral sources, then make changes based on their opinions.

b. Ask for *written feedback* by sending patients a self-addressed, stamped envelope with a note asking for their thoughts on your service.

c. Hire a *mystery patient* to visit your facility, make observations, and write a report.

I once sent a staff member to "mystery-shop" at a skilled nursing facility that was a client of mine, and at its local competition. The administrator of the facility for whom we consulted told me that the competition was getting all of the business because its facility was newer. She thought her facility was better because the staff was more professional. When we put the two facilities to the test, the client facility was not as professional as we expected. The administrator was surprised and enlightened when we told her that the mystery shopper preferred the competition. How many residents did the facility lose before it realized its problem? Probably three to five per month. Asking patients to tell you what they think may hurt your feelings at first, but their replies can help to significantly improve service later on.

d. Draft a *patient satisfaction survey* and distribute copies to patients regularly. Use short-answer or yes/no questions. If you ask patients to rate services, use a small range. For example, "Please rate the following services on a scale of one (excellent) to five (unsatisfactory)." Allow space for patients to write in comments and assure them that you will keep all information confidential.

I have put together several opinion surveys for my clients; writing them is not difficult. Check with other practices to see what they have put together, and contact your national medical organization for a sample survey you can purchase. Also, refer to Chapter 14 for more tips on writing for patient audiences.

The sample survey in Figure 12.1 (pages 290–292) was designed for an obstetrics and gynecology practice. The questions were tailored to meet the needs of that medical office. Your survey should include similar questions, tailored to *your* practice. Keep the questions simple and brief and always allow extra space for comments. Also, you can adapt these questions to a telephone survey or a short survey to include in your quarterly newsletter or website.

Thank you for your time and sincerity in completing this patient satisfaction survey. Because we value your opinion, we have written these questions to determine what you need and expect at Better Health Women's Clinic.

Please return your questionnaire to us by placing it in the locked survey box in the reception area. *Your answers will be kept completely confidential.*

1. When did you last visit Better Health Women's Clinic? Please circle one.
   a. Within the past year
   b. 1–2 years ago
   c. 2–5 years ago
   d. Over 5 years ago

2. Which doctor did you see at your last visit?

3. If you are no longer a patient of BHWC, are you currently under the care of another physician?

The following questions have a rating system to follow. Please circle one.
   5   Excellent
   4   Very good
   3   Satisfactory
   2   Below average
   1   Unacceptable

4. Please rate the accommodation given when scheduling appointments over the phone or in person.

                              5   4   3   2   1

5. Please rate the courtesy given from the following staff at BHWC.

   Receptionist: 5   4   3   2   1
   Nurses: 5   4   3   2   1

| Lab technicians: | 5 | 4 | 3 | 2 | 1 |
| Checkout staff: | 5 | 4 | 3 | 2 | 1 |

6. How satisfied were you with the treatment you received from your doctor?

5   4   3   2   1

7. What rating would you give your doctor on answering your questions adequately?

5   4   3   2   1

8. Please rate your satisfaction with the amount of time the doctor spent with you.

5   4   3   2   1

9. How well did the doctor explain treatment options?

5   4   3   2   1

10. How would you rate the comfort of the waiting room?

5   4   3   2   1

11. How would you rate the examination rooms?

5   4   3   2   1

12. How well maintained was the rest room?

5   4   3   2   1

13. How would you rate the amount of time you had to wait before you saw the doctor?

5   4   3   2   1

14. How would you describe your care at BHWC to your friends?

5   4   3   2   1

15. Would you prefer to talk to the doctor while you are fully clothed prior to your exam? Please circle one.

    Yes   No   Only on the first visit

The following questions ask you to rate importance. Please circle one.

  5 Extremely important
  4 Very important

3   Somewhat important
2   Not very important
1   Not important at all

16. How important is it to see the same doctor at every visit?

              5   4   3   2   1

17. How important is it to have a follow-up contact concerning your test results, regardless of outcome?

              5   4   3   2   1

18. How important is the delivery and labor area of the hospital in influencing your decision regarding obstetrical care?

              5   4   3   2   1

19. Please rate the importance of a nurse-midwife as an option in your OB and/or GYN care?

              5   4   3   2   1

20. We welcome comments on your care, please tell us how Better Health Women's Clinic could better serve you.

Thank you again for participating in this survey. Your suggestions will make a difference in our practice.

Figure 12.1 Sample patient satisfaction survey.

13

Running an Effective Meeting

Stephanie Barnard

With all of the changes in managed care and health systems, health care professionals are spending ever more time in meetings. Yet many professionals dread meetings. Why? Usually they begrudge time away from more pressing concerns, dislike small-group discussions, and see the meetings as unnecessary. Two key elements in creating a successful meeting that participants will not resent are an *agenda* and an *action plan*. Send out the agenda ahead of the meeting, so that participants can prepare. Ask the recorder to create an action plan with assignments and deadlines rather than the traditional passive-voice minutes.

Many managers and professionals feel the need to call a meeting to discuss issues that could be resolved more efficiently by phone, fax, letter, or e-mail. Before you set up a meeting, ask yourself *Do we really need a meeting to accomplish this task?*

PLANNING A PRODUCTIVE MEETING

Brief, productive meetings generate higher morale, greater participation, and better ideas. Follow these steps when planning a meeting:

1. *Determine if a meeting is necessary and what kind of meeting is best.* Ask yourself:

   What is the purpose of this meeting? By establishing a purpose (whether to inform, to motivate, to plan, or to make decisions), you will determine if the meeting is necessary and pinpoint your objectives *before* you meet.

   How long should the meeting last? Most meetings should not exceed an hour. Surprise your colleagues with a meeting that lasts forty-five minutes and they will happily attend your next meeting. Shorten your meetings by removing the chairs from a room. Discussion tends to be succinct when participants cannot sit down.

   When is the best time of the day, week, month, year to meet? Monday morning at eight o'clock seems like a logical day and time to meet. However, most people prefer a Tuesday–Thursday mid-morning meeting, which gives them more time to prepare. Always start and finish on time. Your participants will catch on quickly and appreciate that you respect their time. Avoid catering to latecomers by "bringing them up to speed" with a review upon their arrival.

2. *Call participants for help with planning.* Ask yourself:

   Who should attend the meeting? Participants will be focused and prepared if they have control over the date and agenda of the meeting. Avoid inviting people to your meeting who have no decision-making power. If your purpose is to inform or to motivate, you can invite a large number of people. For a planning meeting, invite between five and twelve people. For a decision-making meeting, invite the minimum number of people (eight or less). A pharmacist who plans Pharmacy and Therapeutics (P&T) meetings told me that he feels obligated to invite the chief financial officer of his hospital to these meetings. It is fine to include influential people in your planning. However, most of them would be just as impressed if you sent an action sheet or a summary after your meeting instead of an invitation to attend.

What goals do we need to accomplish and how can we achieve them? Write these down before you meet.

What roadblocks will we encounter? Will the participants disagree on an issue? After running a few meetings, you will have a sense of who will participate heavily, who will skip your meetings, and who will usually disagree with the group. Plan ahead. If you know that certain participants will disagree, ask each to prepare to speak on the topic. Participants who prepare ahead will likely use fact-based rather than opinion-based arguments. Fact-based arguments usually garner stronger support with less discussion.

3. *Reserve the room, equipment, and refreshments.* Ask yourself:

How should we set up the room? Most meeting rooms are conference rooms that house a large table with chairs around it. For meetings where you will train the participants or have guest speakers, classroom style works best.

What kinds of refreshments and breaks? The postprandial surge will hit the participants after you serve a heavy meal. Try light food and snacks, and take at least one break per hour.

What equipment will I need? Make sure *before* the meeting that you have the appropriate equipment—slide projectors, overhead projectors, flip charts, and the like—and that everything operates. Ask any speakers to arrive early to make sure they know how to work the equipment.

4. *Prepare an agenda.* The key to an organized, productive meeting is an agenda. Ask yourself:

What information should I include/leave out? Include only the items that are most relevant to the meeting. Do not rehash the topics of the last meeting unless you have new information. Assign time limits to each subject and ask a participant (in advance) to serve as timekeeper.

How can we prepare for this meeting to make it run smoothly?

For maximum benefit, send the agenda to the participants at least one week in advance and ask them to contribute to the discussion. Prepared participants are less likely to waste time in your meetings and more likely to make decisions.

5. *Send assignments* to the participants and be sure they prepare their presentations in advance. Ask participants to contribute to the meeting by acting as timekeeper, recorder, or facilitator. The *timekeeper* will watch the clock to assure that the meeting stays on track. The *recorder* will take minutes and prepare an action sheet. Make sure the recorder knows how you want the minutes and action sheet prepared and when you want them distributed. The chairperson usually acts as *facilitator,* but may ask a participant to facilitate the meeting. Having a participant facilitate your meeting will allow you to observe the dynamics of the group.

6. *Prepare visual aids.* The best visual aid is an articulate speaker. Sharpen your presentation skills and practice your contribution before the meeting. Choose visual aids that suit the audience, room, and presentation. Wait until after you explain your idea to present handouts with supporting evidence. You may also want to use flip charts or dry-erase boards for brainstorming. Many meeting facilitators use an extra flip chart as the "parking lot" for issues that are not on the agenda. When a participant suggests a topic that is not relevant, the facilitator writes it on the extra flip chart for future reference. The meeting stays on track, the topic is not forgotten, and the participant feels included. For tips on designing slides and other visual aids, see Chapter 8.

7. *Prepare to answer difficult questions.* If you are presenting an idea to your colleagues, practice before the meeting so that you will sound articulate. As a facilitator or chairperson of the meeting, you should be prepared to deal with participants who hinder progress. If you are organizing a meeting for your staff or colleagues, you can probably guess who will ask difficult questions. Prepare for them by planning and practicing your answers, or prevent

such questions by meeting with the difficult participants in advance.

A continuing education director and surgeon at a major university hospital told me his technique for dealing with participants who waste time is to have an earlier meeting with them to discuss issues. The participants thereby have an opportunity to speak to the chair and offer advice without interruption. By the time the meeting takes place, this surgeon has usually garnered enough support so that any motion he makes will pass.

8. *Document assignments with minutes and an action plan.* Even though most people do not read the minutes of a meeting, minutes are still crucial documentation for joint commission surveys, hospital records, and legal documents. For greater productivity in your meetings, add an action sheet with clear, accountable assignments to your documentation. You should design an action sheet that meets the needs of your group and includes the following headings: agenda topic, speaker, discussion, action, accountable, and resolution date. The action sheet in Figure 13.1 illustrates the outcome of a P&T meeting. Repeat the series of headings for each action item. The recorder should distribute action sheets no later than a week after the meeting. If your minutes are usually long, you may ask a different person to record and distribute the action sheet.

Another popular technique is to create a grid that the recorder can fill in during the meeting, then copy and distribute immediately.

LEADERSHIP SKILLS

Learning how to persuade other attendees at a meeting to adopt your ideas will help you emerge as a leader. Achieve competence, confidence, stage presence, and control by sharpening your public-speaking and interpersonal communication skills.

Action Sheet
Pharmacy and Therapeutics Meeting
May 24, 2001

Agenda Topic
Adding Superdrug to formulary

Speaker
Kevin Richards, PharmD

Discussion
Dr. Richards presented scientific evidence that Superdrug was a cost-effective and efficacious antibiotic. Dr. Moore of Infectious Disease questioned the drug's side effects.

Action
Obtain more information on Superdrug's side effects.

Accountable
Dr. Richards will get information from journals.
Dr. Moore will meet with pharmaceutical representative.

Resolution date
Premeeting data to committee members by June 21.
Final discussion and vote at June 28 meeting.

Figure 13.1 Sample action sheet.

Delivery

1. *Stand up when you present.* A physician told me that in her hospital meetings the participants usually sit around a conference table and remain seated even while presenting their agenda items. At one meeting, however, a pharmacist stood up to give her presentation. The entire group was so impressed that it changed its tradition from sitting to standing while presenting. Not only did this pharmacist capture the attention of her peers, but she also gained

power within the group. Standing up allowed the speaker to achieve better eye contact, the key to power in a meeting.

2. *Speak clearly and loudly.* Unfortunately for soft-spoken people, those who speak the loudest often get the most attention at meetings. If you are soft-spoken, ask to be scheduled for time on the agenda and always stand up before you speak.

3. *Strive to make eye contact with everyone in the group.* Many researchers and organizations have studied meetings to make them more productive. One of the most interesting findings is how seating affects leadership. People who sit in centrally located seats (at the end of the table or in the middle of one side) tend to emerge as leaders.[1] I believe it is because they have the most eye contact.

   Once, on the way to a speaker program, I stopped at a restaurant with the pharmaceutical sales representative sponsoring my presentation to check catering prices. She and the catering manager sat in a booth as I used the pay phone. While I was gone, the catering manager went to her office to collect some papers. I returned and sat *across* from the sales rep. When the manager returned, she sat *next* to the rep, pulled out her papers, and proceeded to direct all of her comments to me! Why? I had better eye contact. The rep was seated beside the manager, making it difficult for the manager to see her. I gained power simply because I was seated in the right place; I who had no decision-making power received all of the attention.

   If you want to gain power in a meeting, sit where you have the most eye contact with members of the group. And sit next to the people you expect to disagree with you. They will have a harder time arguing if they cannot look at you directly.

4. *Listen actively by paraphrasing what others have said.* Paraphrasing or echoing what others have said before you speak shows that you have been listening and that your comments are thoughtful. Once you rephrase what others have said, avoid connecting it to your comments with "but." That approach negates what the other per-

son has said and can appear patronizing. Choose "and," or just end the sentence.

Example

Instead of

"I agree with Kevin that we should consider adding Superdrug to our formulary, *but* I think we should check into side effects before we vote."

Say

"I agree with Kevin that we should consider adding Superdrug to our formulary. I also think we should check into side effects before we vote."

5. *Monitor nonverbal signals* such as slouching, looking away, and doodling on a notepad. Your colleagues are watching and will not take you seriously if you do not seem attentive. As a courtesy to your colleagues, turn off beepers and cellular telephones. If you expect a page during the meeting, sit near the door.

6. *Prepare your comments in advance and practice delivering them.* You may not think you have time to practice, but you do. Try practicing in the car, the shower, the gym, or some other place where you have a few minutes to spare. Nothing dissuades an audience more than an ill-prepared presenter. Chapter 8 gives more public-speaking tips.

Content

1. *Speak only when your contribution is relevant.* Speaking up often on irrelevant matters can diminish the power of the important items you wish to convey.

2. *Make one point at a time.* If you offer two effective arguments and one mediocre argument to support your idea, the group will ignore the strong ones and attack the weak one. Offer enough to persuade the others to adopt your idea only.

3. *Persuade others by focusing on benefits rather than features.* We have seen that benefits motivate others by offering "what's in it for

them." For example, in a P&T committee meeting, a participant may say, "As you can see from this chart, Superdrug is a more cost-effective choice for our antibiotic formulary, which translates into an annual savings of x dollars for the pharmacy and our hospital." When you are persuading others in conversations, meetings, and other interactions, always focus on benefits. Two ways to add benefits to your ideas are—

- Summarizing your statement with, "What this means to you (our organization, the department) is . . ."
- Using *if, then* or *when, then* statements such as, "*If* we adopt this idea, *then* we can save approximately x lives in the emergency department next year."

4. *Anticipate meeting attitudes and positions.* You can probably predict who will agree with your idea, who will comment on your proposal, and who will adopt your plan immediately. Gain the approval of everyone by anticipating, before the meeting, what others will say. Nothing sounds more professional than a physician who says, "Great question, Dr Rusevlyan. As a matter of fact, I can answer it with my next slide."

5. *Speak the language of participants.* Learn and use the terminology that best clarifies your points to a particular audience. A pharmacist once told me that she worked with a practitioner who referred to the "half-life" of a drug as the same thing as its "duration in the body." In pharmacy, she explained, these terms are not interchangeable and must be clarified. Rather than embarrass the erring physician, she simply clarified the difference in pharmacy terms.

6. *Be specific and offer evidence to support your points.* As with a scientific study, a meeting should contain valid evidence to support a claim. For example, in a meeting where you want others to adopt a new administrative policy, you may present statistical evidence from the accounting department and anecdotal evidence from other departments.

7. *Present materials simply and concisely.* The biggest complaint about meetings is that they last too long. Presenting your ideas in a

simple, concise fashion will give you the advantage of appearing focused and prepared. Of course, do not compromise content for simplicity.

GROUP DYNAMICS

People often act differently in a small-group situation. If you are facilitating a meeting, you may encounter participants who overparticipate or underparticipate. Participants who may hinder progress include the following.

- Time wasters. Keep these participants busy with an assignment such as timekeeper or recorder.
- Distracters. These individuals usually want attention. Before the next meeting, ask them to prepare an agenda item or act as timekeeper or recorder.
- Conversationalists. Since these participants enjoy talking, ask one of them to be the facilitator. You may also separate the talkers with assigned seats, or ask them (in private) to save personal conversations for the break.
- Silent types. Most introverted people prefer to listen and digest information rather than comment on it. Asking them to speak without advance warning may make them uncomfortable. Instead, ask them ahead of time to prepare an agenda item or to plan to discuss an issue at the next meeting.
- Critics. Ask critics to offer a reason why they disagree, to research and support their ideas at the next meeting, or to meet with you beforehand to discuss issues.

Dealing with Conflict

Conflict is a natural part of the decision-making process. Yet many people avoid conflict because it makes them uncomfortable. Enter your next meeting or discussion knowing that some people thrive on conflict and that a difference of opinion often leads to a more advanced solution. Use differences to develop the best solution possible.[2]

- Avoid polarization. Try not to take sides on an issue. If you feel strongly about a decision prior to the discussion, ask someone else to facilitate the meeting. Some meetings run more smoothly if the facilitator is a neutral nonmember of the group.
- Clarify goals by restating them. Many times a heated discussion loses focus. As the leader of the meeting, you should help the group involved in a heated debate to focus on its goals by restating them. For example, "Dr Rosenberg has an excellent point; let's remember that for the next meeting. Meanwhile, back to our issue . . ."
- Seek increased communication by paraphrasing what others have said. Echoing what others have said will help the group focus on the issues and how they relate to one another.
- Offer alternative choices. Many times the group will try to select only one solution when a combination of ideas is the best choice.
- Have a fallback plan. If the group discussion becomes too aggressive, be prepared to table it, ask participants to investigate and report new findings, or revote at the next meeting.
- Handle some issues one-on-one. After a particularly negative meeting, you may need to meet with the participants individually to discuss solutions.

Probably the best advice on running a more effective meeting is to solicit participant help. Participants will gladly adopt a new meeting time, agenda style, or timekeeper if they can see the benefits. Encourage participants to be on time by asking them before the next meeting to "arrive on time so we can get out on time." Add one new technique at each meeting until you have accomplished your goal. For example, add the agenda and timekeeper first, then try the action sheet, then ask for each participant to echo what others have said before they speak, and so on. Be creative. Ask the participants, "What can we do to make this meeting more efficient?" and incorporate their suggestions into your next meeting.

NOTES

1. Mosvick, R. K., and Nelson, R. B. How to manage conflict in a meeting. In *We've Got to Start Meeting Like This: A Guide to Successful Meeting Management*. Indianapolis: Jist Works, 1996, pp. 180–184.

2. Ibid.

14

Business Writing

Stephanie Barnard

Whether you are drafting a request letter to an insurance company or a referral letter to a colleague, clear and concise business writing can determine if the reader will read your document and—more important—respond to it. Much of this book has been devoted to scientific writing: manuscripts, grants, peer review articles, and curricula vitae. The writing tips come from authors with a variety of writing backgrounds, yet the advice throughout is the same. The most successful writers know their audience and give this audience what it wants in an understandable, organized document.

Knowing your audience, writing with clarity, and organizing your thoughts are particularly important in business writing. Educated professionals in health care say that they do not have time to read lengthy, complex documents. Give them what they want: short, uncomplicated letters, e-mails, and memos. You need not compromise content, just take extra time to develop what you write into a comprehensible message.

CLARITY AND READABILITY

Most health care professionals have sitting on their desks a two-inch stack of documents to be read. How do they select which to read and which to toss? Most choose the path of least resistance. A short memo with white space and bulleted points looks easier to read and usually gets read first, whereas a long "giant paragraph" memo may just get discarded. Follow the grammar and style suggestions in Chapter 2 and add the following suggestions for business writing.

1. *Begin business letters and e-mail messages with "thank you," and use "please" before making requests.* Remember when you asked your mother for a treat when you were a child? What was the magic word she asked you to say before giving you the treat? *Please.* Then after she gave you the treat, what did your mother teach you to say? *Thank you.* These are still magic words. Starting letters with "thank you" gives you a concrete starting point and avoids the unnecessary warm-up paragraph. For example, "Dear Dr Hill, Thank you for referring Mary Duncan to me for surgery." Using the polite "please" in a letter softens a request.

2. *Review samples of good writing.* Save well-written letters and memos as references. For example, one of the most difficult letters to draft is a reference letter. If you receive one that is clear and concise, use it as a template when one of your colleagues asks you to write one.

3. *Outline your documents before you start typing.* Have you ever completed a task at work from start to finish without interruption? Probably not. Outlining will help you organize your thoughts, overcome writer's block, and create a "road map" for your document in case you have to return to writing it later. There is no need to draft an elaborate outline; a few ideas on scrap paper will go a long way.

4. *Remember that less is more.* Flash back to your eighth-grade history class. When your teacher assigned a paper on some historical event, you were probably concerned with two things: due date and length. After you heard the due date and waited until the night

before to work on the paper, you had to deal with length. So you exhausted the family encyclopedia and came up with seven and a half pages of your ten-page paper. How did you stretch it to ten pages? You probably widened the margins, double-spaced the lines, and still made only eight and a half pages. What to do next? Add unnecessary words. Change "now" to "at this point in time." Add hedging words such as "perhaps" and "indeed." Eventually you could add enough unnecessary words to build ten pages and receive a good grade, even if you compromised clarity. Most health care professionals have been taught and rewarded for writing *without* clarity. You are no longer writing for a grade; you are writing to be read. Cut to the chase.

5. *Use the active voice.* Active voice is the best way to add clarity and purpose to your business documents.
   Example
   Passive voice:
   "It would be greatly appreciated if you would attend the meeting."
   Active voice:
   "I would appreciate your attendance at the next meeting."
   Which sounds more sincere and persuasive? Readers want to know who the subject or doer is. Put that person at the beginning of your sentences and you will achieve the active voice.

6. *Use bullets to create white space.* Throughout the preceding chapters, I have used numbers and bullets to create white space. The text would take more time to read if I had not clarified my points in this manner. The best way to employ bullets is to use a verb at the beginning. Notice that the start of each numbered item is a verb such as "use," "remember," and "outline." These verbs imply action and make the sentences stronger.

E-MAIL MESSAGES

How many e-mail, voice-mail, telephone, and other messages do you receive per day? Most professionals tell me that at least half of what they receive is trash. But how do they choose which messages to read? With e-mail messages, they probably look for two key elements: the "from" line and the "subject" line. If you receive lots of irrelevant messages from the same person, you probably delete some of them without ever reading them. If you receive an e-mail with a general subject line such as "new policy," you may delete that message because you think the writer has nothing new to add. When you write e-mail messages, make them count by following these tips:

- Be specific in the subject line. Say something specific that will entice your readers to open the e-mail. Instead of "New Formulary Addition," write "Superdrug Added to Formulary."
- Draft your message in a word-processing program first, then import it into your e-mail program. Your word-processing program will enable you to spell check the document. Because you are not rushing to free the telephone line, you will probably make fewer mistakes.
- Limit your e-mail message to one screenful. We have all received the unnecessarily long e-mail message that took lots of time to download but only a few seconds to throw away. Make yours worth reading.
- Write with clarity by using bullets, active voice, and a minimum of words to convey your message.
- Avoid discussing confidential patient information on a nonsecure system or putting anything unprofessional in your e-mail. I once received an e-mail from my family physician in response to a call I made to him. He had prescribed a medication that was not approved by my health maintenance organization (HMO). When I tried to fill the prescription, my pharmacist told me to call my HMO to get a preapproval form. I called, and the HMO faxed the form the next day. But two weeks later, my doctor had not completed it. I called and left voice-mail messages at the nurses' desk inquiring about the form. No one ever called me back. When I finally spoke to a person, she claimed the office had never received

the form. I asked her to look in my chart for the form and, as I suspected, it had been there for ten days. I asked her to have the doctor call me. Instead of calling, he sent a poorly written, patronizing e-mail that probably took longer to write than making a simple phone call. This doctor should have responded in the way I requested. A telephone response would have allowed him to get both sides of the story before forming an opinion. What a shame. Because this physician did a poor job of writing, he lost a patient.

- Send copies to others only when they need or request them. You may think that sending your boss a copy of every e-mail you receive will keep him or her informed. In fact, it will not. Imagine if someone doubled your e-mail messages every day! Consolidate the important information at the end of the week and send a synopsis to your boss.

PATIENT EDUCATION LITERATURE

One of the best ways to increase understanding and compliance is to offer patients literature that explains in detail a diagnosis and its treatment. From practice brochures to tips on preparing for surgery, patient education literature can encourage compliance while also marketing your practice. For example, in the reception area of a cardiology office, I saw a freestanding display of patient education literature. These cardiologists probably hired a consultant to help them design and print a series of brochures on smoking cessation, diet and exercise, hypertension, diabetes, and other diseases and diagnoses that they treat. What a clever idea! The benefits of custom-designed educational literature are numerous:

- Patients in the reception area have something informative to read.
- Knowledge of the side effects of a procedure or treatment is readily available (excellent malpractice prevention).
- Patients have information to take home that will help them adhere to your instructions and gain positive outcomes.

- Patients may take the brochure to the treatment room with questions that they otherwise would not ask.
- The custom design for your office (rather than a bulk order from a supply house) enables you to incorporate your techniques and personalize the information.

Remember that all practice forms and patient instructions should be simple and reader friendly. Patients who have difficulty completing forms from your office will either waste time struggling with them or become frustrated with your practice.

Writing for the Patient Audience

The primary consideration for anything that you write should be the reader. When drafting instructions for prescriptions, directions to your office, or articles for your community newspaper, consider who will read them and why. For example, patient education literature from a pediatrician will differ from that from an internist. Why? The patient at a pediatric practice is a child but the responsible party is a parent. The patient at an internal medicine practice *is* the responsible party. In both cases, most of the literature is geared toward the responsible party or an adult audience. In the pediatric practice, however, older children undergoing complex treatments or surgeries will want literature also. This information should be written for children or adolescents as the audience.

The best model to use for educational literature is an existing piece. Collect brochures from pharmaceutical companies and practitioners in your area. Look at the instructions enclosed in over-the-counter medications and direct-to-consumer advertising in magazines and newspapers for ideas. Refer to Chapter 2 for additional writing advice and follow the tips below:

1. *Draft patient literature at a grade-school reading level.* The average patient may not comprehend a document written on a higher level than grade-school reading. Even patients who read beyond that level appreciate a clear message. Documents written at grade-

school level look easy to read because they have shorter words and sentences. Have you ever drafted a letter on your computer and activated spell check, only to find that your letter is written at a twelfth-grade reading level? Here's how to scale back to grade-school level:

- Select words that have few syllables. Words become more complex with each additional syllable.

  Example: Use "some" instead of "proportion."

- Use laymen's terms to describe medications, diagnoses, and treatments.

  Example: Choose "fluid pill" instead of "diuretic."

- Use the fewest words possible to illustrate a point. Sentences in business documents or patient-audience documents should not exceed seventeen words.

  Example

  Instead of

  "If you need to change your scheduled appointment with our office, call our staff at 803-555-0000."

  Write

  "To change your appointment, please call 803-555-0000."

2. *Use charts, graphs, pictures, and cartoons to illustrate a point.* You do not need to get fancy with your drawings. A podiatrist client of mine has a bulletin board in each treatment room of his office. Tacked on the board are small charts and photos illustrating parts of the foot and ankle, and in the corner is a small chalkboard on which he draws examples of surgical procedures and other patient information. Procedures that you treat often deserve their own information sheet or pamphlet, with illustrations on them.

   - Use charts to map out schedules for taking medications, exercising, and sleeping.
   - Use line graphs to explain long-term results and pie graphs to illustrate diet.
   - Use pictures and cartoons to demonstrate treatments.
   - Avoid unnecessary graphics such as boxes, lines, and clip art.

3. *Design literature that is reader friendly.* Chapter 8 offers tips on designing slides and overheads that are easy to read. Sans serif type is more effective in projection forms such as slides, overheads, and liquid crystal displays; serif type is easier to read in printed materials (newspapers, magazines, and brochures). Three easy-to-read serif fonts (typestyles with "feet" on the ends) that work well for brochures and other printed materials are Palatino, Times Roman, and Garamond.[1] Here are examples of a serif font (left) and a sans serif font (right):

H
Palatino
20 point

H
Helvetica
20 point

You can also make the design reader friendly by:

- Choosing type that is at least 12 point in size. Readers with presbyopia (most people over age forty) will appreciate large type.
- Allowing white space to cushion the text and make it easier to read. Some computer programmers buy desktop publishing programs believing that no design skill is needed; but most programs that aid in designing slides, graphics, and brochures offer so many features that you will need design skill just to wade through the options. Many of the extras on these programs do little to enhance design. For example, a pharmacist at a national pharmacy meeting asked me to proof his company's promotional newsletter. Every story was surrounded by a box, giving the newsletter a kind of "horse corral" look. Removing the boxes gave the stories a cushion of white space and made them more appealing. Other ways to create white space in your documents are by starting new paragraphs often and by allowing wide margins.

4. *Do not rush any printing project.* In your haste to get a brochure

finished, you may overlook a typo. Ask a few key patients to proof your piece *before* you go to press, and photocopy a trial run of black-and-white brochures.

5. *Do it yourself and save money.* You can save lots of money by designing and printing your own patient education literature. Office supply stores are loaded with inexpensive desktop publishing programs and colored papers. Resist the desire to use every feature on the program, and know when to call for professional help. Among the professional helpers you should call are the following:

- A photographer to take pictures (even the best scanners and computer programs cannot repair poor photos).
- A local design student to help with layout (a much cheaper option than a professional designer).
- A local English or communication student to help with writing (most designers do not have both design and copywriting experience).

A radiologist once asked me how to get patients to come to their appointments prepared for the procedures he performs. He said that while the referring physicians were sending him lots of patients, they would arrive for their appointments and say "I'm not sure why I'm here. The receptionist at Dr Hannah's office sent me." These unprepared patients often did not allow enough time for the visit and did not prepare for the procedure by avoiding certain foods, arriving with a full bladder, and so on.

I recommended that he draft educational literature to send these patients prior to their visits. To start, I suggested that the radiologist choose the top five procedures he performs and write a one-page summary of it in question-and-answer format. The first headline might read, "How long will this procedure take?" followed by a brief answer. Then I suggested that he add a simple line-art graphic such as a drawing of a glass of water for a procedure that requires a full bladder. Next I recommended that he add his practice name, address, telephone number, and directions to the office.

I advised the radiologist to design this patient education literature in a faxable format (white background, no shading, large text, no photographs), then ask his staff to fax the form to the referring practice upon receiving the appointment phone call. I also recommended that he take a stack of copies to the referring practices so that their staff could hand them out easily. For a busy practice, a project like this might seem ominous. However, once you design a template with the first procedure, the rest of the job is simply cutting and pasting new information for each different procedure. You and your staff will save lots of time explaining procedures, giving out directions, and answering questions. You will also increase the number of referrals, because you will make referring patients to your practice an easy task.

BROCHURES, NEWSLETTERS, AND WEBSITES

One of the most economical and ethical ways to promote your practice is to develop a brochure, newsletter, or website. With minimal effort, you and your staff can draft a practice brochure and import the information to a website. Take your website a step farther by changing the text every month or quarter, and transform it into a printed newsletter. These marketing pieces can be valuable resources for patients, referring practices, or other departments in your organization. Many practices mail brochures to new patients before their first visit. These practices thereby save time and prevent miscommunication, while offsetting the cost of designing and printing the brochures. Providing easy-to-read directions to the office saves your patients time in calling and saves your staff time in answering calls.

For example, you could save $250 per year by publishing a brochure and/or maintaining a website. If five new patients a week call your office for directions, if your staff spends about six minutes per call, and if your average staff member makes $10 per hour, then a brochure or website will save you $5 per week or $250 per year (based on a fifty-week year). Similarly, a pharmacy that designs a monthly newsletter with formulary changes and other therapeutic issues can save money and improve patient outcomes by keeping hospital staff informed of more cost-effective and efficacious treatments.

Doing the Writing

Creating a promotional brochure or website will take some extra time and money, but the payoff is worth it. Professionally printed brochures and newsletters and well-designed websites can give your practice a professional edge. These marketing pieces allow you to share your expertise with patients and colleagues, provide important information in a convenient format, and promote your practice. You can save both time and money by doing some of the work yourself or by hiring a local college student to help you. Start by collecting brochures and newsletters from other practices in your area or departments in your facility. Notice what information these documents include and the style in which they are written. Plan what information to include in your own piece, based on the following tips:

Include the following if appropriate:

- Name, address, phone number, fax number, website address
- Education and experience of all providers and key personnel with *professional* photos
- Office hours
- After-hours and emergency numbers
- Directions to office with a map and parking instructions
- References (quotes from patients)
- Insurance and payment plans you accept
- Services that you offer
- Your practice philosophy or mission statement
- Other pertinent information or frequently asked questions
- Feature stories on anything newsworthy: new therapies, important policies, promoted employees, interesting patients (for newsletters and websites)

Remember your audience and purpose. Your audience and purpose are the most important considerations for anything you say or write. Without an audience to listen to your talk or a patient to read your brochure, your efforts are futile. Pinpoint your audience and purpose by asking yourself the following questions as you plan and write:

- Who is the target audience?
- When will I use/give away this brochure or newsletter?
- How will I publicize this website?
- Can grade-school students understand these documents?
- Is this design too complicated?
- Is this design convenient to mail/download?
- How will I display this brochure or newsletter at the office?

Focus the information on the benefits to the patient. Most people are motivated when they think they have something to gain. In describing your location, for example, give a benefit: "Conveniently located adjacent to ABC Memorial Hospital."

Tips on Brochures and Newsletters

While brochures, newsletters, and websites can use almost the exact same text, they cannot use the exact same design because the brochures and newsletters will be printed materials and the website will be computer generated. All three should be designed in an easy-to-read style. Remember the design concept: *Form follows function.* Do not complicate your design with graphics that conflict with your message. Besides keeping it simple, design brochures and newsletters that patients will read by avoiding reverse type and shading behind text and "cute" clip art, poor-quality photographs, and unprofessional graphic design.

Here are some tips when you are ready to have your materials printed:

- If you plan to mail the piece, check with the post office for bulk mail and other postal regulations *before* you print.
- Ask a key patient, your friends, your staff, and an English teacher to proof your document before you print. Once the ink is set, you cannot turn back. The last thing you want on your brochure is a typo.
- Choose a light-colored paper that feels crisp in your hand and dark-colored text inks that are pleasant and readable (blue, black, bur-

gundy, and purple). Avoid red and green inks, as color-blind people have difficulty seeing them.

- Print enough brochures to last approximately one year (five hundred to a thousand) and enough newsletters to last about three months (based on your newsletter circulation). Most organizations need to update brochures every year, so do not let the printer talk you into printing thousands with the lure of a price break.

Tips on Websites

Do not let a website design intimidate you. To start, you can import the text from your practice brochure and convert it to hypertext markup language (HTML). Like the brochure design, the website design will do more with less. Cut the clutter by using only necessary graphics. Your design will look sharper and it will be easier for patients to download your website. As with the brochure, avoid dark backgrounds with reverse (white) text because it is difficult to read.

DOCUMENTS THAT PROMOTE YOUR PRACTICE

Even if you already work in an established practice, you can still promote your practice economically and ethically. Whether you are an internist or a nurse practitioner, promoting your practice is the key to your future.

News Releases

News releases are mini–news stories written to entice the local media to cover a story in their radio program, newspaper article, or television news show. News editors at all media sources will tell you that the key to getting your story covered or published is drafting a well-written release, having a story that is timely and interesting, and knowing where to send it (which specific editor). You may even want to call the local medical editor to introduce yourself. You will then be the first source the reporter calls when a medical story requires a quote from a local physician, physical therapist, or director of nursing. Send news

FOR IMMEDIATE RELEASE
Dr Susan Redding Joins Springfield Heart Specialists
Date: January 11, 2001   Contact: Bill Rogers, Office Manager
123-555-1212

Susan Redding, MD, has joined Doctors Jack Smith and Beth McCall at Springfield Heart Specialists. Dr Redding received her Bachelor of Science degree from Wake Forest University and her medical degree from Bowman Gray School of Medicine, both in Winston-Salem, North Carolina. She completed a residency in internal medicine and a fellowship in cardiology at the University of North Carolina at Chapel Hill.

Dr Redding specializes in the prevention of heart disease.

Springfield Heart Specialists, located at 123 Hospital Drive, offers board-certified cardiologists. These physicians specialize in the prevention, diagnosis, and treatment of cardiac diseases.

Figure 14.1 Sample news release.

releases to local media contacts when you hire a new employee, attend a conference or other educational seminar, and organize contributions to the community (fundraisers, board memberships, free health screenings). The sample news release in Figure 14.1 is written about a new staff member. The best model to follow is a news story that comes from the paper you are targeting.

Announcements

Announcements are printed notices explaining that you (or your organization) are doing something different or offering something new. Have these announcements professionally printed as you would if announcing a marriage or birth. Send them to referral sources (colleagues, medical practices, other patient sources) when you hire a new employee, have a special promotion, or buy a new piece of equipment. Figure 14.2 shows a sample announcement of a new employee.

East Carolina University Surgery Practice
is pleased to announce that
James Raines, MD
General Surgeon
has joined the practice

123 Healthy Lane • Greenville, NC 27834 • 919-555-1212
David Jones, MD, FACS • Callie Roberson, MD, FACS
Bruce Mitchell, MD, FACS

Figure 14.2 Sample announcement.

Offers to Speak

Learn how to be a better public speaker and offer to give talks to local clubs and organizations. (See Chapter 8 for tips on preparing a presentation.) Send local clubs a letter or memo offering your services as a speaker. Figure 14.3 gives a sample memo for a urology practice.

BECOMING A BETTER COMMUNICATOR

While Part V has been packed with practical tips, suggestions, and challenges, perhaps the best advice I can offer on communication overall is to become solution focused. Many times I have overheard staff members in a hospital or clinic say, "That patient really is a pain," or "The people in that department really have a problem," without considering that *they*, the complaining staff members, may be the cause of the problem. Annoying patients would not be so annoying if they received lucid answers to their questions. The department that seems to have a problem may think that you have the problem, since you have not communicated your ideas effectively. To be solution focused in your communication, whether written or verbal, remember to know your audience, listen to others before you respond, and communicate clearly.

Date: January 10, 2001
To: Area Clubs and Organizations
From: Betsy Moore, Office Manager

Do you have your spring speaker programs lined up? As you plan these meetings, consider having a physician from Chapel Hill Urology as a guest speaker. Our well-trained physicians can speak on many medical topics including—
• Prostate enlargement/cancer
• Male and female incontinence
• Stone disease
• Advantages of lithotripsy
• Male infertility issues
• Advantages of vasectomy
• Preventing sexually transmitted diseases

The following highly qualified people are available to speak to your club:
• Jack Smith, MD, FACS
• Beth McCall, MD, FACS
• Stephen Phillips, MD

For more information, please call our office at 919-555-1212. Thank you for your interest in Chapel Hill Urology.

Figure 14.3 Sample memo.

To know your audience means that in anything you say or write, you should consider what information is important to that audience. Does your boss prefer e-mail messages to voice-mail messages? Does your high-maintenance patient need written instructions in order to comply? What issues are important to the chief financial officer that may not be so important to the medical director?

In this fast-paced world of medicine, listening to others has almost become a forgotten art. Listening does not mean just nodding your head, acting as if you care, and echoing what others have said. Listening means processing and using the information you receive. The only way to improve outcomes in any field is to listen to others and adapt your behavior accordingly.

Communicating well is probably one of life's greatest challenges. Many of us have given what we thought were clear instructions to someone else, only to find those instructions disregarded or misunderstood. A typical interpersonal communication model shows an exchange of ideas between two people: both people must listen, understand, and respond in order to make the model complete. Communicating clearly means offering an understandable message *and* making sure the message is received. The best scientific education, practice experience, and career talent are wasted if the person who possesses these abilities does not cultivate communication skills by striving daily to improve them.

NOTES

1. St. James, D. Other writing projects. In *Writing and Speaking for Excellence.* 2nd ed. Sudbury, Mass.: Jones and Bartlett, 1998, p. 122.

SUGGESTED READINGS

Baum, N. *Marketing Your Clinical Practice.* Gaithersburg, Md.: Aspen Publishers, 1992.

Communication Briefings newsletter. 700 Black Horse Pike, Suite 110, Blackwood, N.J. 08012.

Hoffmeir, P., and Bohner, J. *From Residency to Reality.* New York: McGraw-Hill, 1988.

Levinson, J., and Godin, S. *The Guerrilla Marketing Handbook.* Boston: Houghton Mifflin, 1994.

Lloyd, M., and Bor, R. *Communication Skills for Medicine.* New York: Churchill Livingstone, 1996.

Myerscough, P., and Ford, M. *Talking with Patients.* Oxford: Oxford University Press, 1996.

Nelson, B. *1001 Ways to Reward Employees*. New York: Workman Publishing, 1994.

Pachter, B., and Brody, M. *Complete Business Etiquette Handbook*. Paramus, N.J.: Prentice Hall, 1995.

Rantucci, M. *Pharmacists Talking with Patients*. Baltimore: Williams & Wilkins, 1997.

Sewell, C., Brown, P., and Peters, T. *Customers for Life: How to Turn That One-Time Buyer into a Lifetime Customer*. New York: Pocket Books, 1998.

Contributors

Stephanie Barnard is the owner of Business Image Consulting, a public relations firm in Wilson, North Carolina. She offers marketing and public relations advice to physicians, pharmacists, long-term care administrators, and other health professionals. Ms Barnard's articles on communication skills have been published in several trade journals and she recently wrote patient education literature for a surgical device company. A speaker for ArcMesa Educators, Ms Barnard presents seminars to health professionals throughout the United States at local, regional, and national meetings. Those programs are certified for Continuing Medical Education credits. Her undergraduate degree in communication is from the University of North Carolina at Chapel Hill.

Paul J Casella, a founding member of the Health Care Communication Group, is a graduate of Dartmouth College and the Iowa Writers' Workshop. Although most of his formal training is in literature, creative writing, and filmmaking, for the last ten years Mr Casella has worked with health professionals on their manuscripts for publication, formal presentations, posters, and videos. His poetry has appeared in more than twenty academic journals. Mr Casella is the founder and producer of "PTV: Poetry Television," a video magazine in which a series of poems are presented with images. His current work consists largely of the Writing and Speaking for Excellence seminars through his association with ArcMesa Educators. He is also a consultant to the faculty at the University of Iowa College of Medicine, identifying and serving the advanced communication needs of the faculty.

Catherine Coffin joined the Health Care Communication Group in 1992 and has since taught more than five hundred writing and speaking seminars for health professionals in forty states and five Canadian provinces. She worked as a freelance communication consultant and trainer for the Bayer Pharmaceutical Division from July 1992 to July 1999, and thereafter as a consultant for ArcMesa Educators. Ms Coffin has been a medical research assistant, a writer, and an editor at several New England biotechnology companies and medical centers, including her six years as manuscript editor for the Department of Surgery at the Dartmouth-Hitchcock Medical Center in New Hampshire. She currently lives in Wakefield, Rhode Island.

Kirk T Hughes, a founding member of the Health Care Communication Group, directs an international communication consulting firm specializing in medical publishing, presentation skills, and professional leadership development. His clients include university departments, medical schools, physicians, and corporations in the Americas, Europe, and Asia. Currently associated with ArcMesa Educators, Dr Hughes has directed Bayer College, served as a consulting administrator with the American Council of Pharmaceutical Education, and taught English, science writing, English for speakers of other languages, and advanced communication skills at the University of Pennsylvania and Yale University.

J Willis Hurst trained in cardiology at the Massachusetts General Hospital with Dr Paul Dudley White. Dr Hurst was professor and chair of the Department of Medicine at Emory University School of Medicine in Atlanta from 1957 to 1986. Since that time he has been a consultant to the Division of Cardiology at Emory and has devoted his time to teaching and writing. Among his previous positions Dr Hurst numbers the presidency of the American Heart Association and the Association of Professors of Medicine, membership in the National Advisory Heart, Lung, and Blood Council, and chairmanship of the Subspecialty Board of Cardiovascular Diseases of the American Board of Internal Medicine. Along with receiving numerous teaching awards, he created and edited seven editions of the internationally accepted scientific book *The Heart*. For eighteen years Dr Hurst was the personal cardiologist of President Lyndon Baines Johnson.

Janet S Rasey holds degrees from the University of Michigan (BS in zoology), Oregon State University (MS in radiological health), and the University of Oregon (PhD in biology). Her principal research interests are cancer imaging, radiation biology, and the role of tumor hypoxia in cancer therapy and tumor progression. In 1989, Dr Rasey, professor of radiation oncology at the University of Washington, founded the Research Funding Service there, which she continues to direct. This service helps investigators in the health science schools (medicine, dentistry, nursing, public health, pharmacy, and social work) find sources of research funds, understand the art of grantmanship, and learn to write effective grants.

Diane Redding is continuing education associate at Bayer Corporation. She joined the company's pharmaceutical division in 1986 and has had a variety of job responsibilities in marketing, sales, and editorial services. Ms Redding currently works in Bayer College, a service group within the Scientific Relations Department, and is responsible for coordinating educational seminars and workshops for health care professionals across the United States.

Renée J Robillard has taught writing, editing, proofreading, and medical communications for twenty-five years at the undergraduate, graduate, and postgraduate levels. She has worked as an author's editor and research project manager in teaching hospitals and industry and as a manuscript editor for several medical journals, including the *New England Journal of Medicine*. She is currently the owner of Medical Writing and Research, a medical communication consulting firm. She holds degrees in English and technical writing from Boston

University and the University of British Columbia, and a certification from the Board of Editors in the Life Sciences.

Deborah St James is vice president of continuing education at ArcMesa Educators. She is former director of the Writing and Speaking for Excellence seminars at Bayer Corporation, former editor of *Better Health* magazine, and has taught English for speakers of other languages, and technical, business, and medical writing at both the graduate and postgraduate level. She is the author of *Writing and Speaking for Excellence: A Guide for Physicians* and coeditor of *Empathy and the Practice of Medicine* and *Doctors Afield.*

Steven C Ullery holds a BA in statistics from the University of California, Davis, and an MS in statistics from the University of California, Riverside. For the past twelve years, he has worked in the medical device arena, including four years as manager of a biostatistics department. Mr Ullery lives in Flagstaff, Arizona, where he works in the Medical Products Division of W L Gore and Associates.

Index